A COMPARATIVE STUDY OF PROGRAMMING LANGUAGES

BRYAN HIGMAN
Professor of Computer Studies University of Lancaster

COMPUTER MONOGRAPHS
Editor: J. J. Florentin, Ph.D., Birkbeck College, London

ELSEVIER NORTH HOLLAND INC.
52 Vanderbilt Avenue
New York, New York 10017
ISBN 0-444-19495-9
Library of Congress Catalog Card No. 77-83814

© Bryan Higman, 1977

First published 1967
Second impression 1968
Third impression 1969
First published in paperback 1969
Fourth impression 1970
Fifth impression 1973
Second edition 1977

Macdonald and Jane's Publishers Ltd.,
Paulton House, 8 Shepherdess Walk, London, N.1

Macdonald ISBN 0 354 04068 5

Printed in Great Britain by
REDWOOD BURN LIMITED, Trowbridge & Esher

CONTENTS

iii

PREFACE TO SECOND EDITION

In bringing out this revised edition, my first duty is to thank many unknown individuals for the encouraging reception they have given over a period of years to the first edition. This reception has convinced me that I ought to maintain its style, which I conceive as having two sources, first the significant but not dominating position given to personal attitudes which are not always orthodox, and secondly the general presentation in terms of a switch from theory to historical development at about a third of the way through. Accordingly the bulk of the revision consists of an extension to Chapter 7 bringing the theoretical part up to date, and a complete rewriting of Chapter 13 so that it now covers the developments of the intervening ten years in the ideas lying behind the main line languages. Chapter 14, which has dated more than most, has received the same treatment in miniature as the book as a whole, the original text being rewritten as history whenever possible, and otherwise brought up to date by additional sections. In Chapter 15 the lollipops have been left untouched, the rest drastically revised.

To avoid undue expansion, selection has been inevitable, and it is my own failure in not maintaining the necessary breadth of reading that has confined the new material to what I have termed the main line. To those who are disappointed that on-line languages, simulation languages, languages for computer graphics and so on have not received comparable treatment I can only apologize. For the same reason, in Chapter 7 I have avoided incorporating material on the mathematical theory of parsing that is readily available elsewhere and have concentrated instead on developments that combine semantic interpretation with practical parsing. Contrariwise, I have expounded the theory of Markov algorithms at some length because I believe in it and because it is *not* readily available to the student of Computer Science anywhere else.

'Every scribe that is instructed into the kingdom of heaven is like unto a householder, who bringeth forth out of his treasure things both new and old'. No-one who reveres the name of Babbage should scorn ideas that failed because they appeared at an inopportune moment technologically. Those that remember the computer known as the Deuce may like to speculate on how far its programming principles were so well matched to *serial* memory that they will prove ideally suited to laser storage when it comes in the future, grotesque though they may be at the moment. With such thoughts in mind I have cut out whatever time has shown to have been mistaken, and have allowed certain sections to be absorbed into their own subsequent development, but otherwise I have refrained from pruning anything simply on the ground that it looks antiquated. By this means I hope I have produced a work worthy of 1977 but not disappointing to those who expect to find in it the features of an old friend.

Forton, Lancaster,
January 1977.

1

INTRODUCTION

To non-specialists in the field, the phrase 'a programming language' is usually held to mean 'one of those things like Autocode, Fortran, Algol or Cobol, which are supposed to make programming easier'. Programming is drawing up schedules of instructions for a computer, to make it able to carry out a specified task correctly. Given a programming language, the instructions can be expressed in terms more like the English, or more like the mathematics (whichever you prefer), that we are accustomed to use, and there is a program already written called the 'compiler' or 'translator', which will turn this painlessly into what you would otherwise have had first to write and then to punch for yourself with great difficulty. In some cases the translator does not even bother you with the translation, it just carries on and obeys it; this is called a 'load-and-go' translator. An alternative procedure — usually too slow to be practicable, but of value in special cases — reads what you have written straight into the machine, and there is an 'interpreter' also in the machine which is continuously looking at what you wrote and carrying out the processes implied by it.

If, ten years after the above words were written, the balance of this picture has altered considerably, its component parts are still the same. The picture is a true one, but too narrowly blinkered. The machines' own codes are just as much programming languages, and the writer of a compiler is accustomed to say that it translates from a 'source language' into a 'target language'. Buried inside some compilers there are 'intermediate languages'. Most translators do more than translate; they report back on anything ungrammatical or meaningless in the original text, and also arrange for reports on difficulties which arise during execution, such as division which looks (and usually is) all right, but which on some particular occasion turns out to ask for division by zero. These reports are known as compile-time and run-time diagnostics, respectively. A language has also the right to be judged *per se*, as a means for the communication of programming procedures between human beings, divorced from any translation or running systems; at this last level, natural languages should not be excluded.

The writer of a work on comparative linguistics has always to

1

compete with the fact that few of his readers will be familiar with *all* the languages he refers to, and yet many of them are likely to be more familiar with some one or more of them than he is himself — but not always the same ones. Since natural languages have their place in our study, and English has a sort of neutrality in this respect, we have not hesitated to use it as a source of illustrations when possible. Where something more mathematical is essential, it will be useful to have an equally neutral source.

1.1 A language for illustrations

For this purpose we may use a language which consists of the conventions of algebra, supplemented by the following symbols to provide the programming element:

$$: \quad ; \quad := \quad \textbf{go to} \quad \textbf{if} \quad \textbf{then} \quad \textbf{else}$$

The symbol $:=$ is the imperative equals, and occurs once in each assignment statement. That is, $x := -b + \sqrt{(b^2 - 4ac)}$ is an assignment statement which is to be obeyed, and when it has been obeyed then whatever value x originally had, it has now been given the same value as the expression on the right has. To obey $x_k := y_{k-1}$ we first see what value k has and then, for that value of k only, give x_k the value which y_{k-1} now has. The statement $x := x + 1$ means that x is to be given a value one greater than its present value. Assignment statements are to be obeyed in the order in which they are written. A statement **go to** P means that the next statement to be obeyed is the one that has $P:$ in front of it. The symbol ';' separates statements from one another, and **if** . . . **then** . . . **else** may be taken at their face value. For example, we can calculate the value of e correct to p significant figures by

$$
\begin{aligned}
&\text{x} := 1; \quad \text{y} := 1; \quad \text{k} := 1; \\
\text{Q:} \quad &\text{x} := \text{kx} + 1; \quad \text{y} := \text{ky}; \quad \text{k} := \text{k} + 1; \\
&\textbf{if } \text{y} < 10^p \textbf{ then go to } \text{Q}; \\
&\text{e} := \text{x/y}
\end{aligned}
$$

This language is a subset of Algol 60 with concessions to algebraic notation.

From time to time we shall use the phrase 'a higher-level feature' about some aspect of a language. By this we mean that it can be defined in terms of simpler concepts already in the language, and is introduced as a convenience rather than as a necessity. For example, we can define

if B then begin X; Y; Z **end**; W;

where B is a condition and X, Y, Z, W are assignment or go-to statements, as meaning

2

if B′ **then go to** C;

    X; Y; Z;

C: W

where *B′* is the inverse condition to *B* (assumed available — i.e. if '=' is in the language then so is '≠'). **begin** and **end** are *statement brackets*.

1.2 Preliminary definitions

The foregoing paragraphs may be held to contain the definitions of such terms as 'diagnostics', 'load and go', as we shall use them. Certain other definitions will have to be discussed at length. But it will be advantageous to define here our use of certain terms which belong to the underlying subject of data representation; the following definitions are equivalent for most practical purposes to those in the standard glossaries, but the form in which we give them has certain advantages from the formal point of view as regards their logical relations. (It may be worth recording that in this form they were drafted as part of a legal contract whose interpretation might be later subject to determination by the courts. The starting point was, what is this thing called a 'letter a' that, typed on a keyboard, preserves its identity while going all through the machine, to emerge finally on a line printer?)

A *digit* is
1. A mental concept with the property that it can assume any one of a finite number of states, or
2. Any representation of such a concept in physical form.

A *character* is
1. One of the states of a digit. When 'digit' is given the first of the above meanings, then the word 'character' in this sense may be qualified by the word 'abstract'.
2. Any representation of a digit in a particular state.

An *alphabet* is a complete set of associated representations of the states of a digit, i.e. a set of characters all in the same medium (or abstract) and with a one to one correspondence with all the states which the digit can assume.

A *numeral* is a character which has the semantic associations commonly given to the characters *0, 1, 2 . . . 9*

A *character string* (often simply *string*) is an ordered sequence of characters — i.e. a sequence of digits, each in a determinable state — with a first and a last member and in which each member except the last has a unique successor and each member except the first has a unique predecessor.

3

A *message* is a character string in a semantically defined context — i.e. in a context which provides rules for determining a meaning for the string. If the rules are unsuccessful, we may refer to an illegitimate or abortive message.

A *code* is
1. A correspondence between two ways of using the alphabets of two digits or two ways of using one or more alphabets of the same digit such that corresponding messages convey identical information.
2. The rules stating such a correspondence.
3. *Machine code* is that use of strings in a certain alphabet which is interpreted directly by the control mechanism of a computer. This expression should be 'machine language', but is in too general use to be abandoned altogether.

Note that the effect of these definitions is to make '365' a three-digit number, each of its digits being decimal (having a ten-character alphabet). On a cricket scoreboard, digits are rectangular windows or cup-hooks; characters are distinctive marks on cloth or on pieces of tin (possibly including the blank as a character). Omitted from the above are those definitions which refer to the interpretation of strings of numerals in a place-significant manner; these are too universally understood to give rise to possible difficulties, though their application gives rise to problems.

One other term and its associated notation warrants inclusion here, though hardly required until Section 7. In order to talk *about* a language it is usually necessary to go outside the language, and particularly so when the language in question is a specialized one designed for a limited purpose. If the talking about is to be done with mathematical precision, it may be necessary to invent another language for the purpose, with symbols over and above those of the subject language. Such a language is called a *metalanguage*, its characters metacharacters, and so on. Just as our illustrative language in Section 1.1 used English words in heavy type to create some of its new symbols, so, as far as possible, we shall use English words in special brackets, $\langle$ and $\rangle$, for variables in the metalanguage; other types of metasymbol will be introduced as and when required.

1.3 Objectives
Even in April 1963 it was possible for Automatic Programming Information (Goodman (1963)) to produce a list of over thirty languages which had been implemented in Britain. Six years later, in a monumental work, Sammet (1969) described 120 languages in varying but often considerable detail, but this work was confined to languages actually useable in the U.S.A. It also suffers, from our point of view, by a concentration on differences in superficial detail

(such as character sets) which obscures the underlying relationships. Despite these weaknesses, it is an invaluable work of reference, often written with first hand knowledge of the way development took place. Since then, other languages, including Algol 68, have appeared. In the light of all this evidence it is not good enough for a comparative study of programming languages to confine itself to the compilation of statements like 'Algol allows you to mix integer and floating point numbers but Fortran does not'. It must attempt to lay bare the underlying principles which distinguish a 'good' language from a 'bad' one. At this level there is room for differences of opinion. Consider that one speaker (Sproull, 1964) has told an American Congressional Committee that 'our goal is to permit the computer to accept English as we speak it', whereas most workers in the field insist that a programming language should be unambiguous. A writer once praised the summation convention in tensor calculus on the grounds that 'it makes you do useful things you wouldn't have thought of doing for yourself'. How many programmers would deem that a virtue in a language? (Maybe only users of APL).

Perhaps the best that can be said is that a good language will

1. Use a standard character set;
2. Allow you, somehow or other, to do anything you want to do which can be defined in the context of your problem without reference to machine matters which lie outside this context;
3. Make it easiest to express the solution to your problem in terms which conform to the best practice in your subject;
4. Allow such solutions to be expressed as compactly as possible without risking the obscurity which often accompanies compactness;
5. Be free of any constructions which can give rise to unintentional ambiguities;
6. Permit the sort of ambiguity which is resolved dynamically, if the nature of the problem calls for this;
7. Take over without change as much as possible of any well-formed descriptive language which is already established in the field in which the problem originated;
8. Permit transcription — e.g. reading aloud, hand or typewriting as well as punched cards or tape;
9. Allow of easy apprehension, i.e. it should be possible to read other people's programmes *more* as one would a novel and *less* as one does an examination set book, than most *current* programming languages permit one to do;

and so on. These concern mostly the user. The compiler-writer is in the position of mediator between the machine designer and the user

5

(except that he is terribly at the mercy of a *fait accompli* by the former). The features which make a language seem good to him are quite different. For example, it is advantageous to him if a message in the language can be interpreted without retracing one's steps. ('Two pages of the book . . .' seems clear enough, but has to be reconsidered if it continues '. . . of Psalms'. This sort of thing on the grand scale is very bad for the morale of a compiler.)

1.4 Maintenance

It is an advantage of an artificial language that its inventor can say exactly what its rules are. If, after experience with it, it appears that it can be improved, or conversely that some of its users are abusing it, then it is necessary that somebody should be responsible for deciding what changes are justified, or how ambiguities should be interpreted, and for publishing its decisions. Frequently the inventor is unsuited, for one reason or another, to undertake this task, and if the language is an important one it may be passed to some committee at a national or international level. The committee is then said to be responsible for the maintenance of the language.

2

THE NATURE OF LANGUAGE IN GENERAL

A precise definition of language is an elusive thing, but we come fairly close to one if we say that a language consists of a set of objects called its vocabulary, which can be combined into linear strings in accordance with certain rules known as its grammar, for communication to a recipient with the intention of inducing activity in the recipient relative to certain specific features abstracted from a general situation. Any such string is, according to our previous definition of the term, a *message*. The activity to be induced in the recipient may be internal to it, a mere 'awareness' of the features communicated, in which case the message is said to be in the *indicative* mood, or it may involve external activity, in which case the message is said to be in the *imperative* mood, but this is a crude and inadequate distinction. 'Think on these things' is indicative by this definition, though technically imperative. A lot depends on where the dividing line between internal and external is drawn. Subject to one rider, however, it will serve for the moment, the rider being that it must be possible to communicate *potential imperatives*, with more of a 'briefing' than a 'command' character about them, the recipient being immediately 'aware' of them but acting on them only in response to an overt imperative at some later time.

This distinction is one that is only partially respected by natural languages. It is respected in the command

On the word 'fire' raise rifles, pull triggers, reload and order arms ... fire!

It is ignored at one's peril in telling a small child to 'Go into the kitchen and fetch ...', since the child may well be out of earshot before it knows what it is to do when it gets there. An adult would realize the semantic incompleteness of 'Go into the kitchen', and, even though willing to do so, would probably say, 'What for?' before obeying. But one has seen a computer behave like a small child in this respect when presented with an incorrectly punched tape. One can even buy, as a practical joke, an object resembling an electric plug which has inscribed on it 'The Little Wonder Fuse Blower: Insert in Mains Socket and PRESS'; people have been known to read this inscription, hypnotically 'obey' it, and be surprised when the lights fail.

2.1 Natural and artificial languages

The associations which tie the vocabulary of a language to the features of the situations with which it deals, and thus determine the meaning of a string, are known as its *semantics*, and are usually completely conventional, even though the history of the language may show them to have a natural origin, and to this extent all language is highly artificial. However, it is usual to refer to some languages as natural and to others as artificial, meaning by the former those which possess the power of growth, and whose present form is the result of much evolution, and by the latter, ones which were created at a stroke and do not have this power of evolution. This is one sense in which Esperanto is an artificial language. Alternatively, we may define a natural language as one which is, or was, used somewhere, sufficiently for children to acquire its use in the natural course of development, without a conscious learning process. This raises interesting questions. Most children in civilized countries learn the numbers 0 . . . 9 in this way, and there may be more children in the world who have picked up elementary arithmetic in this way than there are children who have picked up, say, the language of some small African tribe. The language of elementary arithmetic is, in fact, a borderline case under this definition.

The relation between the above two approaches to the distinction between natural and artificial languages is not coincidental. Every language which is used as a means of communication between human beings will inevitably be required, sooner or later, to deal with situations of a hitherto unforeseen nature. As long as the two human beings understand each other they will not be put off by pedants complaining that they have dealt with the new situation by means of illegitimate extensions' of the language. Each intercommunicating group will force the language to meet its own needs, whether or not it has received formal instruction as to what is legitimate and what is not. In particular, each successive generation of children picking up and using a natural language in the second sense, will introduce evolutionary changes and make it a natural language in the first sense.

So a language is bound to change, but change is not always for the better. Any change which tends to cut us off from the established corpus of literature is bad, and extensions which arise unnecessarily, because the language already has the means to deal with the new situation, come under this head. So do careless blurrings of finer distinctions, which have the result that one half-baked idea is now expressed where two crisply expressed ones existed before. Against changes like this, the pedants should have our support.

2.1.1 Evolution in programming languages

Programming languages are not exempt from this process, much though this may be deplored in some quarters. But where programming languages are concerned, there is the complication that some of the communicating individuals are human and some are mechanical, and the latter are unable to apply the sensibility which the former possess in order to keep themselves abreast of evolutionary changes. Thus, on the one hand, use of these languages between human beings tends to enlarge and develop them, while on the other, the difficulty of 'teaching' a machine to 'understand' every idiom in a language has led to subsets and dialects of languages too numerous to mention.

A further complication introduced by the machine derives from the variety of card readers, tape readers, teleprinters and the like which are their organs of communication, and the author has met at least one machine which 'could not read its own handwriting' — that is to say, its output was in a code different from any of those which its input was designed to accept. This complication we shall regard it as our duty to avoid as much as possible, except in Sections 6 and 14.6–14.8 where we consider it in some detail.

2.2 Syntax and Semantics

The complete description of a language involves its grammar and its semantics, the former often being divided into accidence and syntax. There is no hard and fast dividing line between these three. Accidence recognizes a possible internal structure to the vocabulary, as when 'come' has variants 'comes' and 'came'. So far, those programming languages which have not tried to base themselves on English have been very successful in avoiding anything of this sort. One might, perhaps, think that in a programming language numbers were the equivalent of words, and their internal structure certainly matters, but Algol 60, for example, builds numbers up from numerals, etc, in its formal syntax, and only in the ACM input/output proposals for this language (in the identifiers 'output1', 'output2', etc) does anything even resembling accidence find a place.

Again, considering syntax and semantics, one might think that meaning played no part in determining the grammatical structure of a sentence, yet meaning determines our immediate analysis of

Time	flies	like	an	arrow
noun	verb	adverbial	article	noun
subject		preposition		

as is shown (Pfeiffer, 1960) from the fact that we equally immediately apply a different analysis to

Fruit	flies	like	a	banana
noun	noun	verb	article	noun
used adjectivally				

9

A somewhat different situation which we shall discuss again in Section 7.1.1 occurs in the different interpretations in

1. Your son hates games; John's hates work.
2. Your hates are ineffective; John's hates work.

2.3 The communication of algorithms

A programming language is distinguished from other languages in that its purpose is to communicate 'algorithms', that is, organized sequences of instructions. The oldest algorithmic language in the world is probably that used by Euclid for the description of constructions, as in the first proposition in his first book, which runs thus in English:

> To describe an equilateral triangle on the given straight line AB.
> From the centre A at the distance AB describe the circle BCD.
> From the centre B at the distance BA describe the circle ACE.
> From the point C at which the circles cut one another draw the straight lines CA and CB to the points A and B.
> Then ABC shall be an equilateral triangle . . . (here follows a proof of the validity of the construction) . . . and it is described on the given straight line AB.

The subject matter of this language comes very close to that required for machine control, for which the modern programming language Apt has been constructed. The most widely used programming language, if we admit organized sequences of instructions for control purposes as well as for computation, is probably the one in which the following extract is written:

> Using No. 11 needles cast on 130 sts.
> Work in K.1, P.1, rib for $3\frac{1}{2}$ in.
> *Next row* Rib 9, (inc, in next st., rib 6) 16 times, inc. in next st., rib to end (147 sts.)
> Change to No. 9 needles.
> *1st row* P.5, * (K.4, P.3,) twice, K ¹, P.2, K.1, P.3, rep from * to last 16 sts., K.4, P.3, K.4, P.5.
> *2nd and every alt. row* K.5, * (P.4, K.3) twice, P.1, K.2, P.1, K.3, rep from * to last 16 sts., P.4, K.3, P.4, K.5.
> *3rd row* P.5, * (K.4, P.3) twice, C.3, P.3, rep from * to last 16sts., K.4, P.3, K.4, P.5.
> *5th row* as 1st row.
> *7th row*, P.5, * C.7, P.3, C.3, P.3, rep from * to last 16 sts., C.7, P.5.
> *9th row* as 1st row.
> *11th row* as 3rd row.
> *12th row* as 2nd row.
> These 12 rows form the patt.
> Continue in patt. until work measures . . .

Experienced programmers will detect in this extract such features as bracketed sub-expressions, labels, and iterative loops terminating both on counts and on 'computed results', and in one instance a 'built-in check'. It also shows a hint of the 'procedure' or 'subroutine' with parameters, since 'C.3' and 'C.7' are defined earlier as

Work across next 4(11) sts., as follows. Slip next 3(7) sts., on to cable needle and leave in front of work, K. next st. (K.4), slip 2(3) sts. from cable needle on to lefthand needle and Purl, K. the st. (K.4) from cable needle.

2.4 Nature of computation

But although we ought, perhaps, to confine our study to languages which describe computational processes, emphatically we must not be too restricted in our ideas of what constitutes a computation. It is true that there is a tendency to think of computation in terms of numerical work. But viewed against the background of mathematics as a whole, computation takes on a rather different appearance; it becomes that part of mathematics which is concerned with 'getting answers', as opposed to analysing and deepening our understanding of abstract relations in general. Everything now turns on what sort of answers we hope to get. The process by which we obtain $x = (c-b)/a$ from $ax+b = c$ is as much 'getting an answer' as is the one by which we obtain $x = 4$ from $3x+2 = 14$. Furthermore, it is difficult to deny this same status to a successful response to a challenge in the form *Given the axioms . . . find a proof that . . .* , particularly seeing that computers have been programmed to do this. Each new discipline, such as 'Boolean algebra', 'Propositional Calculus', and so on, sets its own slant on what it means by computation. Finally, the processes involved in

$$x = (c-b)/a = (14-2)/3 = 12/3 = 4$$

namely, substitution and reduction, are so close in nature to those which would reduce

Your reply should be addressed to *(the local offices of the appropriate ministry) (your local consular official).
*Strike out whichever does not apply

to the form

Your reply should be addressed to '6, Sunset Gardens, Shortwick'

that again, the same machine can be programmed to do either, and it is manifestly wrong not to see that 'computation' covers both.

For these reasons, we shall regard computation as any form of character manipulation according to prescribed rules, while giving pride of place to those particular rules which, for example, permit the character string '26+5' to be replaced by the shorter string '31'. This still leaves a few details outstanding. Note that as linguists we are not concerned with either the accuracy or the efficiency of any algorithms which may be expressed in any of our languages, but only with the accuracy or efficiency with which the language describes or expresses those algorithms. Thus we have no moral duty to prevent a programmer from getting his machine into a tight loop because, by a slip of the pen, he wrote *R:* **go to** *R;* when he meant *R:* **go to** *P;* although we are concerned with whether, when he has done so, the language makes it easy for him to find and correct such a slip. But sometimes the exterior situation may appear to be wider than our definition allows for, as, for example, when a computer controls an industrial process. Such cases are covered by the definition we have already given for 'character', which allows characters to be followed through a variety of transformations, but effectively defines the limits of the computational system in a control situation as at the digitizers or digital-to-analogue converters.

2.5 Pure procedures

In one curious way, this extended concept of computation brings us full circle historically. The earliest machines were designed to operate upon numbers, and their instructions were coded into numerical form; now we write our instructions in a larger and more convenient character set, but permit the whole of this character set as potential participants in our operands. It used to be claimed that *because* instructions were numerically coded, the machines could operate upon their own programmes, but we can now see that this is only a half truth. It was the numerical coding which led us to appreciate the possibility, but the possibility itself is of wider application.

However, although most programs are modified by the system into a more convenient form while still in the potential imperative state, it seems that it is unnecessary to be able to modify a program which has become overtly imperative, provided that our languages possess a certain flexibility (which the earliest ones did not), and modern practice is all in favour of the *pure procedure*, or sequence of instructions which does not modify itself. Many languages admit no other. The original reason against impure procedures was the pragmatic one that if errors have been made in writing them, these errors are far harder to track down if the procedure has been allowed to alter itself. Later, a more compelling reason has appeared in the possibility that certain routines may be simultaneously in use by different users, who cannot be allowed to change them in ways detrimental to each other. It may therefore be worth while spending some time in considering the nature of the flexibility required. Although it appears in various guises in different contexts, essentially it would seem to be the power to select an operand which cannot be named explicitly at the time of writing the program. For a formal

12

investigation which covers this point see Elgot and Robinson (1964).

By the time a program comes to be obeyed by a machine it is in 'machine language'. The early machines used a language whose grammar was simplified (to make the engineering simple) to the point of considerable inconvenience. In effect all such grammatical devices as pronouns and relatives were eliminated, also dependent clauses of any kind. The use made of the power to alter the program most often took a form which we can paraphrase as follows (though the analogy must not be pressed too far). Faced with a question like

On what river does the capital of England stand?

this question would be broken into the two steps

What is the capital of England? . . . On what river does it stand?

and then, being up against the lack of any equivalent to 'it', into the following three steps

What is the capital of England. . . . Write your answer in place of 'Erewhon' in the following sentence. . . . On what river does Erewhon stand?

so that by the time the machine came to answer the final question, it had been modified into 'On what river does London stand?'. An example in actual machine code occurs in Section 9.1.

A number of devices introduced into machines at various times would all seem to be alternative ways of overcoming this difficulty. It must be remembered that the directions taken by these developments were often dictated by engineering considerations not easily reflected in this paraphrase. The B-line technique amounted to the two-step system:

What is the capital of England (write your answer on your scratch-pad)? On what river does . . . stand (fill in the blank from the scratchpad)?

The *obey* technique involved writing the modified *order* on the scratchpad (not modifying it *in situ*) and replacing the final instruction by 'Answer the question on the scratchpad'. Finally there was the indirect address technique, which, by giving access to the contents of the contents of an address, allows the programmer to write 'the name of the name of' whatever it is he requires, and in this way comes much closer to the form of the original question. Of these three, the B-line technique has been the most popular, probably for two reasons. First, it takes little or no time to implement, compared with the extra store accesses required by the other techniques. This could change with the state of the art in engineering. Secondly, it is wider in scope than our present description would imply, though it is less flexible in this respect than the 'obey' technique. In particular, as is well known, owing to the additive process which it employs, it can be used to select the *kth* member of a set (e.g. the component x_k of the vector x) by storing the set in consecutive locations and writing its initial address in the instruction and the suffix in the B-line (or *vice versa*). Here we return to the realm of linguistic study, for we may remark that the abilities of oblique reference (or indirect addressing) and of being able to write an algebraic suffix, are properties which belong to a language rather than to the machine it is implemented on, although if the machine code does not also possess them, then the implementation may be exceedingly inefficient.

2.6 Classification of Languages

The newcomer to the subject may well ask why there are so many languages. The primitive languages *had* to take into account how the machines worked. When broken down into steps at this level, 'Eat your breakfast' starts with 'Open your mouth' if talking to a child, but with 'Open your beak' if talking to a pet parrot. But for this very reason, these languages could express everything that the machine was capable of doing. Nevertheless, it is because man has the ability to absorb detail into more generalized expressions (thus avoiding being bogged down by it) that man has made progress, and so it was inevitable that more sophisticated languages should arise. When they did, a problem arose to which the following is an analogy. Suppose a typewriter were produced which had words instead of letters on its keys. Then it would be much faster and more accurate in use, but limited to the subjects covered by the chosen vocabulary, unless the ability to fall back on the letters was retained. So it was with programming; either the ability to do *everything* that the machine could do was sacrificed, *or* a loophole was left to fall back on machine language. And correct though the latter was in principle, in practice it meant that one still had to know whether one's machine had a 'mouth' or a 'beak', and while one was learning this (if one did not give up instead) it was almost easier (and often more congenial) to write a new language for the new subject.

With developments in other areas, the situation changed. In a multi-user situation, complete freedom at machine level may mean the ability to interfere with another user. For a few years a generation of prudes held sway, who considered it the function of a high level language to prevent you from saying, even in private, what it might be socially or politically undesirable to say in public. The development of minicomputers ended the credibility of this extreme position but we do have to add to the description of a 'good' language that it should make it easy to preserve a flexible attitude towards environmental taboos.

Again, every language is to some extent multi-purpose — because, for example, in a language designed for numerical calculations it still pays to be able to manipulate letters in order to produce an output which carries a few words of explanation and is not just a maze of numbers, while in a purely literary language it is still as well to be able to compute that the fifth line is three after the second! Should we not then work towards a genuinely all-purpose language? There are objections to this, but they are mostly met if the language is so designed that users need not learn more of it than they require for their particular type of problem, and if behind the language there is an underlying structure which guarantees that systems need not waste time eliminating alternatives which such a user will never avail himself of. But this is not the only efficiency problem; there is a more serious one which we can illustrate by an example. Most machines represent integers in binary form, or in binary coded decimal using a 1,2,4,8 weighting. On such machines much the quickest way of determining whether a number is odd is to form the logical 'and' function between unity and the number; this will be zero for even numbers and unity for odd ones. But this will not work if the machine uses a 1,2,2,5 weighting, or 'excess three' representation. The programmer is supposed to be protected from the need to know which representation the machine uses, and the language will probably forbid him to use logical functions on numerical data in consequence, so that he will be reduced to the exceedingly inefficient process of seeing whether double the integral part of half the number is equal to the original number! One answer to this is to make the function $odd(n)$ a system defined routine, implemented in different machines in different ways. But it is a slow process working out which are the operations whose efficiency is so system dependent that they ought to be defined in this way.

Another reason for the multiplicity of languages is that different attitudes to the problems involved have produced different types of languages. Some have groped their way towards the same methods of expression as are already familiar in natural languages, including among the latter the language of mathematics. These have tried to make their semantics completely independent of the machine. Others have aimed more at a generality of expression within the limitations of a particular machine or group of machines. Others have given particular attention to making allowance for the fact that computation is not exactly a *typical* everyday activity, and that therefore the best grammar for a computational language is likely to differ from that of natural languages. Two subdivisions must be recognized here, *procedural* languages, which recognize explicitly the sequential nature of most computational processes, and *functional* languages, which acknowledge only the one imperative 'evaluate', which can be left implicit, thus

15

(evaluate) ax^2+bx+c where $a = 2$, $b = -3$, $c = 1$, $x = 0,1,2...20$.

In some cases these represent trends, and not all languages have gone to an extreme in these matters. One particular problem was acute enough to give rise to a separate group of languages. In purely numerical work, the length of an operand, whether decimal or binary, can be kept within reasonable limits, but in other problems this is not so; as one example, every sixth-form mathematician knows the outrageously long expressions one can get by differentiating quite a harmless looking function. These problems gave rise to list-processing languages, but more recent trends have been to incorporate list-processing techniques into other types of language. (Giving the 'value' of x as $0,1,2...20$ is an example of this.)

2.7 The role of names in a programming language

Because the 'external world' to which a message in a programming language is related by its semantics is a peculiar and restricted, not to say introspective, affair, since it consists of character strings like those making up the message itself, certain ambiguities of interpretation which in natural languages lead only to mild irritation become, in this context, a serious source of confusion and error.

There are even two ways (at least) of picturing the external world. Some would argue that it involves abstract 'numbers *per se*', objects independent of the code used to generate representations (octal, decimal, roman etc.) for them. Although this is necessary in the mathematical theory of number, it seems unnecessary and possibly unhelpful in the present context; should it be required, then the definitions in Section 1.2 must be supplemented by *two* more, one for *numeral string* and one for *number*, since these must be kept distinct. On the other hand there are computational situations in which it clarifies matters if the external world is considered to be the store of some actual computer. This introduces the additional notions of a 'location' and its 'address'. Consider the following diagram — programming language on the left, interior of the computer on the right:

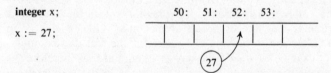

integer x;

$x := 27$;

The function of the compiler is to arrange for the association of the 'name', x, with the *address*, 52, and for the writing of (some representation of) the 'value', 27, in the 'location' so addressed. However, when the extraneous notions are eliminated we find that the interpretation of the high level language side is that (line 1) the new

16

name, x, is 'recognized' and (line 2) 'made' by some unspecified process 'to refer to' or 'to possess' the value, 27. We shall return to this picture in later chapters.

In some languages (Autocode, for example) there is a comparatively fixed set of names, but in others (Fortran, Algol) the message may create them at will, and in this case, in a real computer, it is preferable to regard the name as prior to the external object, which is created by associating a storage location with the name. The exigencies of this situation have led to a confusing multiplicity of uses of the word 'defined', and we shall try to avoid this by introducing alternative terms for some of the uses. We shall say that

1. A string is defined if its semantics are determinable. If the string is a name, its semantics are to that extent already determined, though they can be more precisely determined if we also know what sort of object is referred to. Thus a string may be 'more' or 'less' defined.
2. A name is 'sited' if there exists a corresponding external object otherwise it is 'siteless'. The external object may be called its site.
3. A site is 'filled' if a value has been assigned to its name, 'void' otherwise. A name is 'filled' or 'void' if its site is.

Thus the string $x := y$ is incompletely defined if y is void, and still less defined if y is siteless; it is clear what it intends us to do but far from clear what will happen if we try to do it. In some languages, but not all, it is assumed that void sites contain something that can be recognized as a specific value, 'void' or 'undefined'. In this case we may say that a value is (equal to) undefined. The usage which must be deprecated is that which appears to refer to a 'defined' or 'undefined' value. (Note: when names refer to pushdown stores, the need for care in these matters is even greater.)

Names can also refer to objects which are a part of the message itself — either values which are introduced by being embedded in the message, or more genuine parts of the message as such. Impure procedures are only possible if the grammar of the language (a) makes provision for names of the latter type, and (b) makes provision for assigning new values to these names, and in general, procedural languages need the former provision (for **go to** instructions) but avoid providing the latter. A name which refers to a part of the message as such is, roughly, what is usually called a *label*, although attempts to define this term strictly will reveal variations in its use (e.g. does it indicate a 'part of' the message or a 'point in' the message?). However, the concept of a name in computing theory is more complex than even the foregoing review would suggest, In the following sections we consider a number of subjects of general importance, and return to the theory of names after certain further foundations have been laid.

17

3

RECURSION

Experience in trying to teach the fundamentals of programming and of programming languages suggests that the concept of recursion is one which presents peculiar difficulties. In particular, programmers with considerable elementary experience seem to find it difficult to distinguish recursion from iteration, and, when they succeed in this, they find it difficult to see what the value of recursion is. The latter is not altogether surprising in view of the fact that in numerical work it often happens that a process is most efficiently performed iteratively even when there are advantages in defining it recursively. In other fields, however, this is not necessarily the case.

Iteration is the repeated performance of something until some condition is met, each performance being carried to completion, the condition being examined, and a new performance commenced if the result is unsatisfactory. In contrast to this, recursion involves a self-nesting; the performance is not carried to completion before the condition is examined, instead, the condition is examined within the performance and, if the result is unsatisfactory, the whole performance is asked for again as a subroutine of the as yet uncompleted original one. This description applies to recursive procedures, but the concept is also applied to definitions and structures. If we look at all three we shall have a surer grasp of the situation.

3.1 The nature of recursion

To see the two processes at work procedurally, consider two ways of finding the sum $f(1)+f(2)+ \ldots +f(n)$. In the first we define a subroutine

add term: add $f(k)$ to S, reduce k by 1, and return

Now we write

Set S to zero and k to n.
I: Plant a return link to J and transfer control to 'add term'
J: If k is not zero go back to I.

We thereby perform 'add term' n times, successively and independently, only one link being in use at any time; this is iteration. In the second we define

18

Sum(f, k) as equal to 0 if k = 0,
    otherwise equal to f(k)+Sum(f, k−1)

And now we can simply ask for *Sum*(*f, n*). Consider the case when
n = 2. We plant a return link to whatever we want to do after the
evaluation and transfer control to this definition. This causes us to
evaluate $f(2)$ and then calls for the evaluation of *Sum*(f,1) to be
added to it. So we must store away $f(2)$, plant another link, and re-
enter the definition. This leads to evaluating $f(1)$, again storing it
away and planting a third link before entering the definition a third
time to evaluate *Sum*(f,0). But this is zero, so we come out of the
definition using the link planted for this use of it, add the zero to
$f(1)$, again exit using the second link, add our '0+$f(1)$' to $f(2)$ and
make a final exit. This is recursion; our uses of *Sum* were not successive and independent but nested, and our three links were all
held simultaneously and referred to on a 'last planted, first used'
basis.

A curious feature of this example is that it is much less convincing
if the definition is revised by reversing the order of the addition and
making it *Sum*($f,k−1$)+$f(k)$. The effect of this reversal is far from
trivial in the amount of information which has to be stacked away.

As an illustration of recursive and iterative structures, we may
consider two English sentences. 'I came, I saw, I conquered' is an
iterative structure inasmuch as three similar units occur successively
as parts of the whole. (Inasmuch as the units are themselves sentences,
it is recursive). The sentence 'I said you think he is mad' is a recursive structure. I speak in sentences, so a sentence 'I said . . .' will have
a complete sentence as the object of 'said'; likewise you think in
sentences. The result is that in a sequence of only seven words we
have a sentence within a sentence within a sentence! Some more
horrible examples are given later.

Finally, in the field of definitions, our definition of *Sum*(f,k) is a
recursive definition because it defines *Sum* to a certain extent in terms
of itself. The concept of iteration is less straightforward here, but
generally speaking the iterative equivalent of a recursive definition
would seem to be a form which uses the unsatisfactory device of a
string of dots in the middle. A recursive definition must always
contain one non-recursive alternative, or it becomes circular in the
vicious sense, just as an iterative process must contain some means of
'getting out of the loop' — whether by requiring a number of itera-
tions which can be shown to be finite, or by requiring an exit when a
convergence test has been satisfied which it can be shown will be
ultimately satisfied. This necessary criterion of validity (and a corresponding one for recursive definitions) need not hold, however, for
all conceivable values of the argument of a function; if it does not,
then the function is undefined for values for which it does not hold.

For example, one would not necessarily expect an iterative process for square root to converge for negative values of the argument.

3.2 Applications of recursion

Our summation example is fairly typical of the situation in numerical work, in which the *recursive definition* is often neater, but the *iterative process* both looks and is more satisfactory in use. In consequence we must think of recursion as having two main spheres of importance.

The first is somewhat theoretical, and is that recursive definitions are the basis of the whole modern theory of computable functions (see, for example, Davis (1958)). For the sake of a later illustration, we sketch the beginnings of this. It is assumed that the *successor function* — call it $S(x)$ — exists for every positive integer and zero; it is $x+1$, of course, except that at this stage '+' has not been defined. Then the *predecessor*, $P(x)$, which will equal $x-1$ when '−' has been defined, is defined as

$P(x) = P'(x, 0)$ **where**
$P'(y,z) = [$**if** $S(z) = y$ **then** z **else** $P'(y,S(z))]$

This starts z at 0 and 'successorizes' it until its successor is x and then seizes it as the answer. The sum of two numbers is now

$Sum(x,y) = [$**if** $y = 0$ **then** x **else** $Sum(S(x),P(y))]$

and the difference

$Diff(x,y) = [$**if** $y = 0$ **then** x **else** $Diff(P(x),P(y))]$

But these processes can run into trouble. $P(0)$ will hunt for ever through the positive integers seeking a predecessor to zero, and if $y > x$ then *Diff* will reach a stage at which it calls for $P(0)$. For this reason *Diff* is said to be only partially computable (over the positive integers). There are various ways (which do not concern us here, though see Section 7.7.1) out of this impasse, and it has been shown that it is possible to define in this way every function which a computer can compute (including the rational approximations to transcendental functions, etc), and to provide a basis for demonstrating that there are some things it cannot do. Although most of these lie outside our scope, some of its results concern us here. For example, there is the question of the 'decidability' of a language, which we explain in Section 7.3.

The second important use of recursion arises because the situation in numerical work is not altogether typical. In particular, procedures for analysing structures which may be recursive are most efficient if they themselves are recursive, and they must at least incorporate features which would be unnecessary in the absence of recursion in the data. In brief, we saw that an unlimited, last in first out, store for links and intermediate data is required by a recursive procedure and most translators which are not written as recursive procedures seem to find it expedient to use a similar list or lists for temporary storage of some part of the primary data (i.e. of the message being translated) instead. Thus although recursion may be a luxury, even an extravagant luxury, in languages whose primary field is numerical, this is far from the case in general, and in languages for writing compilers and translators in particular.

3.3 Miscellaneous comments

It may also be worth mention that there are certain functions which are easily defined recursively but which cannot be defined in terms of ordinary algebraic expressions. Newell (1961) cites as an example, referring to Perlis (1959) and Kleene (1952), Ackerman's function, defined over the positive integers and zero by

$$A(m,n) = \textbf{if } m = 0 \textbf{ then } n+1 \textbf{ else if } n = 0 \textbf{ then } A(m-1,1)$$
$$\textbf{else } A(m-1,A(m,n-1))$$

The nearest one gets to an algebraic definition of this function contains exponents connected by a string of dots!

Once a computer is programmed to handle recursive structures as such, and not, for example, as first, second, third level occurrences with no provision for a fourth, it is not worried in any way by the number of levels involved. (Store size sets a limit, of course, but this is never likely to be reached in sentence analysis problems, where limits are set by the length, and not the value of the input data). However, although natural languages have a recursive structure, our ability to handle this feature seems to be restricted, especially when the outer structures surround the inner ones. (In 'I said you thought he was mad' they all end together, and all the return links can be taken in a single jump. See also Section 7.5.) Miller (1965) quotes two examples. In the first, sentences are nested, and only to one level more than in our simple example, but the links have to be recovered one by one. This is

The audience who just heard, 'The person who cited, "The king who said, 'My country for a horse,' is dead," as an example is a psychologist,' are very patient.

In the second, relative clauses are nested. In the form

She thanked the producer who discovered the novel that became the script that made the movie that was applauded by the critics,

each clause drops a level of subordination but is not embedded in the strict sense of being surrounded on *both* sides by its superior. Truly embedded it becomes practically unintelligible, even with the help of two forms of brackets:

21

The movie (that the script [that the novel (that the producer [whom she thanked] discovered) became] made) was applauded by the critics.

Our tolerance limit seems to be at about the second level:

The novel, that the producer (whom she thanked) discovered, became the script. . .

But a little further fooling in this direction suggests that it is rather easier to keep control if, by using distinct constructions (even '. . . that . . . which . . . whom . . .' is slightly easier than '. . . that . . . that . . . that . . .') we can make the burden on the memory less purely quantitative. The moral would seem to be that easy apprehension of the meaning of a text in a programming language will be assisted by the deliberate provision of what Strachey (1963) would have called 'alternative varieties of syntactic sugar'.

4

POLISH NOTATION

A number of languages are based on a concept known as Polish notation; this has advantages for machine codes but is difficult for human digestion. It is so called because it was first introduced by the Polish philosopher Lukasiewicz in connection with the formulae of symbolic logic. A variation more properly called 'reverse Polish' is more popular today in computing circles.

When an operator occurs *between* its operands, as in $a+b$, it is described as *infixed*. Evaluation of an expression such as

$$3 \times 5 + 7 \times 11 \qquad \text{(A1)}$$

must pay due attention to the superior 'binding' of the multiplication sign, and can be performed with the aid of a 'stack' and instructions which affect only the top one or two objects on the stack, thus:

Instruction, leading to ...	Stack ('top' on the right)
Take 3	3
Take 5	3 5
Multiply	15
Take 7	15 7
Take 11	15 7 11
Multiply	15 77
Add	92

The instructions in this form can be abbreviated to the following:

$$3 \quad 5 \quad \times \quad 7 \quad 11 \quad \times \quad + \qquad \text{(B1)}$$

which is a transformation of (A1). A corresponding transformation of

$$(3 \times 5 + 7) \times 11 \qquad \text{(A2)}$$

would be

$$3 \quad 5 \quad \times \quad 7 \quad + \quad 11 \quad \times \qquad \text{(B2)}$$

As can be seen in these examples, and can be proved in general (see Section 7.1.1), the B-forms are unambiguous in spite of the fact that they contain no brackets. They are the reverse Polish notation forms equivalent to the standard notation A-forms.

Reverse Polish is based on an $\langle$operand$\rangle\langle$operand$\rangle\langle$operator$\rangle$, or post-fixed operator structure; direct Polish is based in a similar way

23

on prefixed operators — ⟨operator⟩⟨operand⟩⟨operand⟩ — and in our examples would give

$$+ \quad \times \quad 3 \quad 5 \quad \times \quad 7 \quad 11 \qquad \text{(C1)}$$
$$\times \quad + \quad \times \quad 3 \quad 5 \quad 7 \quad 11 \qquad \text{(C2)}$$

The first of these may be read *sum*(*prod*(3,5),*prod*(7,11)), but, like the inverse Polish forms, they are unambiguous without any need for brackets.

The diagram in Figure 1a is instructive, as it shows the vocabulary elements in direct Polish order when projected on the left and read downwards, but normal order when projected vertically. A topology preserving transformation of the figure gives Figure 1b, which shows reverse Polish order when projected on the left and read upwards.

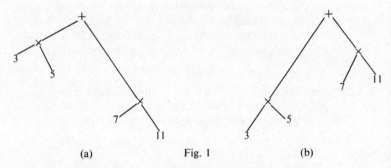

(a)   Fig. 1   (b)

Since the order of the items in reverse Polish is the order in which they have to be considered for manipulation, it will be apparent that the transformation to reverse Polish (suitably generalised) is implicit in every process of compilation. So far as algebraic expressions are concerned, the following algorithm achieves this transformation:

Z: Read next item to A

    if A holds an object, output it and **go to Z else**

    if it holds a closing bracket **then** unload the stack till the opening bracket is met, abolish both and **go to Z else**

Y: **if** it binds more tightly than the item on the top of the stack, or is an opening bracket **then** place it on the top of the stack and **go to Z else**

    output the operator on top of the stack and **go to Y**

and a wide range of syntactic structures can be compiled by suitable further elaboration of this algorithm.

4.1 The Stack

Increasing sophistication in programming languages has made it increasingly difficult to discuss their semantics without some reference to underlying mechanisms, although the less tied these are to a particular implementation the better. The commonest of these mechanisms is a generalization of the 'stack' as described in the previous section.

As there described, there is no need ever to access anything but the top of the stack; an operation such as 'add' can remove two items in succession, add them, and put the result back. For this form of stack, 'push-down store' is a synonym. One aspect of the generalization is that we wish to retain the means to access items deep down, and since there have been implementations in which this is impossible, it is better to reserve 'pushdown store' for the latter cases, keeping 'stack' for the generalizable form. A stack has a solid base, its top moves; the top of a pushdown store stays in the same place. However, a pushdown *list*, as it might be implemented in Lisp (Chapter 12) is one way of implementing a stack as we define it, though not a very efficient one.

Systems vary in the number of stacks they use and in what they use them for. The following is a typical structure for a single all-purpose stack, shown at the moment for executing a statement $x := y$ which occurs in the body of a procedure f called in the course of executing $z := a+b * f(a, b)$ in a block J:

```
Stack TOP pointer SP:
                 value of y        ⎫ working space of f  ⎫
           Z: address of x         ⎭                     │

                 ⋮                 ⎫ locals of f
                                   ⎭

                 pointer to Z       ⎫ information needed   ⎧ region whose
Chain pointer   CH: pointer to W    ⎬ on return to or      ⎨ structure is
                 return address     ⎭ on exit from f       ⎩ known to f
                 entry to f
                 ⋮      ⎫ frozen para- ⎫ closure
                 ⋮      ⎭ meters of f  ⎭ of f

                 value of b         ⎫ actual parameters    ⎫
           Y: value of a            ⎭ of f planted in J    │
                                                           │
                 value of b                                │
                 value of a         ⎫ working space        ⎮
           X: address of Z          ⎭ of J                 ⎧ region whose
                                                           ⎨ structure is
                 ⋮                 ⎫ locals of J           ⎩ known to J
                 ⋮                 ⎭

                 pointer to X
           W: pointer to block below                       ⎭
                 ⋮
```

With this structure, the result of f is formed at Z and must be copied down to Y on exit from f; this is the price paid for the convenience of putting everything into a single stack. This model, by omitting block levels, also assumes that all globals of f are treated as frozen parameters — frozen in the course of processing the declaration of f.

25

5

THEORY OF NAMES

In the first edition it was remarked that 'there is as yet no received theory of names, although there is a great need of one'. Eight years later, the major change has been the appearance of the Algol 68 reports. These have developed their own theory, sounder and more thorough than anything preceding them, and a very satisfactory basis for the language they introduce. But as a candidate for a received theory, this theory avoids rather than answers some of the questions raised by other languages, and it is too early to dismiss these questions as misconceived. We outline their theory in Section 13.3.1, and retain the current chapter with minor revisions as of historical and collateral interest.

5.1 Names and codewords

The first problem arises out of temporary working space for recursively used routines. Each time the routine is entered, a new and independent working area will be required, without abandoning what has already been raised. Dijkstra has coined the happy phrase 'simultaneous *incarnations* of the routine' to describe this situation. What it implies here is that a letter, used to name a working variable of a routine, may have several store locations reserved for it, although all but one of these are very much 'in reserve' at any one time. This shows that, depending on how we handle simultaneous incarnations, it is more or less essential to keep the ideas of the name in the language and the address in the store independent of one another.

Further, when a name is introduced into a mathematical formalism, it is introduced with certain implied properties. We begin with 'let *x* be. . .' . These properties are lost if a name becomes transformed simply into an address. If we restore this information we arrive at (a slight generalization of) what Iliffe (1961, 1962) calls a *codeword*. Using the abbreviation E-object to mean an object external to the program, we may define this as follows

A codeword is an E-object which contains the address of another E-object together with information as to how the contents of this E-object are to be interpreted.

To avoid giving a false impression of Iliffe's own use of the word, it should be added that the second E-object may be composite (a list) and in this case an important part of the information is the number of components, and how to select the *nth* one. Note, too, that compiled machine code is an E-object, and that the above definition does not prevent a codeword from containing the equivalent of a label or of a routine name, or even of a piece of machine code constructed during the running of the programme. In its fully developed form (Iliffe (1971)), this theory becomes one of machine design, one of the unfortunately far too rare examples of language theory feeding back into that area.

An important distinction is made in algebra between 'bound' and 'free' variables in the context of certain constructions. Within such a construction the free variables have the same meaning as they do outside it, but bound variables are completely internal to it, and are dummies in the sense that any other letters will do just as well (excluding such as would lead to confusion). They arise in two ways. (1) In a context like

$$\int_0^\infty e^{-tx}.f(x)dx$$

the letter x could be replaced by any other (except t or f) without affecting the meaning of the expression in any context in which it might be written. (2) In a definition of a function such as

$$\dots \text{ where } g(x) = a.\sin(px+q)$$

the letter x is again a dummy. Computationally these two cases are very different. In the first, x is almost certainly the name of an object created temporarily to assist in the evaluation of the function; in this case it is an object of the same sort as t, and in computational usage it is described not as a bound variable but as a local variable. (Thus a local variable is a piece of explicitly named temporary working space.) In the second case the x is due to be replaced by something more significant whenever the definition is applied. It is called a *formal parameter*, the expression which replaces it during an actual call being referred to as an *actual parameter*. In one sense, therefore, it has no real existence and no storage will ever be required for it. But an alternative point of view could be that it is an object whose value is another name — that of the actual parameter, although this concept still needs further study if it is to cover the case in which the actual parameter is an expression which is not a variable, as in $g(t^2+2)$. Alternative approaches here are (1) that an expression can be a value, and (2) that the value must be an implicit label. On the codeword side the implication is that among the alternative interpretation-cues available there must be two, one of which allows the value found at the address in the codeword corresponding to the formal parameter to be another codeword, and the second of which allows the value of the latter to be a piece of machine code which is to be obeyed in order to obtain the implicit value of the former. The words *argument* and *operand* are both used synonymously with *parameter* and *bound variable* by some writers. The suggested 'name whose value is a name' shows a close relationship between parameters and indirect addressing.

5.2 Lambda notation

Church (1941) introduced a notation for the definition of functions in which the symbol λ plays a special part; in this notation the above definition of $g(x)$ is written

$$g = \lambda(x)[a.\sin(px+q)]$$

and instead of $g(t^2+2)$ one can write

$$\lambda(x)[a.\sin(px+q)](t^2+2)$$

That is, λ is followed by two or three further syntactic units; first there is a list of bound variables, then an expression involving these variables (the *body* of the λ-expression). If we stop at this point, we have a 'function divorced from any operands', such as '*sin*' or 'the Bessel function J_2'. But this may be followed by a list of actual operands; in this case we have the result of applying the function to these operands.

For an alternative notation for implying use of parameters see Section 8.

5.2.1 Recursive functions in lambda-notation

There is no *obvious* difficulty in applying λ-notation to recursive definitions; for example, we can write

$$\text{Sum} = \lambda(x,y).\textbf{if } y = 0 \textbf{ then } x \textbf{ else } \text{Sum}(S(x),P(y))$$

in place of the form given in Section 3.2. But Landin (1964), in his work on the semantics of CPL and other languages, prefers to follow Curry (1958) and make the following further transformation in this case. By a second dose of λ-notation all recursive references are removed from *inside* the definition

$$\text{Sum} = [\lambda f.\lambda(x,y).\textbf{if } y = 0 \textbf{ then } x \textbf{ else } f(S(x),P(y))](\text{Sum})$$

and then the definiend is removed altogether from the right hand side by assuming the existence of an operator **Y** such that if F is a function, then $\mathbf{Y}F$ is the solution of $x = F(x)$.

$$\text{Sum} = \mathbf{Y}\lambda f.\lambda(x,y).\textbf{if } y = 0 \textbf{ then } x \textbf{ else } f(S(x),P(y))$$

Now in this definition f is a bound variable being 'solved for and found to have' the value *Sum*; it can be replaced by *Sum* or by anything else, but to replace it by anything else would be rather foolish. So we write

$$\text{Sum} = \mathbf{Y}\lambda\text{Sum}.\lambda(x,y).\text{if } y = 0 \text{ then } x \text{ else } \text{Sum}(S(x),P(y))$$

And if this seems to be back where we started, then we must point out that what $\mathbf{Y}\lambda$ achieves is (a) to remove all suspicion of circularity, (b) to remove all doubt as to the propriety of ascribing the same meaning to a variable occurring bound inside and free outside the expression in which it is bound, and (c) to permit the right hand side to be used in isolation. What $\mathbf{Y}\lambda$Sum means is that within the expression that follows, *Sum* refers to the whole expression. This transformation has influenced the way in which recursively defined routines are handled in CPL; it would appear to be the origin of the somewhat retrograde step (Dijkstra, 1963) of *requiring* recursive routines to be explicitly declared as such by the prefix *rec*, instead of *permitting* a routine to be declared non-recursive when this will permit more efficient translation.

5.3 Assignment as an all-purpose imperative

The effect of Church's notation is that definition of a function is brought under the form of an assignment statement (the '=' is certainly not relational, even if it is more definitional than imperative). And by implication, *g* is an object whose value is $\lambda(x)[a.sin(px+q)]$ in spite of the fact that it is not a variable in the algebraic sense. It is a type of object whose value is, in a sense, its meaning, in which it also resembles the variable whose value is an expression. One result of this is that the concepts of 'literal', 'constant' and 'variable' which we shall shortly discuss must be held to apply to functions as well as to any other sort of value.

In view of the way computers work, it would not be surprising if statements in a 'primitive' language, such as might suffice for definition of formal semantics (Section 7.6), were all assignment statements; it is therefore gratifying to observe that *go-to* statements can also be brought under this form by assuming the existence of a special variable called **control**, whose value does not remain constant, but points continually to the 'active spot' in a program. To explore this, consider a particular case of the program quoted in Section 1.1, namely,

$$x := 1; \quad y := 1; \quad k := 1;$$
$$Q: x := kx+1; \quad y := ky; \quad k := k+1;$$
$$\text{if } y < 100 \text{ then go to } Q; \quad e := x/y$$

We could rewrite this in several ways out of which we choose the following only because it best illustrates the points we want to make.

29

$$x := 1; \quad y := 1; \quad k := 1; \quad z_1 := S;$$
$$z_2 := \text{control}; \quad x := kx+1; \quad y := ky; \quad k := k+1;$$
R: $\text{control} := \text{if } y < 100 \text{ then } z_2 \text{ else } z_1;$
S: $\quad e := x/y$

Note that alternative forms for the statement labelled R are

R1: **if** $y < 100$ **then control** $:= z_2;$
R2: **control** $:=$ **if** $y < 100$ **then** z_2 **else** S;
R3: $i :=$ **if** $y < 100$ **then** 2 **else** 1;   **control** $:= z_i;$

and that using either R1 or R2, the statement $z_1 := S$ is unnecessary. This concept is valid enough that some machines (the Atlas being one) have no jump order, but have one address (store or accumulator) which plays the part of the variable we have here called **control**.

5.4 Implications of assignment

As a second method of approaching the subject, consider what happens when we simulate this program manually. What we do is to write out something like

x:	1		2		5		16		65		326	
y:		1		1		2		6		24		120	
k:			1		2		3		4		5		6
e:													2.717

it being understood that in each line whenever a value is inserted the previous one is crossed out. Now most languages require the complete form of a program to begin with the equivalent of 'let x, y, and k be integers...'. Many computers are so organized as to deal differently with integers and with numbers which may contain a fractional part (rational approximations to real numbers); indeed the latter often require a greater storage space than the former. So 'let x ...' becomes an indication to the computer to allocate an appropriate amount of storage and to associate the letters x, y .. with the storage so allocated. This corresponds fairly closely to our action in putting these letters as the 'titles' to successive lines, but since computers are relatively less efficient at searching and association than we are, and since their storage locations are all numbered (with addresses), the compiler usually makes a transformation in the programme equivalent to

1: line4 $:= 1;$ line5 $:= 1;$ line6 $:= 1;$
2: line4 $:=$ line4.line6 $+ 1;$ line5 $:=$ line5.line6;
    line6 $:=$ line6$+1;$
3: **if** line5 < 100 **then go to** line2;   **stop**;
4: 1   2   }   etc, inserted during running
5:   1   1   }   of program
6:     1   }

Note that optionally the compiler can render line 3 as

3: **if** integer in line5 $<$ 100 **then go to** instruction in line2;

it is now combining information about the nature of the contents of the addresses with the addresses themselves; in other words it is adopting something nearer the codeword approach. If x and y were bound variables something more elaborate would be required; possibly line4 might be preloaded with 'use line27' or something to that effect. However, it is much more satisfactory if line3 can read 'if integer whose address is in line5 . . .'

But having once introduced the inside of the computer, we can make a third approach. For this purpose let us suppose that ':=' is but one of many symbols of the general form '?='. Then x $?=$ y is only valid if x refers to an object (is sited), and its effect is to change the value of that object — the various forms changing it in different ways. What can it change it to? Possibilities, not all applicable in every context, are

1. The literal 'y'. E.g. after x $?=$ cat, the value of x is a string of three letters, c, a, t, copied from the string in the instruction and belonging uniquely to x.
2. The name of the literal 'y' in the program. E.g. if x $?=$ cat is stored in locations 50–54, then the value of x becomes '52–54', or some equivalent like 52(3) (meaning three characters starting in location 52).
3. The name of a unique literal 'y' elsewhere in the program. This, with minor variation only, must be what happens at 'z_1 := S' in the illustration program.
4. The value of the object of which 'y' is the name. This is the usual interpretation by which, after $y := 2; x := y;$ the value of x is 2.
5. The name (inside the computer as an address) of the object whose name (outside the machine, in the program) is 'y'. (I.e. the codeword for 'y'.)
6. In case the value of y should be a name (as it will be if it was assigned by a $?=$ of type 5), the value of the object whose name is the value of y. This is a form of indirect addressing, and as the result may be another codeword, we must add
7. As (6) but 'fully transparent', continuing until a value which is not a codeword is reached.

These seven possibilities apply when the right-hand side of an assignment statement is a single name, and they are not exhaustive, because we still have not considered complications such as names which have λ-expressions as their values. But the right-hand side may be an expression containing several names, in which case the possibilities apply to them independently. This shows that the '?=' notation has served its usefulness in directing our thoughts, and must now be

31

abandoned. Also options (6) and (7) apply equally (with slight modification) to the left-hand side — another pointer in the same direction.

It is tempting to argue that 'what goes on inside the computer' ought to be eliminated from the semantics of a good programming language, but it is not quite as simple as that; the computer in the abstract serves as a model of the semantics of the language (cf. Gilmore, 1963). For example, we can clarify the semantics of a possible instruction of the form 'let x mean y' by saying that it involves $x \ ?= y$ in sense (5), with all subsequent references to x in the context $z := \ldots x \ldots$ bearing interpretation (6) so far as x is concerned; the value of x becomes the codeword for y and subsequent calls for x yield the value currently associated with the codeword which is the current value of x. The peculiarity required of the subsequent calls need not be compiled into them, it can be the result of including a suitable mark in the information part of the codeword at the time when it is assigned to x as its value — a mark which says to the world at large 'treat me as transparent'.

5.5 Literals

A constant is an object whose value never changes. In the written language advantage can be taken of this to use its value as its name; it is then called a literal.

It is unfortunate that letters are usually not literals whereas numbers are, but this is due to the fact that x usually stands for a number whereas 12 is 'literally' 12. Consider the character π. This is conventionally a constant with the value 3.14159 . . . and therefore not a literal. Convention can be broken in either direction. Greek scholars, or mathematicians who want their results in algebraic form, will require it to be a literal; conversely one can use π as a variable just as one does x or any other letter.

Within a machine the address of an object is unlikely to be its value, and a rather different concept of a literal is required — if, indeed, there is much use for it at all. Since an address is an integer, many machines permit some economy in storage by making available instructions of the form 'add the number n' as well as of the form 'add the contents of address n', but this is so restricted a 'literal' usage that it may well have to be ignored during compilation and introduced later during an optimization process. (Option (2) in the interpretation of '$?=$' is a somewhat similar device; its main virtue is that it saves copying when circumstances permit such an economy.) In a more general way, whenever a value is stored within the program and subject to the 'write-protection' which guarantees pure procedures against accidental alteration, then there is some point in referring to it as a literal.

If the same literal occurs at several places in a program (as, for

32

example, '1' in '$x := x+1;$ $y := y+1$'), each occurrence can 'be itself', though some compilers in fact prefer to regard them all as names of a single external value, probably because it facilitates a standard treatment. (All codewords will require the same storage space, and the variable element, which is the length of the literal itself, is taken outside the program.) But this is not so of other constants. A constant, unless system defined (as π might well be), must occur as a literal once in a program, at that point where it is defined, and other uses must name the object which is in the definition. This is outstandingly true of labels, and hardly less so of definitions of procedures, etc. An awkward fact is that one of the 'other' uses can easily occur before the 'defining' one; compiler writers are all too familiar with the various ways of getting over the difficulties this gives rise to.

5.5.1 Notation for literals

In natural languages, quotes are used to mark the distinctions we have been discussing, but the usage is not entirely consistent, and the only universal rule is that surrounding a character string in quotes signals a departure from the interpretation which would otherwise be in force. Usually in programming languages it converts the contents of the quote from non-literal to literal. This is the same as the usage in English by which

Jack is singular

means that a certain boy (whose name is 'Jack' and who is, in a sense, the value of this name) is rather odd, whereas

'Jack' is singular

means that the four-letter string is (a noun which has the property of being) singular. But English can also provide precedents for the converse usage. Thus we may write any one of the following sentences:

1. He was elevated to the chair.
2. He was 'elevated' to the chair.
3. He was literally elevated to the chair.

Where (1) is neutral in tone, in (3) any metaphoric usage in (1) is removed — i.e. he not merely went up to a superior position in the hierarchy but was caused to go up physically in space. But in (2) the effect of the quotes may be either the same as that of 'literally' in (3), or may be precisely the opposite, making it sarcastic (he was removed to a place where he could no longer be a nuisance) and even less literal. The pitfalls of trying to ignore the distinction altogether can be seen in a sentence such as

Jack is a noun, and is a conjunction.

A further complication arises from the fact that early computational work was numerical; this has given rise to the convention that sequences of numerals are literals even without quotes. But then, perversely, many languages which adopt this convention break it by allowing integers as labels. In Algol, compiler writers have gone on strike over this point, and have generally refused to implement integer labels. The issue became acute in Algol because it was the first language to combine bound variables of label type with call by name (actual parameters not being reduced to a value before entering the procedure), with the result that in an actual parameter list a situation could arise in which it was not clear from the immediate context whether an integer was a literal or a name.

5.6 A formal theory of names

It is obvious that up to this point we have been collecting a scrapbook of matters which cannot be overlooked in a more coherent theory. Can such a theory be presented?' What follows is merely a sketch which tries to avoid both the less necessary constraints and the more grievous traps.

One fairly clear-cut approach is suggested by a paper of Gilmore (1963), and although it generalizes his presentation somewhat, we take the liberty of applying his name to it, and defining a Gilmore system as one in which

1. Any string of characters is eligible to be a name. Names may be valid, invalid or intrinsic.
2. Each name has (potentially) an intermediate value and a final value.
3. A result is the final value of a 'program' — i.e. of a character string supplied to a machine for interpretation as a name.
4. Rules exist by which certain names are assigned immediate final values — e.g. there are rules for determining that a string is a literal.
5. A definition is a subsequence of a program whose semantics is that a certain literal is the final value of a certain name.
6. For names to which a final value cannot be assigned in either of the above ways, there are rules for transforming a string into its intermediate value. The result of this transformation is a sequence of names of which one is an operator and the remainder are operands. (There are some degenerate cases. Note that it is the transformation rules which distinguish when a name is eligible to be an operator.)
7. There are rules by which the result of operating by any operator on appropriate final values as operands can be evaluated.
8. When the final value of a name is not immediate (under (4) or

34

(5)) it is recursively defined as being the result obtained by applying the operator to the final values of its operands.

9. A name is valid when the application of the rules leads to a final value. An intrinsic name is one which has no value but is permitted under (6) and (7) as an operator. All other names are invalid. The set of all valid names under a given set of rules is a language.

10. Note that when the program is in a Polish notation the transformation under (6) consists merely of splitting the string into substrings; in other cases it may be more complicated. In a language using λ-calculus, a name whose final value (however derived) is a λ-expression without parameters ranks as an operator.

But this approach as it stands applies only to function languages. Something more, bringing in the external world more explicitly, and relating names to codewords, is required in general.

We therefore define a value as a string of characters held at an address in store. Input and output values are included by a suitably wide definition of store, and the notion of address includes that of a sequence of addresses to accommodate values of various lengths. A program is a particular example of a value once it is in the machine. There is a pre-grammar whose function is to divide any string of characters into 'words'. It may be trivial — e.g. 'spaces separate words' — but it is also flexible and can alter its interpretation according to circumstances — e.g. it might first determine whether certain conditions hold under which the rule is that 'full stops separate words'. However, one invariable rule is that from an opening quote to its mating closing quote is indivisible. This rule is tempered by the fact that the value on which the pre-grammar is called upon to operate can begin inside outer quotes.

There is a dictionary, which is in (at least) two parts, a system part and a part which can be added to or subtracted from by a program (if several programs are running at once each has its own second part). The dictionary consists of a 'lexicon' or series of 'entries' (character string plus associated material) and a 'rubric' or set of rules for applying the lexicon. The function of a dictionary is 'to record the interpretation of words', and in our case the dictionary may record that a word

(a) is an intrinsic name, and provide details of the effect of using it as an operator, or

(b) is a sited name, and provide means for obtaining its codeword.

The second of these is deliberately a little vague to allow room for alternative ways of handling, e.g. a name which refers to the top of a push-down list or stack, some of which might involve a short calculation to obtain the codeword. The first might also provide a codeword

35

to a section of program. If a word is not 'found' in the dictionary, the rubric may invoke the pre-grammar to split the name and re-enter the dictionary recursively. (This provision allows for such features as subscripted names.) Any word which can neither be found nor analysed is treated as a literal — this will usually be the case with strings of numerals.

One of the most difficult aspects of this approach is that it requires generalization of the concept of evaluation. There is a sense in which it is fair to call 'it will produce 2.717 as the value of e' an evaluation of the program in Section 5.3. I.e. the number is the value of e, but its production is the outcome of the evaluation of the program; evaluation is a process which, applied to imperative strings, means obeying them, with results that are important but do not include the assignment of a value to the string. In generalizing the Gilmore system to include procedure languages it is necessary to permit the process of evaluation to include such operations as adding to and taking from the dictionary (both lexicon and rubric, in general) together with the storage allocation actions which these operations imply.

This problem is the same as is dealt with by Landin (1965, Pt. II), and it also arises in the use of the word 'evaluation' by Ross (1962; see Section 15.4). Here we are concerned primarily with the nature of a 'name'; the theory as we have sketched it is thought to be complete and sound at an abstract level, but to call for much work on, for example, how to keep the rubrics consistent. Interpretations which cannot be brought within its scope run considerable risk of running into trouble through inadequate definition of the relation between the names of the language and the codewords which correspond to them in the external world.

6

SYSTEMS ASPECTS

English is English whether spoken by a soprano or by a bass, with an American or British accent, and a poem is the same poem whether printed in a large and sumptuous library edition or a small-print paper-back. One may ask how far differences of this sort are permissible in programming languages. In fact, there is considerable divergence between what the various programming languages will tolerate in this respect.

The normal input to a computer is either 80-column punched cards or punched paper tape. A large computer will have both. The former has twelve rows, and therefore twelve punching positions per column, whereas the latter has five, six, seven or eight punching positions across the tape. In theory, therefore, alphabets ranging from 2^5 ($= 32$) to 2^{12} ($= 4096$) characters are in use, but in practice, cards used this way are rarely punched with more than three holes per column, while on the smaller paper tapes some characters are reserved for functions similar to the 'shift lock' and 'shift release' of the typewriter, so that alphabets of between forty and eighty characters have been the rule. Alongside any computer installation there will be separate equipment which can read cards or tape and produce therefrom paper printed with normal alphabetic and other signs, colloquially known as 'hard copy' (or as 'listed copy' — a shibboleth for detecting the card user). In the case of card equipment, one card produces one line of print made up of eighty characters; from tape each character corresponds, as it were, to pressing one key of a typewriter (shift keys counting as separate depressions). A line of hard copy from tape is thus whatever occurs between one 'carriage return' symbol and the next; it is of no particular length, and the number of tape characters is only loosely related to the number of characters (including blanks) on the hard copy, since the former includes shifts. However, a line longer than the width of the paper will not produce a satisfactory hard copy, and any paper tape which is to produce good hard copy must be divided into lines less than a certain maximum which can conveniently be put at eighty characters. With this convention the distinction between card and tape practice effectively disappears.

It should be added that, notwithstanding growing standardization on to the I.S.O. character set, the situation is complicated by the fact that different codes are in use by different equipments, which do

37

not agree even on shifts and carriage returns, so that tape produced by one yields gibberish, often overrunning margins, on another. Nevertheless, a computer ought to be able, by means of a 'dictionary program', to accept any code, and should not be prevented from doing so by premature interpretation of any punching as a control symbol.

It is becoming an acknowledged principle of 'good practice' that what matters is the appearance of the hard copy — produced, of course, on an appropriate equipment. This was not always so. In many systems using Autocode, for example, if 3.14159 were punched with an unnecessary figure shift in the middle (which of course would not show on the hard copy) it would be rejected as improperly punched. One result of accepting the principle is that if a program is printed in a book like this, and a tape punched and its hard copy checked against the book as correct, then the tape is a good one. In some languages facsimiles of the hard copy are preferable because in true print (and some modern typewriters) the characters are not all the same width, so that there is no guarantee that characters on successive lines which are vertically aligned are, in fact, on the same column of the cards they represent. This is a tiresome complication in languages where it is important, and one may hope that future languages will avoid it.

6.1 Semantics of layout

Where languages differ considerably is in the semantic or grammatical content of page layout. In natural languages it is usual to distinguish units known as words, separated by spaces. A new line is equivalent to a space unless precautions are taken against this; otherwise, in prose at least, a new line has neither semantic nor grammatical content. There is, however, a vague semantic content in the paragraph. In natural languages grammatical analysis often takes place with 'semantic reinforcement' (See sections 2.2, 15.3 and 15.4), and such vague semantic implications can have a significance not required in languages with less ambiguous grammars. Nevertheless, page layout is sometimes pressed into service. Algol dispenses with it altogether; neither space nor newline symbols convey anything whatever and they are, from another point of view, noise symbols, though they are normally used to provide that redundancy which human beings like and computers prefer to be without. (Cf. Dickens (1837)). Languages at the autocode level usually demand one instruction per line; that is, the newline character has the semantic function of sentence separator.

Cobol, which in some respects prides itself on a relative freedom of expression, has certain very rigid format requirements in the matter of page layout. The first six characters in a line constitute a line number (and line numbers if present must be in ascending sequence but not necessarily consecutive) or they may be blank; the seventh is either blank or contains a hyphen to indicate that a word has been 'run over' from the previous line; the next word (or part word if hyphenated in Col.7) begins either in the 8th or the 12th space, according to whether it starts a new paragraph (or section) or not. In some parts of the program successive further indentations by four spaces at a time may be used in certain circumstances to improve readability. Once the main contents of a line have been begun, freedom comes back, and, for example, any 'run' of several spaces is linguistically equivalent to a single space.

The development of filing systems as a basis for an operating system, initiated by M.I.T's 'Project MAC' (Corbato 1961), produced revolutionary changes (now too commonplace to detail) in the environment in which a program might be run. The immediate effect was that line numbers were used not only for checking but also for editing; thus they became the property of the system and not of the language. The new standard Fortran, voluntarily tying itself to 80-column cards, bowed to the inevitable and set 72 characters as the maximum length of a line. The subsequent development could be described as a phase in which systems and languages struggled for maximum freedom in their own spheres coupled with minimum interference with each other, except for certain areas where smooth cooperation is the goal. One of these is the possibility that well-proved parts of a program could be separated out and compiled once and for all. This is known as program segmentation.

Several issues impinge on one another here. In a multi-user context, it is necessary to be able to vary the area of store used by a program according to the needs of the moment. If the requirement is to be able to move a program when it is halfway through a run (dynamic relocatability), then this is a matter for *machine design* and rather outside our scope; if it is only a matter of varying the location from one run to another (static relocatability) then it is a matter for *system software*; the program must be held on file in a form known as relocatable binary, in which each machine language word is tagged with extra bits to indicate whether any apparent addresses are true or relative. Some additional details about this 'language' are given in Section 9.2.1; here our concern is with the fact that incorporated binary sub-routines will need this feature in any case, because they will vary in location from one program to another even if the system is not multi-user and the location of a particular complete program never varies. So it is necessary that compilers shall convert the high-level text into relocatable binary and that a subsequent phase (variously known as the consolidator or the linking loader, and probably a common service for all languages) shall combine this with the library routines. Finally it becomes a *language feature* whether or not a notation is provided by which the same facility is available for user fragments.

None of the older languages (except possibly Algol 60) possess such a notation but most implementations now extend the standard language to incorporate one. What Algol 60 did was to recognize that a routine might be more efficient if written directly in machine code, and for this purpose to include the productions

$$\langle \text{procedure body} \rangle \; ::= \; \langle \text{statement} \rangle | \langle \text{code} \rangle$$

and to say that the development of $\langle \text{code} \rangle$ is implementation dependent; throughout the report there is no reference to a library, and apart from the predeclared identifiers (*sin, sqrt* etc.) it appears to assume that a program must be self-contained and self-sufficient. According to this picture, $\langle \text{code} \rangle$ should read $\langle \text{string} \rangle$ and *in this syntactic position* the string should be taken by the compiler to be in assembly language. What is usually done in the presence of a filing system is to replace $\langle \text{code} \rangle$ by **external** (or **external** $\langle \text{title} \rangle$) and to require that the procedure identifier (or the $\langle \text{title} \rangle$) be identical with the name given to the relocatable binary version in the library (or in some user file that can be associated with the library). Implementation is then completed by a provision that procedure declarations, as well as complete programs, are acceptable to the compiler. (But the linking loader does not care, of course, whether a segment in relocatable binary started life in Algol or in assembly code). Similar provisions are made in other languages. For a different approach, see under 'pragmats' in Section 13.1.4.

Another impact of systems development on programming languages arises from the ability of a system to handle several programs simultaneously. Should a program, in its turn, be given the power to call several procedures in parallel? It requires a notation such as

> **parbegin**   A: **begin** ... **end;**
>
>   B: **begin** ... **end**
>
> **parend;**

to indicate that this section commences simultaneously at A and B, and ends only when both processes are either completed or abandoned. But being parts of the same program, these processes are liable to use the same data, and thus to require an intercommunication protocol. The introduction of semaphores by Dijkstra (1968) provided such a protocol. English readers may understand the use of this word more readily by knowing that the word originally applied to the semaphore arm of a railway signal (horizontal for stop, inclined for go) has, on the continent, had its meaning extended to cover red and green lights carrying the same information. Dijkstra's semaphore is a non-negative integer (s, say) to which two special operations may be applied, V(s) or *up*(s), which is $s := s+1$, and P(s) or *down*(s), which is

40

if s > 0 **then** s := s—1
        else wait until some other process executes a V(s)
        then try again **fi**

These operations are such that two processes can only execute them successively, thus if two or more processes are waiting on a P of the same s, only one can actually execute it following one V(s). If the program is such that s never exceeds 1, then s is called a binary semaphore and we may mentally equate 0 and 1 with red and green respectively of automatic railway signalling.

A system of the sort we have been describing inevitably poses the question whether languages can be mixed — to state a more specific case, whether an Algol program might call a subroutine already present in the machine but in Fortran, for example. As a general question this must be considered to be beyond the scope of this book, but those interested could consider the problems involved by noting the explanations given later of the different ways in which parameters are called in the two languages mentioned.

6.2 Traps

Next we must consider the implications on a language of being used within a system that is capable of interfering. This includes the subject of 'traps'. The earliest computers did what they were told, however absurd, and produced some sort of answer, however unrealistic, unless they got into a loop. The cautious programmer would see that before asking for x/y say, he inserted an order **if** $y = 0$ **then go to** . . . , thereby wasting time and space in 99% of the times it was executed. In most cases there was nothing he could do but stop, so later machines saved him the trouble by stopping for him. But then attention focussed on the cases when there was something he could do, and the outcome of this was the trap, which we can define as a jump instruction not in the program but imposed by the hardware as a result of certain conditions arising, and made in such a way as to preserve all information necessary to return to the interrupted program at the point from which the jump was made.

There are two rather different implications of the trap for the designer of programming languages. First, the writer of the program does not know when the trap will occur, and must therefore give *advance* instructions as to what to do if and when it does occur. Secondly, the programmer is no longer writing a self-contained story, in terms of quantities solely of his own choosing and naming; he has to take account of things not of his own creation, and therefore with names not of his own invention. Actually the latter is a wider matter than traps, since the same comment applies to items like console switches, but these have played little part in language development because until the advent of time-shared machines their

41

use by programmers was deprecated more and more as computer time became more and more expensive.

If a programmer does not anticipate a trap, it will usually lead into a system routine which reports its nature and terminates the programme. The earliest trap-like feature in a high-level language was probably in Mercury Autocode, where 'label 100' was a system routine unless set in the user's program, and was invoked in case of overflow, division by zero, etc. A more developed use of the concept came in Cobol, but it was ignored in Algol (unless incorporated in procedures in machine code). It is perhaps worth noticing that the concept of a trap is best allowed to be level independent; that is, it may be a feature of the hardware of the machine, but the high-level programmer really has no need to know whether this is so or whether it happens as a result of the way his program is compiled.

6.3 System programming

System routines are generally lengthy or involved enough to encourage the development of higher-level languages in which to write them, but they are also highly machine dependent. Consequently, although languages have been developed for this purpose, they tend to lack the generality of interest which warrants dissemination and they also tend to be involved in commercial security. An exception to the latter is Imp, an 'Improved Mercury Autocode' which was used to develop the system for the Edinburgh Regional Centre. That these languages keep pace with developments elsewhere is shown by the close resemblance of S3, the system language for the ICL 2900 series, to Algol 68.

A development in another direction arises from the use of active terminals, though this merely underlines a need which already existed. Programs may be required to run consecutively, the output from the first being the input to the second — and more complicated situations than this can easily be designed. These call for what is known as a Job Control language, and clearly this is related to, though by no means identical with, the sort of language required by a terminal user. A highly developed language for these purposes is associated with (and has no distinct name in) the ICL George system, and IBM/360 provides similar facilities. It is not unreasonable that these should be specialized to the manufacturers concerned. However, in practice, users mostly avoid the need to learn these languages by relying on professionally written macros, and there is no justification for the long delay which has occurred in developing a standard language in this area.

Also associated with the use of active terminals are conversational (or interactive) compilers. The demands which these make may one day affect language design, but as yet they do not fall within the scope of this work except for a few remarks for which the reader is referred to the introduction to Chapter 13.

42

7

FORMAL LANGUAGE STRUCTURE

We use the phrase 'formal language structure' to cover two subjects, formal grammar and formal semantics. The former was initiated by Chomsky (1956 and 1959) and has led to a veritable explosion of work. By the latter we mean formal techniques for deriving, from any given statement in a language, a rigorous description of its effect in all conceivable environments; development on this side has been slower, even when only programming languages are considered. The most widely understood item in this field is the development from Chomsky's notation due to Backus (1959) and used in the Algol report edited by Naur (1960), often called Backus Normal Form or Backus-Naur Form (Knuth 1964B). In this work we shall use the abbreviation CBNF to cover any notational form which can claim to belong to this family. For a number of reasons we confine our attention to the linguistic approach and ignore the considerable body of related work in the theory of automata.

7.1 Basic principles of formal grammar

Chomsky initiated the mathematical study of grammatical structure by the following abstraction. A grammar, on his definition, consists of two vocabularies and a set of 'production rules'. One vocabulary is the vocabulary as we already know it, from which the language is constructed; this is the *terminal* vocabulary. The other, or *non-terminal* vocabulary, consists of the names of structural units. The two are distinguished by using lower-case letters for the former and upper-case letters for the latter. The *production rules* are permissive replacement rules. One of the non-terminal symbols, usually denoted by S, has a unique status. The language consists of all terminal strings which can be obtained by suitable choice of production rules from S. (These, and the intermediate stages, are often called 'productions' in the language.)

The very simple grammar

$$S \rightarrow AB$$
$$A \rightarrow a$$
$$A \rightarrow ac \qquad \text{Language 1}$$
$$B \rightarrow b$$
$$B \rightarrow cb$$

43

leaves one no choice but that S must be replaced by AB, but then allows two alternatives in each case for replacing A and B, both of which result in eliminating non-terminal symbols with the result that this grammar permits just the four derivations

1. $S \to AB \to aB \to ab$
2. $S \to AB \to aB \to acb$
3. $S \to AB \to acB \to acb$
4. $S \to AB \to acB \to accb$

Note that

$$S \to AB \to Ab \to ab$$

is equivalent to (1), because it differs only in the order of performance of independent substitutions. On the other hand, (2) and (3), which both lead to *acb*, are different. By incorporating a notation to indicate the derivation they may be written

$$[ac][b] \quad \text{and} \quad [a][cb]$$
$$A \ \ B \qquad\qquad A \ \ B$$

respectively. In this language the string *acb* is ambiguous, with two interpretations depending on whether *c* is assumed to be derived from *A* or *B*. (Note that the expanded forms may be regarded as being in a metalanguage — Language 1a — related to the original one by a simple modification of its replacement rules. Not every grammar can be so modified, but context-free grammars (see below) always can.)

The grammar

$$\begin{aligned} S &\to aT \\ T &\to bT \qquad\qquad \text{Language 2} \\ T &\to c \end{aligned}$$

includes a recursive production, and can lead to strings of any length, viz., to *ac*, *abc*, *abbc*, *abbbc* ..., which we can write as $ab^n c (n \geqslant 0)$.

Backus and Naur, by introducing the metalinguistic symbols $\langle, \rangle$ and $|$, made it possible for the non-terminal vocabulary to be more helpful. They also replaced $\to$ by $::=$, the sole (but real) merit of which seemed to be that this symbol was unlikely ever to occur in the terminal vocabulary of any language (at one stage Algol 68 seemed set on destroying this advantage, but ultimately it thought better of it). The metalinguistic brackets allow the capital letters of Chomsky to be replaced by descriptive words or phrases, so that, for example, instead of $S \to AB$, we can write

$$\langle \text{sentence} \rangle ::= \langle \text{subject} \rangle \langle \text{predicate} \rangle$$

44

The third symbol is a metalinguistic 'or else', which allows us to compress Language 1 into

$$S ::= AB$$
$$A ::= a|ac$$
$$B ::= b|cb$$

In an interesting formalism due to Chomsky and Schutzenberger (1963) this symbol is replaced by '+', leading to

$$S = (a+ac)(b+cb) = ab+2acb+accb$$

When this formalism is used, any coefficient greater than unity implies ambiguity in the language.

It is not clear whether Chomsky intended his terminal symbols to be quasi-numerical (i.e. literal) or quasi-algebraic (i.e. nominal), but Floyd (1963) made this distinction explicit by introducing a third element of vocabulary for which he used Greek letters; this is 'representative' vocabulary, consisting of symbols whose replacement rules confine them to replacement by a single terminal character. Examples of representative symbols are λ for $\langle$letter$\rangle$, and ν for $\langle$numeral$\rangle$; formally they rank as terminals at least so long as the sets they represent do not overlap.

7.1.1. Illustrations

As immediate applications of these concepts we may note first that $S = a+SbS$ and $S = a+bSS$ express the grammar of mathematical expressions (a) with infixed operators and (b) with prefixed operators, if a is representative of simple operands and b of operators, and that expansion of these (by repeated substitution of the right-hand side into itself) confirms earlier statements about their ambiguity.

Secondly, the ambiguity in Language 1 is precisely that which we noted in the sentence 'John's hates work' in Section 2.2, where interpretation depends on whether 'hates' belongs to the subject or to the predicate. It is interesting to note that the ab form in this example is valid — 'Your hates are ineffective; John's work!' — but that the $accb$ form runs foul of the agreement-in-number which English demands — contrast 'John's fish fish flounder' (presumably John's fish are large and carnivorous!). Another interesting feature of this example is that in natural languages a principle of style would seem to rule that an ambiguity of this sort may be resolved when possible by choosing the structure which matches that of a previous sentence. No such principle has so far been invoked in any programming language.

Similarly, if b is effectively a representative symbol, Language 2 reproduces the structure of the sentences in 'The house that Jack built'. We have only to set

$$a = \text{This is the}$$
$$b = \langle\text{noun}\rangle \text{ that } \langle\text{verb}\rangle \text{ the}$$
$$c = \text{house that Jack built}$$

to see in a general way how it works (obviously a more accurate analysis is possible by going into greater detail).

7.2 Further developments

Iverson (1964) suggested a notation which achieves a compromise between the verboseness of Backus and the uninformative anonymity of Chomsky. Basically this consists in listing the non-terminal vocabulary in a three-column table, the columns being (a) line number, (b) Backus left-hand side, and (c) a right-hand side in which the line numbers and not the Backus forms are used. It also incorporates further higher-level features in addition to the Backus vertical line, but these are not altogether felicitous and were supplemented and modified by Burkhardt (1965). Burkhardt quite rightly makes a sharp distinction between the symbols of the language being described and those of the metalanguage, but his method (using heavy type for the former) has its own disadvantage. He also fails to appreciate the value of the 'representative' concept, which Iverson distinguishes by means of letters instead of line numbers. The following grammar illustrates most of the features involved:

a	letter	a|b|c|d|e|f|g| etc	Language 3
d	numeral	0|1|2|3|4|5|6|7|8|9	
e	empty		
s	sign	+|—	
1	identifier	a|*{a|d}	
2	integer	$1 d	
3	number	{s|e}{2|$0 d.$1 d}↑1{$_{10}${s|e}2}	
4	primary	1|3|(7)	
5	factor	4|*↑4	
6	term	5|*{×|/|÷}5	
7	expression	{s|e}6|*s6	

Here black type has been suppressed in the representatives. The asterisk indicates the thing being defined and thus shows the occurrence of simple recursion of the sort in Language 2. Braces are metalinguistic brackets. Thus the last item indicates that an expression is a term preceded by either a sign or nothing, or is an expression followed by a sign and a term. The sequence is deliberately arranged so that occurrence of a number higher than the one currently being defined implies a more elaborate recursion, as in the definition of a primary as an identifier, a number, or any expression enclosed in brackets. The ↑ in 'factor' is the exponentiation sign. The ↑ and $ in 'number' (and elsewhere) are Burkhardt's additional metasymbols; in words, this definition reads

46

a number is an optional sign ('sign' or 'empty') followed by either an integer or 'at least no digits "point" at least one digit' followed by at most one . . . (exponent part).

Note that 'at most one' is equivalent to 'optional', and other synonymous constructions of this sort can be found; this is an inevitable result of introducing higher-level features. The value of a specific notation for 'at most' appears in dealing with languages like Fortran, where, for example, names are restricted to six letters in length.

Language 3 was constructed by adapting a part of the syntax of Algol. Note first that a term *can* be a factor, which *can* be a primary, and that an expression can be a term but can also be an expression followed by + or − and a term. So

$$35$$
$$x$$
$$x-35$$
$$x-35+k$$

are all possible expressions, and in the last $x-35$ is an expression and k a term; we cannot misunderstand and think that $35+k$ is an expression to be subtracted from x, because the grammar provides no option that way round. But a primary can be an expression in brackets, so that

$$x-(35+k)$$

is possible. Similarly, $-a{\uparrow}2+b/c$ is defined by the grammar to mean $-(a{\uparrow}2)+(b/c)$, and not, for example, $(((-a){\uparrow}2)+b)/c$. Thus this syntax controls the interpretation of algebraic expressions (or such of them as involve no further symbols or notation) of any length and complexity. At least, it does so in so far as it is unambiguous, but in fact it has been badly constructed, since although it provides only one analysis for $-a{\uparrow}2$, it provides two for $-3{\uparrow}2$. It is a very simple but useful exercise to revise this grammar to remove this ambiguity.

7.3 Context-free and other grammars

Chomsky showed that within his basic concept, four nesting categories of language could be distinguished, with corresponding nesting types of grammar. In the outermost, which he called Type 0, production rules are very free, permitting, for example, replacements like

(a) aAbCD→aHD   i.e. AbC→H in the context a . . . D
(b)   PQ→QP

Such grammars he showed rather despondently to be (a) so free as to be of little use, and yet (b) lacking the means to characterize natural languages. His Type 1, or *phrase structure* grammars, restricted productions to those in which a single non-terminal was replaced by a

47

non-null string; this banned all rules which *shorten* a string to which they are applied, but a rule like (b) above, though technically banned, may be retained as a mere shorthand for the permitted sequence

$$PQ \rightarrow PZ \rightarrow QZ \rightarrow QP$$

where Z is a new non-terminal used only in these three rules. In Type 2, or *context-free* grammars, the single non-terminal must stand by itself on the left-hand side of a production, i.e. the replacement must be freely available in any context. In Type 3, or *one-sided linear* grammars, only rules of the form

$$A \rightarrow a \quad \text{or} \quad A \rightarrow aB \quad (B \neq A)$$

are allowed. It is important to realize that 'context-free' has become a technical term with the meaning defined above, and may not be used with the freedom of natural English.

A language, defined as a set of terminal strings, may be produced by several grammars, and these may differ in ways which may or may not be trivial for a given purpose. (1) The replacement of one rule by three as above, while theoretically interesting, is a needless complication in practice. In a similar way we can show that a rule $A \rightarrow acB$ is only a technical violation of the Type 3 restrictions, whereas a right-hand side with more than one non-terminal would violate them fundamentally. (2) Gorn (1963) cites the language $a^m b^n$ $(m+n>0)$ to show the effect of choice of grammar on presence or absence of ambiguity. It is generated by either of

1. $S \rightarrow a|b|aS|Sb$ 2. $S \rightarrow AB|AB$
$\qquad\qquad\qquad\qquad\qquad\qquad A \rightarrow a|aA$
$\qquad\qquad\qquad\qquad\qquad\qquad B \rightarrow b|bB$

If a and b are representatives for ⟨adjective⟩ and ⟨noun⟩, then (1) permits 'binary electronic coder decoder' to be interpreted in six ways, including ways like 'binary electronic-coder decoder'; whereas (2) insists on 'binary and electronic, coder and decoder'.

A language is said to be *decidable* under a given grammar if it is possible to write an algorithm which will determine whether any arbitrary string of its terminal characters is in the language or not; in practice this will probably mean to display at least one derivation of the string or to prove that none can exist. (E.g. it is not difficult to prove that no string of a's, b's and c's beginning with b or c can belong to Language 2.) One virtue of the Type 1 restriction is that it makes it possible in theory to write down *all* the strings of a *given length* in the language; this restriction is therefore sufficient to make a language decidable. On the other hand, if the insertion of ⟨empty⟩ between any two characters may open up new vistas, life is clearly going to be very difficult, and in fact it can be shown that there are undecidable languages. In practice, it is much more important to

48

have an efficient 'parsing' algorithm; one, that is, which will lead quickly to a structural analysis in the majority of cases. More recent study of grammars has aimed at isolating features which will help this.

7.4 Breaking the context-free barrier

First, however, let us return to the fact that natural languages transcend phrase-structure grammars. There are ways in which even the higher *programming* languages show features outside those of context-free languages. These appear on detailed examination to be curiously interdependent, and to repay study at the formal level first.

7.4.1 Context sensitive formal languages

The simplest formal language to resist generation in context-free terms is probably 'Thrush'; a user of this language, according to Browning,

> sings each song twice over
> Lest you should think he never could recapture
> That first fine careless rapture.

Its sentences are doubled character sequences like 'tomtom', or 'waggawagga'. In Chomsky terms, a sentence like 'tomtom' is generated via the intermediate forms 'tToOmM' and 'tomTOM'. Let us write

$$\langle small \rangle ::= a|b|c \ldots |z$$
$$\langle big \rangle ::= A|B|C \ldots |Z$$
$$\langle double \rangle ::= aA|bB|cC \ldots |zZ$$

then the grammar of Thrush might be written (A)

$$\langle sentence \rangle ::= *\langle doubles \rangle +$$
$$\langle doubles \rangle ::= \langle double \rangle \langle doubles \rangle | \langle double \rangle$$
$$*\langle small \rangle ::= \langle same\ small \rangle *$$
$$\langle big \rangle \langle small \rangle ::= \langle same\ small \rangle \langle same\ big \rangle \quad \Big\} \ 728\ \text{rules in all}$$
$$\langle big \rangle + ::= +\langle corresponding\ small \rangle$$
$$*+ ::= \langle empty \rangle$$

or possibly (B)

$$\langle sentence \rangle ::= \langle word \rangle \langle same\ word \rangle \qquad \text{how many rules?}$$
$$\langle word \rangle ::= \langle small \rangle \langle word \rangle | \langle small \rangle$$

In A, the word 'same' is used only to tailor the presentation to easier comprehension (like the tricks of the Burkhardt-Iverson notation); in B it involves an *unlimited* number of rules and breaks the concept of a grammar as a *finite* expression of a language. Yet not only the number of rules, but also the process involved in A strike one as absurd. B goes straight to the heart of the matter, so far as the

49

process is concerned, and for practical purposes 728 might as well be infinite.

The implications of the word 'same' can be realized in a formal way by introducing λ-notation into CBNF, and writing the grammar (C)

$$\langle \text{sentence} \rangle ::= \lambda(X)[XX](\langle \text{word} \rangle)$$
$$\langle \text{word} \rangle ::= \langle \text{letter} \rangle \langle \text{word} \rangle | \langle \text{letter} \rangle$$

This ability to specify identical choice of replacement for two or more occurrences of the same non-terminal is a definite requirement. Cobol grammarians introduced a notation for it (section 10.3) from the beginning, and Rose's (1964) modification of the 'definite sets' of Ginsberg and Rose (1962) into 'extended definable sets' was an equivalent move. It was only the fascination of the possibilities within context-free structures that temporarily obscured this fact.

Just as the Algol 60 report introduced CBNF and context-free development, so in the Algol 68 reports A. van Wijngaarden introduced a metalanguage which recognized these needs. We can illustrate the working of his notation by developing the grammar of another formal language, a^{n^2} (the language consists of sequences of a's but only those in which the number of a's is a perfect square). A sequence of $(n+1)^2$ a's can be regarded as made up of a head of n^2 a's and a tail of $2n+1$ a's. This is not the only way of looking at it, but we choose this one and call it the structure postulate.

A van Wijngaarden grammar provides two levels of production rules. The upper level is finite and context-free, and it generates *domains* for lambda-forms in the lower level — i.e. it generates the sets (sometimes finite and sometimes infinite) of permitted actual parameters to be substituted for what are in effect formal parameters in the finite expression of the lower level. As it is desirable to be able to distinguish the two levels at a glance, they are expressed in different modifications of the Backus notation, namely

	BNF	upper level	lower level
is made up of	::=	::	:
followed by	(concatenation)	space	,
meta-or	|	;	;
to terminate a rule	(lacking)	.	.
non-terminals	in $\langle \rangle$	*capital letters	phrase not as below
terminals	(literal)	small letters	phrases ending in 'symbol'

* and digits for one specific purpose (see end of section)

As in BNF, the meta-or is merely a notational convenience. Lower level productions consist of lists of phrases separated by commas; the production rules provide for replacement of complete phrases. The clumsy form of terminal phrases is designed not to prejudice the 'graphological' component of the final representation (e.g., 'begin symbol' can be 'BEGIN' or **begin**, etc., 'letter a symbol' can be upper or lower case, roman or italic).

On this basis we can secure the introduction of n into our grammar by the single upper level rule-pair

$$\text{TALLY} :: \text{TALLY i; i.}$$

which makes TALLY any member of i^n $(n>0)$. The structure postulate can now be written into the lower level grammar, or grammar proper, in the form

$$\text{TALLY i head: TALLY head, TALLY tail.}$$

which is a hyper-rule standing for the set of rules obtainable by replacing TALLY consistently throughout it by each of its terminal productions from the upper grammar — viz. for the rules

$$i^{n+1} \text{ head: } i^n \text{ head, } i^n \text{ tail.} \quad \text{(every } n>0\text{)}$$

The complete grammar can then be written

sentence: TALLY head.
TALLY i head: TALLY head, TALLY tail.
i head: letter a symbol.
TALLY i tail: TALLY tail, letter a symbol, letter a symbol.
i tail: letter a symbol, letter a symbol, letter a symbol.

It is to be noted that premature use of either the third or the fifth line results in a sequence containing irremoveable i's. This phenomenon is known as the occurrence of a dead end and is a feature of these grammars. In Algol 68 this has been developed into a positive asset, certain unwanted productions being steered into dead ends by 'predicates'. These can be recognized by their first word, which is either 'where' or 'unless', and they disappear if they evaluate to 'where true' or 'unless false', but lead to a dead end otherwise (see Section 13.6 for examples).

When two independent 'parameters' from the same domain are required, digits are appended, as TALLY1, TALLY2, which represent independent productions from TALLY.

7.4.2 Syntax and semantics

What appears at first sight to be a different matter is the fact that in natural languages syntax and semantics can and do overlap. The ambiguity in

The driver of a lorry that is full of gin ...

can be semantically resolved (on the basis of the *meanings* of 'driver' and of 'lorry') if 'that' is replaced by 'who' or 'which'. A similar situation occurred in Algol 60 over the construction

51

if B **then** C **else** D $=$ E

which would be (**if** B **then** C **else** D) $=$ E if C was of type integer or real, but **if** B **then** C **else** (D $=$ E) if C was boolean. Since C could be a formal parameter it might be impossible to determine the choice until run-time. This ambiguity was removed in the 1962 revisions, an obviously sound change taking the short view, but more dubious on the long view since it may have been the first appearance of a challenge that cannot be expected to disappear.

The essential feature in both of these examples is that some quality, less of the word or symbol than of the object referred to by it, is required to match a corresponding quality elsewhere in the sentence. Such 'matching' can be ensured by a van Wijngaarden grammar, but the reference to the object represents an intrusion of semantics.

Floyd (1962) 'proved' that Algol 60 is not context-free by considering programs like

begin real xx. . .; xx. . . := 0 **end**

which is valid Algol 60 if both the *xx. .*'s are of equal length, but otherwise either invalid or grammatically correct nonsense according to your point of view. The Algol 60 syntax contains the following productions among many others

$\langle$variable identifier$\rangle$ ::= $\langle$identifier$\rangle$
$\langle$simple variable$\rangle$ ::= $\langle$variable identifier$\rangle$
$\langle$type list$\rangle$ ::= $\langle$simple variable$\rangle$|$\langle$simple variable$\rangle$,
$\langle$type list$\rangle$
$\langle$type$\rangle$ ::= **real**|**integer**|**boolean**
$\langle$type declaration$\rangle$ ::= $\langle$type$\rangle\langle$type list$\rangle$

The last three of these define, straightforwardly, the structure of a type declaration, but the first two are nonsense except that they imply that $\langle$identifier$\rangle$ could be written instead of $\langle$simple variable$\rangle$ on the right hand side of the third. This is because they are trying to say something which the notation cannot convey, namely, that a simple variable is an identifier which has occurred in a type declaration. What is required is that the third production should be revised to read $\langle$identifier$\rangle$ instead of $\langle$simple variable$\rangle$ and that the first two should be cut. This will create a gap, since $\langle$simple variable$\rangle$ is used elsewhere in the syntax. Means to bridge this gap must be supplied by a means of saying that, because of the semantics of a declaration, the gap will be bridged at compile time by converting the type declaration into a temporary production in which $\langle$simple variable$\rangle$ may be any of the identifiers in the type declaration. On this view, which is substantially identical with that put forward by

Caracciolo di Forino (1963), there are two levels of Chomsky-grammar in Algol 60, an outer or formal grammar whose terminals are the characters used in Algol 60, and an inner, or semi-semantic grammar, whose terminal vocabulary consists of identifiers (phrases to the outer grammar) and whose productions must be provided as part of the program. Declarations are rules to the inner grammar but phrases to the outer one. Both the inner and outer grammars are context free but the combination is not. Alternatively, one may replace ⟨simple variable⟩ by ⟨identifier⟩ throughout, and leave it to the semantics to say that certain strings are grammatically correct but meaningless. There are precedents in natural languages, both for grammatically correct nonsense (e.g. 'the corner of the round table') and for defining one's usage as one goes. (This paragraph is unchanged in substance from the corresponding one in the first edition; the Algol 68 solution is a different one again, for which see section 13.6.)

However, the earliest occurrence of this overlap between semantics and syntax is the Hollerith constant of Fortran. In BNF this is

⟨hollerith constant⟩ ::= ⟨integer⟩H⟨character sequence⟩

but to put it this way omits the absolutely essential information that the only way of determining where the ⟨character sequence⟩ ends is by a decimal interpretation of the characters comprising the ⟨integer⟩. From the point of view of formal context-free syntax one can only say that a language employing such a feature should be given an 'H' certificate (as used to be used to protect immature minds from the impact of 'horrific' films). Suppose, however, that one starts with

hollerith constant: decimal TALLY form, letter h symbol, string TALLY form.

then

string i TALLY form: CHARACTER symbol, string TALLY form.
string i form: CHARACTER symbol.

generates the character sequence, and a lengthier, but not particularly elaborate companion set of productions can generate the characters of the integer, thus

NUMERAL:: zero; one; ... nine.
LPART:: LPART NUMERAL; decimal.
RPART:: NUMERAL RPART; TALLY RPART; form.
decimal RPART: decimal zero RPART.
LPART zero i RPART: LPART one RPART.
LPART one i RPART: LPART two RPART.

LPART nine i RPART: LPART i zero RPART.

53

LPART NUMERAL form: LPART form, digit NUMERAL
   symbol.
decimal form: EMPTY.

So even this horror is not outside the range of these grammars.

7.4.3 Transformational and other models

What is particularly alarming about the above demonstration is that
it does not take much imagination to realize that a mechanism that
permits counting opens the way to the whole of mathematics. Does
this ruin its usefulness? When we construct a model of a natural
phenomenon, its function is to explain, to improve our understanding. But it can do this in either of two ways, deterministically
or stochastically. In the former, the presence or absence of certain
features in the phenomenon is explained by showing their possibility
or impossibility in the model. In the latter, everything may be
possible, but absence or extreme rarity of occurrence in the real
world may be related to improbability in the model. There is room
here for a qualitative interpretation of probability in which one says
that anything for which the model provides a simple explanation is
credible in the model, but anything which the model provides only
as a result of some unlikely or tortuous sequence of events is described as incredible. Judged deterministically, context-free grammars exclude too much and the unrestricted grammars exclude
nothing. Stochastically, too, Chomsky's original proposal is disappointing; as we have already remarked, the process in grammar A
for Thrush, with its 731 rules, and its * and + which fuss around
marshalling into correct order a string of characters which come
into being initially in the wrong order, is grotesque and incredible
in comparison with any of the parameterized models.

Confronted with this situation, Chomsky made the fatal mistake
of seeking a solution in what he called 'transformational grammars'.
These grammars assume a context-free basis known as 'deep structure', the terminal productions of which may be subject to certain
compulsory transformations to produce the 'surface structures'. The
latter are not context-free, and they involve no change or development in semantics (which are completely determined by the time the
final deep structure form is reached); indeed the usual first illustration is the transformation from the active voice to the passive ('Jack
loves Jill' to 'Jill is loved by Jack'). The MR101 stage of the Algol
68 reports contained a paragraph of which the following is a somewhat simplified version

   "The strong unitary void clause
      begin int J := A, **int** K = B, L = C;
      M: **if** (K>0|J≤L: K>0|J≥L|**true**)

54

                    then int I = J; (D|E; J := J+K; **goto** M) **fi end**
may be replaced by
        for I **from** A **by** B **to** C **while** D **do** E",

which is clearly a transformation in this technical sense (except that
it is not mandatory). But it is significant that the final report dispenses with such devices completely.

What could be regarded as a compromise point of view is the
doctrine propounded by the Vienna group of workers on PL/I,
namely, that word order is a comparatively late phenomenon in the
development of surface structure; according to this point of view
the earlier, deep structure, productions lead to (unordered) sets of
components. All sentences, not only exceptional ones, now require
rules imposing a sequence on the components as they emerge from
deep to surface level.

7.5 Simplifying properties of grammars
We pass now from the point of view of the 'speaker' who uses a
grammar to synthesize sentences, to that of the 'hearer' who uses it to
analyse them and extract a meaning. Much of the work on formal
grammars has been aimed at determining the properties which make
them easy to analyse without robbing them of their power. For the
sake of brevity we summarize this work more or less in the form of a
glossary of the terms which have been used.

The simplest grammars are *polynomial* (because the Chomsky-
Schutzenberger expansion terminates). An example of one is given in
Section 9.3.

Next come *one-sided linear* grammars, the Type 3 grammars, linear
because no term in the expansion ever contains more than one non-
terminal. They are not as narrow as might appear, for Chomsky
showed that every Type 2 grammar can be revised into Type 3
unless it proves impossible to eliminate productions of the form
$A \Rightarrow \phi A\psi$ (neither ϕ nor ψ empty), when the grammar is described
as *self-embedding*. (This may well have some bearing on the differ-
ences between the 'horrible' sentences of Section 3.3.) But since this
condition bans the algebraic use of brackets, it is too restrictive for
most purposes. A language is described as *metalinear* if it contains a
production $A \rightarrow BC$ which cannot be eliminated, but B and C
themselves give rise to linear (or metalinear) productions which do
not interfere with each other.

Within context-free languages, Ginsberg and Rose (1963) distinguished a grammar as *reducible* if some non-terminal other than
S gives rise to a proper subset of the productions, and as *sequential*
if the non-terminal vocabulary can be arranged in order, starting with
S, in such a way that *each* member defines a subset of the grammar
defined by its predecessors — i.e. if in Iverson-Burkhardt notation no
definition contains a line number greater than its own.

Floyd (1963) defined an *operator grammar* as one in which no two non-terminals ever occur on the right-hand side of a production without a terminal between them. In such a language it is sometimes possible, for any pair of terminals occurring consecutively (possibly with a non-terminal between them), to say which emerged first in the derivation. A grammar in which it is always possible to do this he called a *precedence grammar*. Broadly speaking, an operator which emerges earlier in a derivation has a stronger 'binding power' — one can see this in Language 3 —but Floyd's concept is more powerful than that of binding power because it transcends the implications of the fact that binding power is a scalar quantity.

Floyd (1964) has also shown that in some context-free grammars the ultimate origin of a terminal symbol can be deduced from a consideration of a limited number of its neighbouring terminals. These he calls *bounded-context* grammars. (Note that 'context' here refers to the terminal string, whereas it is the non-terminal which gave rise to it whose replacement is context-free.)

No account of the detailed work which has been published in this area since 1967 could be contained in the space we could allow for it. A convenient text covering the material has been produced by Aho and Ullman (1972).

7.6 Formal semantics

All the above features can be shown to contribute something to the problem of creating an efficient parsing algorithm for a language. As soon as we transcend context-free grammars, the situation becomes more dominated by the practicalities of compiler writing, and we propose at this point to introduce the idea of formal semantics. In many areas to which languages are applied, a strictly formal semantics is impossible. This is because semantics concerns relations with a qualitatively different external world. Since the external world of programming is of the same nature as language itself, the situation here is more hopeful.

A 'Gilmore system' as defined in Section 5.6 is a formal semantic once the rules there referred to are supplied. But Gilmore's approach applies only to function languages and our attempted extension is hardly adequate for semantic purposes.

Consider also a new machine for which no compilers have as yet been written. To write a compiler for a language on this machine is to define what the machine will do in response to any valid sentence in the language, and thus the compiler *is* the semantics *vis-à-vis* this machine. To write a program which can transform a suitably expressed description of the language into a compiler is therefore to turn the description into a formal semantic of a sort — but only of a sort unless we can eliminate '*vis-à-vis* this machine'. One answer to this is to design a formal machine with only such instructions as may be regarded as the 'primitives' of formal semantics. Any inefficiency in such a machine would be as irrelevant as is the inefficiency of the definition of *sum* in Section 3.2. Pioneer work in this direction concentrated of necessity on practical work in compiler writing, where efficiency on a particular machine was of overriding importance; it included the Syntax-directed Compiler of Irons (1961 and 1963), the Sequential Formula Translator of Samelson and Bauer (1960), the Compiler-compiler of Brooker (1963), Gargoyle — 'a language for compiler writing' — (Garwick 1964), and the work of Huskey (1961) and Leavenworth (1964).

Somewhat different approaches were made by Landin (1964, 1965), McCarthy (1963), and Ross (1962, 1964), and yet another is used in the formal semantics of Algol 68 (Section 13.6). Landin's work effectively laid bare one possible set of 'primitives'. The approach of the Cambridge CPL team was that a functional language based on lists, λ-calculus, McCarthy type conditionals (see Section 12.4) and certain arithmetic primitives (such as *sum* (x,y)) can be made to express with precision all one wants to do in computing, and that the structures of 'popular languages' are just 'syntactic sugar' over this 'semantic centre'. Thus the semantics of any language can be accurately specified by stating to what 'applicative expression' any given construction in the language is equivalent. Certainly, in one case where Algol 60 interpretation tied itself up in knots — the recursive use of **own** — Landin's approach clarifies what it is reasonable to expect the interpretation to be and how the concept might be revised with advantage. Landin also introduced (as did others) the important concepts of the environment and closure of a procedure (Sections 13.6 and 13.7).

McCarthy's aim was to go somewhat deeper; it was the first in a series of investigations into formal methods of determining when different procedures are equivalent in the sense that they must produce the same result — e.g. a recursive and an iterative solution of the same problem. Subsequent work in this direction has centred on proving the correctness of a program (e.g. by comparing an 'efficient' program with a 'definitive' one); its techniques have relied too heavily on predicative calculus for detailed discussion here. Ross's approach is more in the main tradition but being based on the requirements of natural languages it permits semantics to influence syntactic analysis, and claims that most of its resources are untapped by any programming language. It is discussed further in Section 15.4.

Two features characterize all the early work in this field. (1) The input language is a transformation of CBNF augmented to supply semantic material. (2) The productions are ordered in a definite sequence for consideration, and ambiguities are removed by accepting the first successful parse which is found (thus defining, by the ordering of the productions, which possible meaning of an ambiguous string is to be *the* meaning).

7.6.1 Iron's method

In Iron's transformation of CBNF, where we would write

$$\langle primary \rangle ::= \langle letter \rangle | etc.,$$
$$\langle exp \rangle ::= \langle primary \rangle | \langle exp \rangle \langle sign \rangle \langle primary \rangle$$

he writes

$$letter \rightarrow primary \ \{LDA - \rho_1\}$$
$$primary \rightarrow exp \ \{\rho_1\}$$
$$exp \ sign \ primary \rightarrow exp \ \{\rho_1 ; STA - t ; \rho_3 [t \leftarrow ti] ; \rho_2 - t\}$$

the items in braces being the semantics, and dependent on the machine being compiled for. This particular set would cause an input string $A + B$ to be subjected to the following transformations:

$$letter(A) + B$$
$$primary(LDA - A) + B$$
$$exp(LDA - A) + B$$
$$exp(LDA - A)sign(ADD)B$$
$$exp(LDA - A)sign(ADD)letter(B)$$
$$exp(LDA - A)sign(ADD)primary(LDA - B)$$
$$exp(LDA - B ; STA -- t ; LDA - A ; ADD - t)$$

Each syntactic item has an associated string, that is, and the object is to convert a series of items to a single item, merging their strings according to the rules in braces, where ρ_1, ρ_2 ... are the 'parameter' strings counting outwards from the arrow (i.e. right to left). The reversed arrow in the square brackets implies that in copying ρ_3 every t is to be replaced by ti (thus generating t, ti, tii, ... as temporary working stores). The final string is the machine assembly code which will leave the value of $A + B$ in the accumulator ('load accumulator from B; store accumulator into t; etc'). Had the string been $A + B + C$, the t's derived from $A + B$ would have become modified in the final transformation which would have given

$$exp(LDA - C ; STA - t ; LDA - B ; STA - ti ; LDA - A ; ADD - ti ;$$
$$ADD - t)$$

This is inefficient coding, but Irons showed that by adding redundant syntactical forms with short-cut interpretations, such as

$$exp \ sign \ letter \rightarrow exp \{\rho_3 ; \rho_2 - \rho_1\}$$

the coding can be made efficient. (It would also need modifying from the above to accommodate the Algol rule as to the order of evaluation of primaries.) Provision is also made for generating labels and for error monitoring. The Algol declaration situation is dealt with by a double pass, the first one generating additional syntactic rules.

7.6.2 Parsing and compilation

It began to be realised that the Chomsky model has weaknesses even at the context-free level. Although effective as a generating scheme for randomly chosen sentences in a language, it seems to have something missing when purposeful generation for the expression of specific ideas is under consideration (Higman 1974). And as a tool for parsing, it forces us to exclude certain grammars in favour of other equivalent ones. Thus the syntactic structure of an identifier as given in the Algol 60 report, can be written

$$\langle \text{identifier} \rangle ::= \langle \text{letter} \rangle | \langle \text{identifier} \rangle \{ \langle \text{letter} \rangle | \langle \text{numeral} \rangle \}$$

but for parsing purposes this contains two traps. One is that it invites the compiler to accept the initial letter as the complete identifier in accordance with the second principle in the final paragraph of Section 7.6. The other is that in trying the second alternative the compiler will get into a tight loop by asking whether we have an identifier (defined as an identifier (defined as ...))? The syntax must be revised to read

$$\langle \text{identifier} \rangle ::= \langle \text{letter} \rangle \langle \text{identifier tail} \rangle | \langle \text{letter} \rangle$$
$$\langle \text{identifier tail} \rangle ::= \{ \langle \text{letter} \rangle | \langle \text{numeral} \rangle \} \{ \langle \text{identifier tail} \rangle | \langle \text{empty} \rangle \}$$

(or alternatively $\langle \text{letter} \rangle \$0\{ \langle \text{letter} \rangle | \langle \text{numeral} \rangle \}$) if parsing is to be successful. This difficulty is known as the problem of left recursion; the work by Foster (1970) in this series is largely concerned with this and similar parts of the story.

Compiler-compiler was distinctly oriented to the machine structure of the Atlas (but see Section 15.2). In the University of London Institute of Computer Science, where an Atlas was the local machine, it was used in ways that went far beyond the implications of its name, and amounted to the philosophy that the production of equivalent machine code from input imperatives is only one special case of a more general process. This process is that of receiving statements purporting to be in a certain language, analysing them according to a stored grammar of that language, and reacting to them in any appropriate manner. Students of the semantics of language in general have in fact recognized three definitions of the semantics of a statement. (1) What the speaker intended it to mean. (2) What the hearer understands it to mean. (3) As an extreme form of the latter, but arguably the only objective definition, how the hearer reacts to it. It is not unreasonable to say that a television receiver *extracts a meaning* (there is a choice, depending on channel selection) from the total signal impinging on the aerial, *by its reaction* in displaying a picture. The proposition that understanding and translation have more in common than is generally realized has been developed by Steiner (1975).

59

But Compiler-compiler had a weakness beyond the difficulty of transferring it to other machines — it performed a complete syntactic analysis, storing the results as a tree, before applying any of the semantic routines. This led to a search for simpler ways of realizing the same philosophy. The most complete high-level language along these lines was BCL (a successor to Atlas Commercial Language). Developed by Hendry (1966), its fate seems to have been suffocation by commercial security (cf. the final paragraph of Section 15.3). As a commercial language the idea was to provide a high-level equivalent to BNF in which systems analysts would write the grammar of every document type in a commercial system, and a further set of facilities which programmers could use to generate the desired reactions to the input of a given document. The following fragment (written in 1968!) will serve to illustrate this. It accepts invoice items which start with a currency symbol, F, S or L for francs, dollars or pounds, and then continue with two numbers representing quantity and price, and it prints the total value in pounds on encountering a control card with a C where a currency symbol would be expected.

```
DEFINE
   QUANTITY, TOTAL, RATE, PRICE ARE INTEGER
   OUTFORM IS ('TOTAL = ', TOTAL)
   CARD IS (EITHER
      ITEM IS (EITHER ('F', DO RATE = 13 END)
               OR ('S', DO RATE = 3 END)
               OR ('L', DO RATE = 1 END),
            QUANTITY,
            PRICE)
      OR CONTROL IS ('C',
                     DO OUTPUT(OUTFORM);
                     STOP END)
   DO  TOTAL = 0;
     L: INPUT(CARD);
        TOTAL = TOTAL+QUANTITY*PRICE/RATE;
        GOTO L
   END
```

Note (1) that as ITEM and CONTROL are not referred to except in their definitions, they could be omitted (with the following IS), making the groups here called by these names into anonymous ones; the names serve as helpful comment only. (2) The main program is a loop without exit, the exit occurring as the reaction to finding a 'C' when inputting a card. The story of BCL reverses that recounted above for Compiler-compiler; it was after it had been developed as a commercial language that it was realized that it could function just as well as a generalized compiler-compiler.

In all this there is a tacit assumption that parsing is done from left to right, backtracking if necessary should it appear that a false trail has been started. That is, one parses from the beginning to the end with all the temporal overtones of 'beginning' and 'end'. It is not clear whether this is a near necessity in practice, or a theoretical requirement; the author favours the latter on the grounds of the nature of spoken language.

7.6.3 The Parsing Machine

The problem of deciding whether a string is or is not in a language is that of succeeding or failing in the attempt to display a parse, and is called the recognition problem. Griffiths and Petrick (1965) studied the efficiency of various sequences of attack on this problem. A given parse may be expressed in the form of a tree with S at the top and the terminal string along the bottom. In Compiler-compiler, as we have seen, an actual representation of this tree in store is assumed to be the 'yield' of the parsing process; in BCL the process is 'void' and achieves the desired results as side effects. One may try to build the tree from top to bottom or from bottom to top and this has given rise to the terms top-down and bottom-up analysis. The ultimate value of this distinction may be questioned, since except when explicit construction of the tree is required, a combination of both methods seems more frequent and more effective than either in isolation. Knuth (1967) examined the problem using a near machine-level device which he called the Parsing Machine, with acknowledgements to an earlier version, the Glennie recognizer. An extended parsing machine is perhaps the most straightforward form of generalized compiler-compiler.

The Parsing Machine is so called because one supplies it with a grammar in the form of a program which it obeys. In the basic form of the machine each instruction takes the form 'can I recognize, and accept, a certain syntactic structure?' — terminals by single instructions, nonterminals by subroutine calls — with a branch on the answer. (Accepting consists in moving the input scanning pointer to the terminal following the recognized structure). Thus it defines an identifier by the subroutine

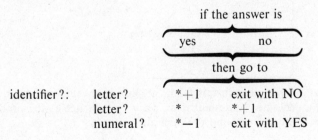

		if the answer is	
		yes	no
		then go to	
identifier?:	letter?	*+1	exit with NO
	letter?	*	*+1
	numeral?	*−1	exit with YES

where the asterisk stands for the line number of the current instruction. In words, if no initial letter is found then the reply to the question 'identifier?' is *No*, otherwise we go to the next instruction. Here failure to find a letter leads on to the alternative of looking for a numeral, but success (in either) leads to repeating the process by looking for a further letter. Failure to find either leads to recognition of the terminals already accepted as an identifier. As a second example consider the following grammar of an English sentence

sentence?:	word?	*+2	*+1
	number?	*+1	NO
	full stop?	YES	*+1
	other mark?	*+1	*+1
	space?	*+1	NO
	space?	*	*−5
word?:	letter?	*+1	NO
	letter?	*	YES
number?:	numeral?	*+1	NO
	numeral?	*	YES

This grammar accepts a sentence like 'In 1509 Henry 7 died.'; it rejects the collapsed form 'Henry7' and it rejects bad typing that puts a space before a punctuation mark. Note that if any characters are accepted by a subroutine which ultimately exits with NO, then the scanning pointer must be put back to the first of these during the exit. This is the process known as backtracking, referred to at the end of the previous section.

We can draw this grammar as a flow diagram, using the convention that acceptance moves down and to the left, rejection down and to the right, thus

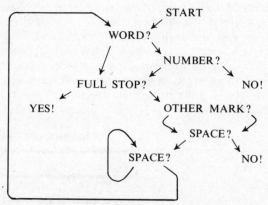

It is noteworthy that in this form the parsing machine program becomes a generative grammar if we regard a sentence as the product of a random walk around the diagram.

Like any other machine, the parsing machine has its tricks and techniques. The technique of replacing

by

	identifier?	a	β
	letter?	*+1	β
	identifier?+1	a	(never called)

improves efficiency by only calling *identifier?* if one is sure that the housekeeping of a subroutine call is time well spent, but it also encourages clean language design. It illustrates a remark made earlier; the parsing machine operates top-down in principle, but this catching of an initial letter has more affinity with bottom-up techniques, and efficiency demands the mixture. By the trick

X?:	*+1	NO	YES
	Y?	NO	YES

it can, by calling *X?*, recognize a *Y* without accepting it, thus leaving it available for re-examination. Although based on a context-free principle, by use of this trick it can decide whether a string belongs to both of the context-free languages $a^n b^n c^m$ and $a^m b^n c^n$ — i.e. whether it belongs to the non-context-free $a^n b^n c^n$. So it is not confined to context-free analysis.

But it cannot, in the basic, purely syntactic form described above, deal with a Hollerith constant; for this the Extended Parsing Machine is required. The extension consists in increasing the repertoire of instructions to include those necessary to generate the reactions to the recognized units. In the case of a numeral string this involves synthesizing the number using the appropriate radix. So we write

integer?:	numeral?	*+1	NO
	i := val(numeral)	*+1	(never called)
	numeral?	*+1	YES
	i := i*10+val(numeral)	*−1	(never called)
Hollerith?:	integer?	*+1	NO
	H?	*+1	NO
	i := i−1; i⩾0?	*+1	YES
	accept any character	*−1	(never called)

Note that *val(numeral)* changes the internal representation of a numeral character to that of the corresponding integer. Other syntactic positions in which *integer?* would be called in a Fortran compiler include labels and integer constants, and the uses made of the contents of *i* in these positions would be different from that shown in *Hollerith?*

It is clear from the free way in which the semantic routines are

63

written that the nature of the Extended Machine imposes no ressrictions on what it can do. As a model it must therefore be judged ttochastically. In the author's opinion it is always credible in its own right, because counter-examples are either badly programmed or dealing with unnatural languages (e.g. a^n, n prime). It becomes a reality by the construction of a program to simulate its operation. This can be written in any high-level language, using techniques simple enough to leave no doubt as to what is happening. (With care this is true even of the semantic routines in the extended machine, which have to be specially written for each application.) In this way the Parsing Machine becomes a practical tool for the expression of a formal semantics. The work of Leavenworth (1964), already cited, foreshadows this approach, being written in Fortran, but is clumsy in requiring each recognition process to be written as a distinct Fortran routine.

A rather luxurious simulator is presented in the next section.

7.6.4 A Parsing Machine Simulator

Of a number of implementations of the parsing machine by the author, all the more worthwhile ones seem to have included machine dependent features; a new version, untested but more self-explanatory, is therefore given here. In order to make the description as implementation independent as possible it is written in a functional notation; thus *val(ins)* could be *val* of *gram[ins]* in one implementation or *stack*[4*ins+1] in another. Because it is impossible to separate the semantic routines necessary to the syntax from those that merely add a meaning to it (the Hollerith constant again!), we ought to start from a structure which we might call a *semiote* (from the word *semiotics*), defining it by

mode semiote = struc(grammar gram, **[]routine** procs)
where

mode grammar = [] instruction
mode instruction = struc(int type, val, good, bad)

Type is defined for $1 \leqslant type \leqslant 4$, as meaning

(1) accept the next character in the text if it is the one whose internal representation is *val*,
(2) accept the next character provided it is *not* the one whose internal representation is *val*,
(3) try to accept a syntactic structure defined by the subroutine starting at the **instruction** whose index in the grammar is *val*,
(4) perform the routine whose index in the []**routine** is *val*.

We should then define a **proc(string, semiote)bool** *parse* which applies the semiote to the string and returns a value indicating success or failure in the operation. However for reasons already stated, instead of defining *parse* this way, we define it as a **proc(proc (int)int** *text, type, val, good, bad*)**bool**, where *text*(*i*) delivers the internal representation of the *i*th character of the string, and the other procedures each select an integer out of the grammar. We leave **routine** partially defined as a **proc(?)int** because of scope problems detailed later; its result determines its method of reentry into the parsing process.

It is assumed that the grammar begins in *gram*[0] with the instruction (3, *n*, T, F); this simplifies the entry procedure and allows T and F to be represented by −1 and 0 respectively. Two features aid debugging. (a) Semantic routines not required by the syntax may be omitted initially from *procs* and appended later. (b) Traces may be obtained by setting either of the booleans (1) *fullparse*, which produces an output in a form exemplified by

0(1T 2F 4(6F 7T 8S 6F 7F 9–15S)T 5T) VALID

(where instruction 8 has called a *proc* that already exists but instruction 9 calls *procs*[15] which does not; 'VALID' is printed in the calling routine after examining the result from *parse*) and (2) *semtrace* which outputs a trace of all calls of missing semantic routines in the form

S15 AT ⟨extract from string⟩ (P=p) DURING 9 4 0

which is particularly useful for ensuring, after the syntax is debugged, that further semantic insertions will be performed in the right order before actually invoking their performance.

The simulator is as follows:

```
proc parse = ( ?)bool:
      (int ins := 0, p := 1, f := 0, sp := 1;
      bool r;
      [1 : ?]int stack c or as described below c;
      proc post = (union(int, char) x)void: (if fullparse then
                        case x in (char s): write(s),
                                  (int i): writef(($zd$, i)) esac fi);
      proc printstate = void: (int g := f;
            writef(($' at '"'5a, '. . ." (P='zzd, ') during 'zzd$,
                  subtext(p−1, p+3), p, ins));
            while g ≠ 0 do writef(($bzzd$, stack[g+1]));
                        g := stack[g] od);
Z: post(ins);
      case int h = val(ins); type(ins) in
        char:  (r := text(p)=h; goto W),
        nchar: (r := text(p)≠h; goto W),
```

65

```
      sub:   (post('(');
               stack[sp] := f; stack[sp+1] := ins;
               stack[sp+2] := p; f := sp; ins := h; sp plus 3;
               goto Z),
      sem:   (int i := 1;
               if h ⩽ upb procs then i := procs [h] (?)
               elif fullparse then writef(($z+d$, −h))
               elif semtrace then writef(($1's'd$, h)); printstate fi;
               case i in goto U, V, W, X, Y, Z esac) esac;
U: r := true;
V: post('S');
   goto Y;
W: if r then (text(p)=endoftext|r := false|p := p+1) fi;
X: post((r|'T'|'F'));
Y: if int t = (r|good(ins)|bad(ins)); t>0
      then ins := t; goto Z
      else r := t≠0 fi;
   post(')'); sp := f; ins := stack[f+1];
   if not r then p := stack[f+2];
   if (f := stack[f]) ≠ 0 then goto X fi;
   r)
```

There are still certain weaknesses in the machine as thus presented.
One is its scope problems; some elements of the array *procs* may
require locals of *parse*, or alternatively some variables shown here
as locals could be globals, e.g. *stack* could be an external stack sliced
(by [*ext.sp* @ 1 : *upb ext.stack*]) to deliver its unused portion.
Additional diagnostics are easier to write if *printstate* is available
to the elements of *procs*. Another weakness is that it deals only with
one character at a time; for an alternative here see Section 13.7.

7.7 The use of Markov algorithms

For the formal description of its semantics, Algol 68 has adopted a
method based (at one or two removes) on Markov (1951) algorithms.
These were originally introduced for the purpose of studying the
basis of computation — an alternative to the Turing machine and
for most purposes far superior to it. They operate on character
strings to produce character strings, using for the purpose (a)
additional 'private' characters not in the ('public') alphabets of
either their operands or their results, and (b) three 'meta' characters,
Λ (used conventionally to denote the empty string), →, and the stop.
Consider the following illustrative example

$$*0 \rightarrow F*$$
$$*1 \rightarrow T*$$
$$* \rightarrow . \Lambda$$
$$\Lambda \rightarrow *$$

This algorithm is intended for application to a binary number expressed as a string of 0's and 1's. The * is a private character. Let us call the following process a *single* application: we search the string from left to right for each of the above left-hand sides in turn, and when we find one we replace it by the right hand side and cease any further search. Then a *complete* application consists in repeating the process of single application until we have applied a 'replacement with a dot', after which we stop. In the above example, the first single application will fail to find *0, *1 or * anywhere in the string, but will (by convention if necessary) find the empty substring at the beginning of the binary number, to which it will therefore prefix a *. Successive single applications will now find either *0 or *1 and will have the effect of moving the * through the number, converting 0 into F and 1 into T until the end is reached. Neither *0 nor *1 will then be discoverable, but the third rule will come into play, its effect being 'delete the * and stop'.

7.7.1 *Markov algorithms*

Markov algorithms have two great virtues. The first is directness. As we operate at all stages on the character string in front of us, there is no translation into another medium (whether computer store or abstract concept of number) to confuse the issue. Let us suppose that we append to a program its input and output files, thus

begin ⟨program⟩ **end file** ⟨name⟩:⟨contents⟩ **file** ⟨name⟩: **finish**

(where we illustrate with one input and one output file). If we can write a Markov algorithm that will transform this string by first placing the results in the output file(s) and then deleting everything else, then this Markov algorithm contains the 'total semantics' of the language in which the program is written.

The second virtue is lucidity; the semantics of a Markov-style algorithm is so simple as to leave no room for misinterpretation. But this is bought at a price, the first intimation of which is perhaps the oddity of a style in which the first instruction to be obeyed is more often than not the last in lexicographic sequence. In the application of Markov algorithms to recursive function theory as sketched in Section 3.2, it is shown (Curry (1963), Mendelson (1964)) that, given algorithms to convert the string s into $f(s)$, $g(s)$ and $h(s)$, there are processes for writing algorithms to implement

(a) $s := f(g(s))$
(b) $s := $ **if** $f(s) = \Lambda$ **then** $g(s)$ **else** $h(s)$
(c) **while** $f(s) = \Lambda$ **do** $s := g(s)$

Together with an algorithm for the successor function, this provides a necessary theoretical foundation for the subject, but the processes are too clumsy to be considered as more than existence theorems.

Consequently we devote the next few paragraphs to techniques more relevant to our immediate purpose.

(1) A notation such as

⟨capital letter⟩→⟨same capital letter⟩

implies an unordered subset of rules; it is permissible provided that the effect of the complete algorithm is independent of the priorities which would be implied by choice of a particular order for expression of the subset in expanded form. A sufficient condition in this case would be that the rest of the algorithm is such that no more than one * can appear in the string at any time.

(2) The following algorithm checks that opening and closing brackets match. In it, π refers to any public character, v (for 'neutral' character) to any public character except the brackets; α and β are private characters.

$\beta\pi\to\pi\beta$	β's follow closely after α as a matter of priority
$\alpha v\to v\alpha$	α moves freely to right through neutral characters
$\alpha(\to(\beta\alpha$	α generates a β on passing an opening bracket and
$\beta\alpha)\to)\alpha$	must lose one on passing a closing bracket
$\beta\beta\alpha\to\beta\alpha$ ⎫ ⎧	α reaches the end of the string with β's still in tow
$\beta\alpha\to.\Lambda$ ⎭ ⎩	Delete them and fail for excess of opening brackets
$\alpha)\to.)$	α cannot pass a closing bracket; fail for excess of closing brackets
$\alpha\to.\Lambda$	Correct!
$\Lambda\to\alpha$	Place the initial α

Note three features of this algorithm. (1) Its first line does not satisfy the sufficient condition of the previous paragraph but is valid, nevertheless. (2) The algorithm stops on different lines according to the result. (3) The α is preceded by as many β's as the current nesting depth of the brackets, and there is no limit on this. A handier form in some respect is

$$\alpha_n v\to v\alpha_n$$
$$\alpha_n(\to(\alpha_{n+1}$$
$$\alpha_{n+1})\to)\alpha_n$$
$$\alpha_0)\to.)$$
$$\alpha_0\to.\Lambda$$
$$\alpha_n\to.\Lambda$$
$$\Lambda\to\alpha_0$$

In this form $\alpha_0, \alpha_1 \ldots$ must be distinct characters and the number of them limits the permitted depth. If we think of the number of α's as unlimited we must consider the alternative form as a convenient abbreviation for the first one.

(3) It is possible, by a process of *reculer pour mieux sauter*, to simplify the writing of large Markov algorithms. Consider the

following version of the (four line) algorithm with which we started, which uses the extra private characters a, ϕ, ξ_n, ζ_n (n ranging over *line numbers*)

$$\phi\langle\text{any}\rangle \to \langle\text{any}\rangle\phi$$
$$:$$
(eight unknown lines; see below)

$$\xi_{10}*0 \to \zeta_{10}F*$$
$$\xi_{11}*1 \to \zeta_{10}T*$$
$$\xi_{12}* \to \zeta_s$$
$$a\xi_{13} \to a\zeta_{10}*$$

the routine in lines 10–13

$$:$$
(other lines)

$$\xi_n\phi \to \zeta_{n+1}\phi$$
$$\xi_n\langle\text{any}\rangle \to \langle\text{any}\rangle\xi_n$$
$$a\zeta_n \to a\xi_n$$
$$\langle\text{any}\rangle\zeta_n \to \zeta_n\langle\text{any}\rangle$$
$$a \to \Lambda$$
$$\phi \to .\Lambda$$
$$\Lambda \to a\xi_{10}\phi$$

Although the eight earlier lines are described as unknown, their left hand sides all contain a ζ subscripted with their own line number. If the reader will follow the operation of this algorithm he will find that it simulates, in great detail, the action of the simpler one, with this important exception, that it concludes by transferring control to the algorithm beginning in line s. We are therefore entitled, without impropriety or loss of rigour, to combine short algorithms by writing them in any order and modifying the dot-replacements to cause transfers; in effect we lose none of the advantages of the Markov approach by writing a large program in block flow-diagram form, each block being allowed a different exit for each of its stopping points. By writing *two* ζ's to an exit, the second (and immediately effective) one to a block that, by omitting to nominate a successor, uncovers the first on exit, a '**goto** X **via** Y' effect can be obtained, simulating a subroutine.

(4) Finally, we offer the following addition algorithm for consideration. p, q and r represent single numerals freely chosen subject to the constraints noted

1:	$\%p \to p\%$	
2:	$\% \to =$	
3:	$9@ \to @0$	
4:	$p@ \to q$	$q = p+1$
5:	$:@ \to :1$	
6:	$°pq= \to =r$	$p+q = r$
7:	$°pq= \to @=r$	$p+q = r$ and carry one
8:	$°pq \to q°p$	
9:	$p:q= \to .r$	$p+q = r$

69

$$10: \quad p:q=\to\ :1=r \qquad p+q = r \text{ and carry one}$$
$$11: \quad\ \ p:q\to\ :q°p$$
$$12: \quad\ \ \ \ :p\to 0:p$$
$$13: \quad\ \ \ \ +\to:\%$$

In following through the action of this routine on the string '183+ 954' every line except the third and tenth will be used. Lines 13, 1 and 2 convert it into 183:954=. Lines 11 and 8 introduce the ° which acts as a sort of 'usherette' conveying the last digit of the left hand operand to a place in the neighbourhood of the last digit of the right hand operand. Lines 6 or 7 perform the addition, according as carry is not, or is, required, stacking the answer beyond the =. Lines 9 and 10 tidy up at the end.

Two features of this algorithm assist our general appreciation of the subject. (1) An understanding of the 'usherette' principle is necessary before the algorithms in the following section become even credible. (2) If '+' is replaced by '−' throughout the above algorithm, and 'carry' by 'borrow', it becomes an algorithm for subtraction, except that $a-b$ is only partially defined; if $b>a$ then the algorithm never stops. What it does is to use lines 10 and 12 to generate an endless sequence of non-significant 9's. To make the definition complete, a notation for negative numbers is required. It is not difficult to modify the above algorithm to make it generate a new character (say **9**) instead of the endless sequence, but it then becomes quite an exercise to make it accept *operands* of either sign.

7.7.2 Nonpareil

The author (Higman 1968) considered the application of these ideas in some detail to five simple languages designed for the purpose. *No grammars were written* for these languages, but the interpretive algorithm ignored everything before a **begin** and after a **finish**, returning a diagnostic if no **begin** was found. Once past **begin**, a private π (effectively a control pointer) passed through everything except certain 'characters' known as 'clause operators', namely, :=, **when** and **do**. On meeting one of these it generated an italic copy, alongside the original, of everything up to the first semicolon on either side of the clause operator. *This action implied a grammar* along the following lines (the distinction between ⟨section⟩ and ⟨clause⟩ arising out of activities still to be described)

```
⟨clause op⟩ ::= :=|when|do
   ⟨clause⟩ ::= ⟨left⟩⟨clause op⟩⟨right⟩|⟨non-op clause⟩
  ⟨program⟩ ::= ⟨title⟩begin⟨contents⟩end⟨files⟩finish
 ⟨contents⟩ ::= ⟨section⟩;⟨contents⟩|⟨section⟩
  ⟨section⟩ ::= ⟨name⟩:⟨clause⟩|⟨clause⟩
```

None of the languages invoked type distinctions; all identifiers were 'declared' in the same manner as labels. A program string like

$$\ldots ; i: ; j: 15; \ldots$$

provides, between the colon and the semicolon following the i, the working space necessary to hold the current value of this variable as the program proceeds; the 15 in the corresponding position after j represents an initial value.

In the simplest of these languages, *Brilliant*, where values were all integers, and names were constructed entirely of letters, the right hand side of the italic copy was evaluated in two stages. First, usherettes took each name with them to find the declaration point and return with a copy of the value. When this was complete, an arithmetic algorithm took over until only a single arithmetic value remained. Finally, if the clause operator was $:=$, another usherette carried the result to the destination, whereas if it was **when**, then if but only if the result was zero, the π was led there. (i.e. 'L **when** M' means '**if** M$=0$ **then goto** L', and the program

> **begin** i: 0; j: 15;
> Q: i := i+j; j := j−1; P **when** j; Q **when** 0;
> P: Out := i **end file** Out: **finish**

should end up reading 'Out: 120'. Brilliant did not use **do**.)

The remaining languages were really more fascinating (and instructive) from the way their facilities developed than from the actual structure of the Markov algorithms. The next language, *Diamond*, was defined by the introduction of a name-evaluation phase into the algorithm. Before being taken walkabout, a presumed name was scanned from right to left; if this scan detected the character \$, then this character, and the name to the right of it, were replaced by the current value of the name and the scan recommenced. In this way $A\$i$ could give rise to $A1, A2 \ldots$; the declaration of names in this form was equivalent to declaring a static one-dimensional array, and $\langle name1 \rangle\$\langle name2 \rangle$ equivalent to $\langle name1 \rangle$ [$\langle name2 \rangle$] of Algol 60.

Pearl explored an alternative extension, that values could be general strings. Now it became necessary to enclose values in quotes, to distinguish them from names. Usherettes had to be trained to keep their eyes shut when traversing these values. The infixed arithmetic operators remained but needed a quote-stripping philosophy and were supplemented by string operators (such as $^{\circ}$ for 'concatenated with').

Ruby threw in both extensions. The result was an explosion of power, and a mess (like dynamic own arrays in Algol 60). *Nonpareil* was an attempt to tidy up this mess. One immediate result was that \$ had to deliver a value stripped of its quotes, and that $\$\langle name2 \rangle$

(with ⟨name1⟩ empty) turned out to mean 'indirect ⟨name2⟩' (cf. the ! operator of BCPL). It was necessary to introduce the operators **D** and **U** (= **down** or **up** one quote level); the former, preceding a name, converted it into a value by enclosing it in an extra layer of quotes. **do** was introduced to provide for subroutine calls, and the following translation of a program given later (Section 11.2) will show what is meant by 'an explosion of power'

begin i: '1' ; A1: '2'; A3: '4';
     initialising at once and omitting the unused A2;
report: 'i := '3'; A1 := '5'; Out := $x; Out := $y; Out := $z;'
   do 'x: 'w'; w:; w := A$i; y:; y := D$A$i; z: 'A$i';'⁰
     report **end**

Reaction to **do** is to reduce the right hand side to a single value as before, then insinuate the π inside the string and attempt to continue. In this case, $w := A\$i$ assigns '2' to w and $y := DA\$i$ assigns $A1$ to y before the body of *report* is entered. The semantics of the parameter calling is complete. Remarkably it can be changed from call to call, which is something few languages allow (though cf. Fortran's $f(x)$ and $f((x))$). With the aid of **U**, dynamic arrays could be handled. Note that under the changed rules of the game, there is no need to make provision for comment in any of these languages; comment does not have to be recognized, all that is necessary is that it contains nothing that will trigger off any reaction.

Although no difficulty was experienced in finding algorithms to perform the searches correctly in block-structure situations, doubt arose over the best way to handle recursive procedures. (1) Could the existing locations hold push-down lists? (2) Should values be held in the italic copies and not in the originals? (3) Should a computer-style addressable store be generated? — i.e. a sequence like

$$; 0 \; ⟨v0⟩; 1 \; ⟨v1⟩; 10 \; ⟨v2⟩; 11 \; ⟨v3⟩; 100 \; ⟨v4⟩ \ldots ;$$

where the v's are values in a normal alphabet (or empty), and may be, in some cases, binary sequences that 'refer to' the corresponding heavy type sequences? There is no problem about doing this, and it has the advantage of providing a direct link with what is likely to happen in a real implementation. What needs careful consideration is the establishment of the connection between the identifiers of the program (particularly their declarations) and the locations in this store. Of course it is quite unnecessary for the addresses in the simulated store to be consecutive, and the locations need not be created until they are actually required; they will most likely be created by the processing of the declaration, and their form may be related to its nature. The use of one extra character, say ★, allows Markov techniques to generate a segmented store (addresses of the form ⟨segment no.⟩★⟨word no.⟩).

Alternatively, if we prefer, we may introduce a 'Markov compiler' which first transforms the program into a more convenient form for subsequent interpretation. This may be 'intermediate code' or 'assembly language'. In the latter case it leads on to the idea of working space as an extension of the program itself, whether both exist as character strings or as words in computer store.

A pilot study of the semantics of Algol 60 using Markov techniques was made by T. W. de Bakker (1967), and students of E. Nixon (Wesselkamper (1972), Cooke (1975), Snidvongs (1975)) have also followed this line. Using the Markov compiler method, their approach is that scanning, creation of store by extending the string, and substring replacement in a context which permits interpretation of a 'value of' operator, are a suitable basis for a *canonical* representation of the semantics of a program, and thus for work on the equivalence of superficially different programs.

The detailed application of this approach to Algol 68 is considered in Section 13.6.

8

MACROGENERATOR

Most programming languages show remarkable complication as soon as one looks at them closely. It will be advantageous to consider first one which is simple enough to survey fairly fully and show how it exemplifies the principles we have set out.

Macrogenerator (Strachey, 1965) is a function language which enables the user to write in abbreviated form anything which involves considerable repetition of certain patterns, even though the repetition is with variations too elaborate to permit simple use of 'ditto'. We shall call the language in which the patterns occur the *pattern-language*. A repeated pattern such as we have described can be given a name by writing

$$\S DEF,\langle name\rangle,``\langle pattern\ in\ full\rangle";\qquad (A)$$

where $\langle\rangle$ retain the metalinguistic significance they have throughout the rest of this book, and "" are used where Strachey would in fact use our metalinguistic brackets. (The quotes in (A) may be omitted if they serve no useful function, but are necessary if, for example, the pattern contains a semicolon.) The variable parts in the full pattern are represented by ~1, ~2. ., read as 'parameter No. 1', etc, and the abbreviated form for the pattern is then

$$\S\langle name\rangle,\langle\sim1\rangle,\langle\sim2\rangle\ldots;\qquad (B)$$

where $\langle\sim n\rangle$ indicates the string which is to be substituted for $\sim n$ on this occasion of use. In serious use the pattern-language is probably a machine assembly code — the affinities with Iron's semantic items are obvious — but the Macrogenerator makes no assumptions at all about it except that it does not use unpaired quote symbols, and at the end of this section (sub-section 8.4) we show it in action on three nursery songs in English; the first of these shows a completely straightforward application.

From the function language point of view, the structure $\S X,A,B,C;$ is equivalent to the structure $X(A,B,C)$ of more conventional mathematical notation, and except when X is *DEF* it may be read as 'function X of A,B and C'. It is important to realize that (A) and (B) above are identical in syntactic structure but differ in semantics; we shall refer to them indifferently as functional forms but shall differentiate them as definitions and abbreviations respectively when it is necessary to do so. Functional forms may be nested, and when a definition is nested this usually corresponds in conventional mathematical notation to the usage '... *where* ... *is* ...'. For example §A,B,§DEF,A,"$Q\sim1$";; is '$A(B)$ *where* $A(x)$ *is* Qx'.

8.1 Syntax

In Backus style, which usually gives the panoramic view before the detail, the formal syntax can be expressed thus:

  1. ⟨complete text⟩ ::= ⟨text⟩⟨endsymbol⟩
  2.   ⟨text⟩ ::= ⟨text unit⟩|⟨text unit⟩⟨text⟩
  3.   ⟨text unit⟩ ::= ⟨quote⟩|⟨function⟩|⟨open text⟩
  4.   ⟨quote⟩ ::= "⟨text⟩"
although this is slightly restricting — see below —
  5.   ⟨function⟩ ::= ⟨function head⟩⟨function tail⟩
  6. ⟨function head⟩ ::= §⟨item⟩
  7. ⟨function tail⟩ ::= ;|,⟨item⟩⟨function tail⟩
  8.   ⟨item⟩ ::=⟨unit⟩|⟨unit⟩⟨item⟩
  9.   ⟨unit⟩ ::=⟨quote⟩|⟨function⟩|⟨plain text⟩
10.   ⟨open text⟩ ::=⟨character⟩|⟨character⟩⟨open text⟩
11.   ⟨plain text⟩ ::= ⟨plain ch.⟩|⟨plain ch.⟩⟨plain text⟩
12.   ⟨character⟩ ::= ⟨any character from the set available to the equipment except §, " or ".⟩
13.   ⟨plain ch.⟩ ::= ⟨any ⟨character⟩ except , or ;⟩
14.   ⟨endsymbol⟩ ::= "

Although these productions suffice to analyse a message, they do not guarantee a semantically meaningful one; in particular, the distinction between definitions and abbreviations is ignored, and the parameter notation. Productions 1, 2 and 3 amount to the statement that a complete text consists of a string of open texts, quotes and functional forms terminated by an end symbol. Productions 4, 12 and 13 show that opening and closing quotes are always paired, and that an unpaired closing quote can only arise from production 14. Since productions 2, 3 and 4 are recursive, quotes can be nested, so that the end of a message will be detected by monitoring when 'depth in quotes goes negative'. Productions 5, 6 and 7 define a function as

          §⟨item⟩;
or   §⟨item⟩,...⟨item⟩;

so that § ... ;, like the quote symbols, have the quality of brackets. Within these brackets, unless further protected by quotes, the comma has a special significance and the semicolon cannot be introduced. An ⟨open text⟩ is simply a sequence of characters not enclosed in either type of bracket, and a ⟨plain text⟩ fulfils the same role under conditions in which the special interpretation of the comma and semicolon must be applied. Production 4 requires the contents of a quote to conform to the syntax of the language as a whole, and in particular inhibits it from containing an unmatched §, an unnecessary restriction which we shall remove in considering the semantics.

8.2 Semantics

Let us next consider the semantics informally. It is semantically *useless* to write a definition which is not used, or parameters in excess of the number required (except for **where** definitions), but *meaningless* to write a functional form with a first ⟨item⟩ which has not been defined or with an inadequate number of parameters; the former are merely silly but the latter, although not syntactically incorrect according to the above productions, should give rise to error monitoring.

To interpret a string in this language the ⟨complete text⟩ is dealt with unit by unit. An ⟨open text⟩ is copied to the final form as it stands, and a ⟨quote⟩ likewise. In copying a quote, the quote symbols that surround it are omitted, but any within it are retained, and also any commas, §, or other symbols which might otherwise have a special interpretation. If a functional form is met, it is interpreted. A temporary copy is made, each ⟨item⟩ being copied according to the same rules as before. This can involve recursive interpretation. When this is complete, the definition of the first ⟨item⟩ (as interpreted, if this differs from the original form) is sought, *the search starting with the most recently acquired definitions.* Unless this is DEF or one of the other 'machine macros' described below, the final copy is made from the second ⟨item⟩ in the definition, copying it *according to the usual rules* (with recursive interpretation if necessary) but with the additional rule that *parameters are substituted for literally* from the corresponding ⟨item⟩ of the temporary copy (literally because they have already undergone interpretation). If the first ⟨item⟩ is DEF, the functional form is interpretated by adding its second and third items to the list of definitions. When interpretation is complete, the temporary copy, including all definitions to which it may have given rise by the interpretation of its parameters, is deleted. (If any definitions arose out of the final copy, these are retained.)

Formalizing these semantics gives rise to some interesting points. It becomes apparent that the definition strings must be regarded as in different languages at different stages! We adopt a compromise notation which retains Backus brackets within an Iverson-Burkhardt framework for syntax and uses square brackets for semantic items. We assume the existence of a push-down list of strings and we use the abbreviation [*] to mean 'concatenate the current symbol with the string on the top of the list'. Then in broad outline, but it seems

76

impossible to fill in further detail, the formal semantics can be written

⟨text⟩ ::= $0{⟨1⟩[*]|⟨n⟩[*]|⟨c⟩[*]|⟨outerquote⟩|⟨function⟩}
{⟨endsymbol⟩[stop]}

⟨outerquote⟩ ::= "$0{⟨1⟩[*]|⟨n⟩[*]|⟨c⟩[*]|§[*]|⟨innerquote⟩}"

⟨innerquote⟩ ::= "[*]$0{⟨1⟩[*]|⟨n⟩[*]|⟨c⟩[*]|§[*]|⟨innerquote⟩}"
[*]

⟨function⟩ ::= §[pushdown]⟨item⟩$0{,[replace]⟨item⟩};[apply]

⟨item⟩ ::= $0{⟨1⟩[*]|⟨n⟩[*]|⟨outerquote⟩|⟨function⟩}

where ⟨c⟩ is 'comma or semicolon', ⟨n⟩ is 'numeral', and ⟨1⟩ is any other character but these and § and quotes. As long as one meets symbols in the ⟨1⟩, ⟨n⟩ or ⟨c⟩ classes, that is, one copies them [*] on to the end of the string; failing this one investigates the possibility of a quote, a function, or the endsymbol. The distinction between ⟨outerquote⟩ and ⟨innerquote⟩ is solely in the absence of the copy sign after the first and last symbols of the former. Immediately on finding a function sign one pushes down the current list and starts a new one; this is the temporary copy. In doing so, one must replace the inter-item commas by some new symbol because others without this status may be uncovered from quotes. On reaching a semicolon which is not a part of an included item (and an item cannot begin with a semi-colon) one performs 'apply'.

Now 'apply' consists in removing the temporary copy from the push-down list, allowing the previous top to emerge, and adding the interpretation of the temporary copy to it. It is here that one feels that the lack of detail is regrettable, nevertheless, three things make it difficult (though probably not impossible) to incorporate further detail into the main formalism. (1) Most of the definitions have been supplied dynamically, so that we have a situation similar to the 'Algol declaration' one. (2) The machine macros, DEF, etc, have to be treated differently. This is part of the third, which is (3) the syntax of the definition strings now differs from that of the input message at least in respect of the character ∼.

The resolution of all these points involves revolutionary developments which go beyond the scope of the present chapter. But a glimpse may be obtained by considering the following revision of the grammar given above.

1. ⟨open text⟩ ::= $0{⟨textunit⟩|⟨int.ch⟩[error]}"[stop]

The only novelty here is the inclusion of a monitor. This induction (it has rather exceeded the notion of a production) means 'carry out the process of looking for a text unit, alternatively (if that fails) look for an internal character and signal an error; repeat this as often as you can, or, when you can no longer do either, then find a closing quote and stop' (This does not prevent [error] from calling halt.)

77

2. ⟨text unit⟩ ::= "⟨quote⟩"|§⟨function⟩|⟨ext.ch not"⟩[*]
3. ⟨function⟩ ::= [pushdown]⟨item⟩$0{,[replace]⟨item⟩};
   [replace] [apply]
4.   ⟨quote⟩ ::= $0{"[*]⟨quote⟩"[*]|⟨not"⟩[*]}
5.   ⟨item⟩ ::= $0{"⟨quote⟩"|§⟨function⟩|⟨not, or;⟩[*]

These have been rearranged in the interests of efficiency; thus (2) will usually amount to 'not an opening quote? not a §? not an internal character or a closing quote? then copy'. One result is to eliminate the separate inner and outer quotes. Replacement of the Comma will be by the internal character ♯. Now we add

6. ⟨definition⟩ ::= $0{∼{⟨n⟩[trans]⟨parameter⟩|[error]}|⟨text
   unit⟩}♯[pop up]
7. ⟨parameter⟩ ::= $0{⟨any character except ♯⟩[*]}♯[pop up]

which will be called by [apply]. (6) means 'look for something beginning with ∼ or for a text unit, the former followed by a numeral or there is an error, but having found the numeral transfer the *n*th item of the temporary copy to the input (pushing down the true input)'. The ⟨parameter⟩ which is then expected is, of course, found and treated according to (7), but *only because* [trans] put it there; it was not there in the original string!

The foregoing analysis, which rather stood on its own in 1967, should be compared with the more general approach to semantics now introduced in Section 7.6.3.

8.3 Further details of the language

The second of the nursery songs in the next section is slightly more complicated than the first, having two levels of repetitiveness, and consequently a little nesting of functional forms; it is not difficult to apply the above rules to follow through the interpretation. The third, with two solutions — one by myself and one by the Cambridge research student who checked my solution on the machine — is more like an exercise in structural analysis than a convenient method of abbreviating, but it illustrates a number of points which we cannot spare space to describe in detail. These include.

1. Careful control of the 'depth in quotes' of the ∼ sign, to determine at which copy it is uncovered, and hence interpreted; this, when definitions are nested, determines whether ∼*n* refers to the parameters of the inner or the outer function. (It solves the 'non-local variable which is a formal parameter of an outer procedure' problem.)
2. The functions *S, P, W* which are the 'successor' 'predecessor' and 'word' functions respectively on the numerals.
3. The introduction of 'variable functions' whose names depend on a parameter, as in §*VERSES∼1*.

4. The use of (3) combined with the rule that definitions are sought beginning with the most recently acquired, to control the 'exit' from a recursive definition, since

$$§\sim1,§DEF,\sim1,``\dots"\,;,§DEF,X,``\dots"\,;;$$

will behave differently when ~1 is X from how it will behave when they are not the same.
5. Various features in connection with lay-out control.

In addition to DEF, the complete Macrogenerator contains a number of other 'machine macros'; these are all late additions to improve the fluency in directions where it was felt to be desirable. A function UPDATE revises an existing definition, where DEF would either override it only temporarily or else waste extra storage space overriding it permanently. A function §VAL,X; allows the defining string of X to be copied without interpretation; in simple cases which do not involve interpretation it is equivalent to §X;. There are also functions to permit arithmetic and radix conversion on numerical strings. To illustrate UPDATE, the functional form §AORB; will output alternately A and B if defined with the aid of a subsidiary function Q thus:

$$§DEF,Q,A\,;§DEF,AORB,\langle§§Q;;\rangle,§DEF,A,\langle A§UPDATE,Q,B;\rangle;,$$
$$§DEF,B,\langle B§UPDATE,Q,A;\rangle;;$$

The author has found a machine macro RAN, not provided by Strachey and such that §RAN,N; provides a random character in the range 1 ... n, to be invaluable — e.g. for providing random examples of sentences in a language from its grammar. One noteworthy property of Macrogenerator is that it is a counter-example to any notion that one can always make do with a single type of bracket, since it shows that a sequence like

$$\langle\dots(\dots)\dots\langle\dots)\dots\rangle$$

may sometimes be both possible and significant, namely, when the semantics depends on the depths in the two forms of bracket independently. The one serious inability of the Macrogenerator in its complete form would seem to be that if the pattern-language includes quote symbols, then it is impossible to derive any part of the interior of an output quote by means of a functional form. To provide this facility, either one must admit distinct metaquotes, or one must add a character which, I have argued elsewhere (Higman, 1963), is a necessary part of any completely self-handling language, namely, c (read as 'the character'), which encloses the immediately following single character in implicit 'super quotes' — even if this is c itself.

79

8.4 Examples

On the following page we reproduce in facsimile the examples already referred to. They were prepared on a Flexowriter (a typewriter incorporating a paper tape punch and reader), and the paper tape fed into the computer. The output tapes to which this gave rise were fed into the reader of the Flexowriter and produced the copy, all but a few lines of which is reproduced on the three following pages. (Note: (1) the local convention which allows the new line and space symbols occurring between *→ and →* to be suppressed, and (2) that the ***Z is a system code signifying the end of the tape.)

1. §DEE,VERSE,<
Old Macdonald had a farm, E-I-E-I-O,
And on this farm he had some ~1, E-I-E-I-O!
With a ~2 ~2 here and a ~2 ~2 there,
Here a ~2 there a ~2 everywhere a ~2 ~2,
Old Macdonald had a farm, E-I-E-I-O.
>;
§VERSE,chicks,cheep;
§VERSE,ducks,quack;   COMPUTER
§VERSE,turkeys,gobble;   INPUT
  etc., etc.,

2. SONG FROM A CHILDREN'S GAME
§DEF,VERSE,<~1~1
Hey do diddledy ho ~1
>;
§DEF,LINE,<
The ~1 wants a ~2>;
§DEF,FORM,<§VERSE, §LINE,~1,~2;;>;
§FORM,farmer,wife;
§FORM,wife,child;
§FORM,child,dog;
§VERSE,
We all pat the dog;

§DEF,S,<§1,2,3,4,5,6,7,8,9,§DEF,1,<~>~1;;>;
§DEF,P,<§N,0,1,2,3,4,5,6,7,8,§DEF,N,<~>~1;;>;
§DEF,W,<§L,One,Two,Three,Four,Five,Six,Seven,Eight,Nine, §DEF,L,<~>~1;;>;
§DEF,HEAD,<
§W,~1; men went to mow, went to mow a meadow,
>;
3. §DEF,END,<
One man and his dog, went to mow a meadow>;
§DEF,TAIL,<§W,~1; men, §~1,§DEF,~1,<§TAIL,§P,>~1<;;>;§DEF,6,<
§TAIL,5;>;§DEF,2,<§END>;;>;
§DEF,VERSE,<
§HEAD,~1;§TAIL,~1;>;
One man went to mow, went to mow a meadow,§END;
§REST,2,§DEF,REST,<§VERSE,~1;§~1,
§DEF,~1,<.§REST,§S,>~1<;;>;§DEF,9,<!>;;>;;

§DEF,VERSES,<§VERSES~1,§DEF,VERSES~1,<§VERSES,§P,>~1<;;>;
§DEF,VERSES1,4.   ALTERNATIVE METHOD;;§VERSE,~1;>;
§DEF,W,<§L,One man,Two men,Three men,Four men,Five men,Six men,*→
      →*Seven men,Eight men,Nine men, §DEF,L,<~>~1;;>;
§DEF,HEAD,<
§W,~1; went to mow,went to mow a meadow>;
§DEF,REST,<§REST~1,§DEF,REST~1,<§W,>~1<;
§REST,§P,>~1<;;>;§DEF,REST1,<One man and his dog,went to mow a meadow>;;>;
§DEF,VERSE,<
§HEAD,~1;
§REST,~1;>;
§VERSES,9;
>
***Z

81

COMPUTER OUTPUT

1.

Old Macdonald had a farm, E-I-E-I-O,
And on this farm he had some chicks, E-I-E-I-O!
With a cheep cheep here and a cheep cheep there,
Here a cheep there a cheep everywhere a cheep cheep,
Old Macdonald had a farm, E-I-E-I-O.

Old Macdonald had a farm, E-I-E-I-O,
And on this farm he had some ducks, E-I-E-I-O!
With a quack quack here and a quack quack there,
Here a quack there a quack everywhere a quack quack,
Old Macdonald had a farm, E-I-E-I-O.

Old Macdonald had a farm, E-I-E-I-O,
And on this farm he had some turkeys, E-I-E-I-O!
With a gobble gobble here and a gobble gobble there,
Here a gobble there a gobble everywhere a gobble gobble,
Old Macdonald had a farm, E-I-E-I-O.

   etc., etc.,

2. SONG FROM A CHILDREN'S GAME

The farmer wants a wife
The farmer wants a wife
Hey do diddledy ho
The farmer wants a wife

The wife wants a child
The wife wants a child
Hey do diddledy ho
The wife wants a child

The child wants a dog
The child wants a dog
Hey do diddledy ho
The child wants a dog

We all pat the dog
We all pat the dog
Hey do diddledy ho
We all pat the dog

One man went to mow, went to mow a meadow,
One man and his dog, went to mow a meadow

Two men went to mow, went to mow a meadow,
Two men,
One man and his dog, went to mow a meadow.

Three men went to mow, went to mow a meadow,
Three men, Two men,
One man and his dog, went to mow a meadow.

Four men went to mow, went to mow a meadow,
Four men, Three men, Two men,
One man and his dog, went to mow a meadow.

Five men went to mow, went to mow a meadow,
Five men, Four men, Three men, Two men,
One man and his dog, went to mow a meadow.

Six men went to mow, went to mow a meadow,
Six men,
Five men, Four men, Three men, Two men,
One man and his dog, went to mow a meadow.

Seven men went to mow, went to mow a meadow,
Seven men, Six men,
Five men, Four men, Three men, Two men,
One man and his dog, went to mow a meadow.

Eight men went to mow, went to mow a meadow,
Eight men, Seven men, Six men,
Five men, Four men, Three men, Two men,
One man and his dog, went to mow a meadow.

Nine men went to mow, went to mow a meadow,
Nine men, Eight men, Seven men, Six men,
Five men, Four men, Three men, Two men,
One man and his dog, went to mow a meadow!

4. ALTERNATIVE METHOD

One man went to mow,went to mow a meadow
One man and his dog,went to mow a meadow

Two men went to mow,went to mow a meadow
Two men
One man and his dog,went to mow a meadow

Three men went to mow,went to mow a meadow
Three men
Two men
One man and his dog,went to mow a meadow

Four men went to mow,went to mow a meadow
Four men
Three men
Two men
One man and his dog,went to mow a meadow

Five men went to mow,went to mow a meadow
Five men
Four men
Three men
Two men
One man and his dog,went to mow a meadow

Six men went to mow,went to mow a meadow
Six men
Five men
Four men
Three men
Two men
One man and his dog,went to mow a meadow

Seven men went to mow,went to mow a meadow
Seven men
Six men
Five men
Four men
Three men
Two men
One man and his dog,went to mow a meadow

Eight men went to mow,went to mow a meadow
Eight men
Seven men
Six men
Five men
Four men
Three men
Two men
One man and his dog,went to mow a meadow

Nine men went to mow,went to mow a meadow
Nine men
Eight men

etc.

84

9

FROM MACHINE CODE TO FORTRAN

The practice of arithmetic is based on the representation of a number by a sequence of digits, each digit taking one of the values, 0, 1, . . . up to but not including a maximum known as its radix, and representing a unit equal to the interpretation of the radix of the preceding digit (reading from right to left in most cases). Occasionally, as in sterling before decimalization, the digits have different radixes; more usually all the digits have the same radix which may then be called the 'scale of notation'. Various methods of mechanization of the radix are possible — e.g. a wheel on a shaft with n detents mechanizes a digit of radix n. Electronically, a gas-filled tube with a central cathode and ten anodes around it is known as a decatron, and embodied in a circuit such that only one anode can carry a current at any moment, it is a representation of a decimal digit. Most electronic devices, however, either change their state smoothly, in which case they are not digital, or are either on or off, in which case they represent binary digits. For this reason most computers operate in binary, but the reason for this is almost purely practical, not theoretical. (Binary does have slight advantages in numerical analysis when numbers have to be expressed approximately, and so rounded off; this also makes precise definition of semantics in terms of character manipulation very difficult.)

Fundamental to the understanding of computers is the idea of the interpretation of a sequence of digits. Consider the sequence *251265*. Arithmetically, this is *251,265* — i.e. two hundred and fiftyone thousand, two hundred and sixtyfive. But thought of as *25.12.65*, it becomes Christmas day 1965! In the form *2.5.1265*, it could mean 'apply operation No. 2 to the contents of accumulator No.5 and store location No.1265', and operation No.2 might be 'add the contents of the specified store location into the specified accumulator'. The dots are implicit, that is to say, if the sequence *251265* is to be added to something it is interpreted as *251,256*, but if it is to be obeyed it is interpreted as *2.5.1265*; the difference lies not in the way the sequence is stored, but in the circumstances in which it is used. This principle does not depend on the use of any particular scale of notation, although immediate application of it is prevented if an integer is presented in an inappropriate radix.

To relieve the sheer burden on the human memory, one gets into the habit of writing *2.5.1265* as *ADD.5.1265* as long as one is writing on paper, and of making the substitution only at the moment of preparing the final version for insertion into the machine. This is the second step away from pure machine language in most cases, the first (unless one's machine already works in decimal) being the use of decimal in place of the actual radix of the machine.

9.1 Machine code

A brief example will serve to convey the flavour of coding in machine language. Let us suppose that we wish to start a vector (x_1, x_2, x_3) at the value $(0, 0, 0)$. Before we can begin we have to decide on the store locations for these three numbers. Suppose that for some reason we have decided on locations 207, 208, 209. It is also necessary to decide where the instructions are going to be stored; let this be locations 50 onwards. The available instruction set is something we have to learn for each machine, but we can choose a fairly typical set for an early machine. The coding in the following sequence uses a method which is independent of the number of components in the vector; when this is three we lose on the deal, but though it is unnecessarily long it is better as an illustration than a shorter version would be:

50:	PutN	1 0000	Put the number 0 in accumulator 1
51:	PutN	2 0003	Put the number 3 in accumulator 2
52:	Store	2 0061	Put the contents of acc. 2 in location 61
53:	JumpZ	2 0062	Jump to the instruction in location 62 if the contents of acc. 2 are zero
54:	Add	2 0060	Add contents of loc. 60 into acc. 2
55:	Store	2 0056	Put contents of acc. 2 in location 56
56:	JumpU	0 0056	See below for explanation
57:	PutC	2 0061	Put contents of loc 61 into acc. 2
58:	SubN	2 0001	Subtract the number 1 from the contents o acc. 2
59:	JumpU	0 0052	Jump to the instruction in location 52
60:	Store	1 0206	See below
61:	JumpU	0 0061	See below
62:	?		First instruction of next sequence

This sequence of instructions starts by putting zero into accumulator No. 1 for storing in the x-locations, and '3' into accumulator No.2 as the suffix of the last component — we shall zeroize the components in reverse order. We then tuck the latter safely away in store because we are going to alter it in the accumulator. In fact, after checking that we have not finished, we convert the suffix k into an instruction 'store contents of acc. 1 in x_k' by adding it to an instruction to 'store contents of acc. 1 in x_0' which we have thoughtfully provided in location

60, and we store this manufactured instruction ahead of ourselves in location 56 so that we shall come to it and obey it. The original contents of location 56 are thus of no consequence, and conventionally we make them something which will be both harmless and useful in case because of some sort of mistake (e.g. 55: Store 2 0156) we fail to overwrite it — namely, 'jump unconditionally to yourself', an instruction which will continue to be obeyed without doing anything at all, but will at least tell us what we have failed to do. We then reduce the index by one and recycle, taking care to leave the loop before attempting to put zero into the nonexistent x_0.

9.2 Assembly code

It may later become apparent that our choices of locations were unsuitable. If the reader will attempt to rewrite this sequence assuming that it is to be stored in locations 74 onwards and that the vector is stored in locations 30, 31, 32, he will appreciate the immense scope which long programs in machine code give for errors due to silly slips and oversights. Most of these are eliminated in the following version:

```
       *      = 0050) These are not instructions but 'directives';
       x0     = 0206) for * see below
       PutN   1 0000
       PutN   2 0003
       Store  2 WS+1  WS means the location labelled as such
       JumpZ  2 WS+2
       Add    2 WS
       Store  2 *+1     * is a special label meaning 'here'
       JumpU  0 *
       PutC   2 WS+1
       SubN   2 0001
       JumpU  0 *−7
WS:    Store  1 x0
       JumpU  0 *
          ?
```

Such a version is said to be in Symbolic Assembly Code, because so many addresses are represented symbolically and not literally. The characteristics of this level of language are

1. It is the language of a particular machine, and in general it is meaningless with reference to any other
2. Its lines are more or less in one to one correspondence with the contents of individual locations in the machine, but,
3. A few of its lines are additional to the machine code and supply cross-referencing information, such as labels of working space,

where the program is to be stored, and so on. These are known as 'directives'. And

4. Some of the more advanced forms of symbolic assembly language permit a limited macro-generation facility (one line corresponding to several machine instructions).

5. Although not illustrated above, symbolic assembly languages always permit alternative formats, namely, instructions and numerical constants, and usually there are alternative forms for constants, e.g. in the above language there might be permitted

DecF	0.271828
Alpha	RESULT=
Octal	000370

and so on. Usually (as here) this is done by means of 'pseudo-functions', that is, apparent functions which are not in the machine code itself.

Before a machine can accept its own symbolic assembly code, it must be provided with an assembly program which will (1) do all conversions from decimal, (2) recognize its own functions and supply numerical values, (3) keep count of where it is putting things and keep a record of the meaning of labels and other symbolic quantities, (4) perform the arithmetic to deal with symbolic addresses such as 'WS+2', '*−7', and (5) recognize and act upon its directive functions and constant formats. It should also (6) include some error detecting facilities.

At an elementary level it is fair to say that if a machine code is such that some sequences of digits are meaningless then it is simply inefficient with no compensating advantages. But symbolic assembly language is redundant, and therefore provides certain scope for error detection and/or correction. It is highly desirable that an assembly program should exploit this potential, and most of them do, at least so far as error detection is concerned. It is relatively easy, for example, for this program to report constants which overflow the registers they are to be put into, references to labels which are nowhere defined, and so on. And usually all accidental misspellings are reported as errors — as 'illegal functions' if they occur in the function part of the format.

Because of this error-detecting facility, there is a lot to be said for making an assembly code, and not the true machine code, the lowest form of input to a machine. In the days when stores were small this meant keeping the assembly program as compact as possible both as regards the space it occupied and in the time it took to do its work, and this meant foregoing luxurious extensions of it, but the increased store capacity of even 'small' computers has deprived this observation of most of its force.

In this case, too, care should be taken that the symbolic assembly language allows one to say everything that the machine can do. Assembly code designers should resist the temptation to be policemen except for overwhelming reasons. A useful trend in design here is to start with the assembly language and to make it cover a range of machines with different machine codes. It is then made to exclude any coding which could produce different results on different machines, forcing inefficient working if necessary to this end.

9.2.1 Relocatable binary

When, as suggested in Section 6.1, the need to relocate a segment of program is a matter of machine convenience rather than human convenience, the details are different but the principles are much the same. *PutN 2 0003* translates into a machine word; *PutN 2 *+3* can be written as *PutN 2 0003**, the same word with the star appended. A program called a loader can accept this form from a file and perform the addition before putting the word into the location from which it will be executed. In practice, addresses are usually relativized to the start of the segment, rather than to the individual location, and distinct tagging symbols are required for normal addresses (as here), shifted addresses (e.g. for byte addressing) and so on, so that the matter gets a bit complicated.

9.3 Grammar of machine codes

Before leaving machine codes for good, it should be pointed out that few machines have a unique format for all their instructions. The grammar of a machine code is usually finite (polynomial) but it is often of a form of which the following is a simple example:

$$
\begin{array}{ll}
S ::= aA|bB & a ::= 0|1|2|3 \\
A ::= dC & b ::= 4|5|6|7|8|9 \\
B ::= DD & d ::= a|b \\
C ::= ddd & \\
D ::= dd &
\end{array}
$$

With this grammar, productions can lead to any of the one hundred thousand numbers 00000–99999, and to nothing else, but those numbers beginning with 0, 1, 2 or 3 are interpreted according to the format *x.x.xxx*, and the rest according to the format *x.xx.xx*; thus format selection must wait on the identification of the first digit.

Machines with variable length instructions are also known; this is commonly the case where the natural word-length is too short to be adequate for every purpose, but also reflects the fact that the amount of information which an instruction has to convey varies. The means for indicating that a given sequence is incomplete and requires extension may or may not be recursive. There is one machine whose grammar as seen by the ordinary programmer can be written

89

$$\langle\text{instrucn}\rangle ::= \langle\text{funcn word}\rangle|\langle\text{instrucn}\rangle\langle\text{parameter word}\rangle$$

the number of parameter words being determined by the function. Character-based machines may operate similarly or may operate in reverse Polish notation.

9.4 Early autocodes

One leaves symbolic assembly languages and enters on autocodes as soon as one (a) places on the compiler the responsibility for assigning storage locations, and (b) abandons the one-to-one correspondence between the functions of the machine and the functions permitted in the language in favour of something nearer to mathematical notation. But at this level the freedom with which mathematical notation may be used is usually firmly, if not narrowly constrained. Autocode is specifically the name of a language designed for use on the Mercury computer (and of a predecessor known as Manchester Autocode). Generically it is extended to a number of consciously similar languages for other machines, and as descriptive of a language level it includes at least the earliest forms of Fortran. The latter, the name derived from 'FORmula TRANslator', was originally an American development for the IBM machines. As Fortran II (Rabinowitz 1962) it spread rapidly. Since then it has evolved to permit the expression of ideas developed in other languages, but the original form is still of interest for comparative purposes.

In the Manchester Autocode (Brooker, 1956), the programmer was required to reduce an expression like

$$x = a+b\times c+d\times e \tag{1}$$

into

$$v1 = b\times c$$
$$v2 = d\times e$$
$$v1 = a+v1$$
$$x = v1+v2 \tag{2}$$

but was saved all truck with actual addresses in the machine, or with matters like initial clearing of accumulators, etc, for which a knowledge of the particular machine code is necessary. Provision was also made for limited instructions of the type

$$v2 = f(v1)$$

e.g. with $f = squareroot$. In Mercury Autocode and in Fortran II the reduction of (1) to (2) was also mechanized subject to certain restrictions which arise fundamentally from the fact that at the time that they were announced the programming techniques necessary to implement recursively defined expressions had not been developed. They also accepted restrictions arising out of the machines for which they were developed (see the quotation from Brooker and Morris

90

below). The appearance of tools of this sort was such a relief from coding in machine languages (even using symbolic assembly techniques) that their limitations were hardly noticed until some time later. By this time large vested interests had grown up, in the shape of users who swapped programs and parts of programs. In consequence, both languages tended to grow by having such additional facilities grafted on to them as could be added without interfering unduly with the basic facilities *in their original forms.*

In the original Mercury Autocode, for example, the letters $i, j \ldots t$ were available as integer variables and the others as real variables, and this rigidity has never been removed. In Fortran there was greater freedom in that multi-letter words could be used as the names of variables, but the initial letter of any name played a similar role (I to N integer, however) in determining its type. In Fortran IV this convention may be over-ruled by Algol-like declarations, but in order to accept, as far as possible, programs written in earlier versions the convention still holds unless overruled. Rather interestingly this has led to a new concept of much wider application (or at any rate it was the first example of the concept). This is the provision of a background of conventions so wide that it provides a 'default interpretation' whenever any statement of a declarative nature is omitted. The great virtue of this is that it eases enormously the preliminary burden of learning necessary to the casual user of the language before he can write a useful program.

Consider also the matter of subscripting. In Mercury Autocode the syntax of variables is built up thus: we first define the following representative symbols

$$\langle\text{a-letter}\rangle ::= a|b|c|d|e|f|g|h|u|v|w|x|y|z$$
$$\langle\text{i-letter}\rangle ::= i|j|k|l|m|n|o|p|q|r|s|t$$
$$\langle\pi\text{-letter}\rangle ::= \langle\text{a-letter}\rangle|\pi$$
$$\langle\text{sign}\rangle ::= +|-$$

and the permitted structures for variables can now be shown as

$$\langle\text{integer variable}\rangle ::= \langle\text{i-letter}\rangle$$
$$\langle\text{real variable}\rangle ::= \langle\text{simple variable}\rangle|\langle\text{subscripted var}\rangle$$
$$\langle\text{simple variable}\rangle ::= \langle\text{a-letter}\rangle|\langle\text{a-letter}\rangle'$$
$$\langle\text{subscripted var}\rangle ::= \langle\pi\text{-letter}\rangle\langle\text{subscript}\rangle$$
$$\langle\text{subscript}\rangle ::= \langle\text{integral number}\rangle|\langle\text{i-letter}\rangle|(\langle\text{i-letter}\rangle\langle\text{sign}\rangle$$
$$\langle\text{integral number}\rangle)$$

Thus, $3, i, (j+2), (k-3)$ are all permitted as subscripts, but not $(i+j)$; the latter must be precomputed by, say, $m = i+j$. Also, whereas ab is a multiplied by b, ai is interpreted as a_i (one must write ia to get the product). In Fortran, because of multiletter names, the multiplication sign must be explicit (and because of the punched card influence it is an asterisk), and subscripts are bracketed. The curious distinction in Autocode between a-letters and π-letters 'is connected' according to Brooker and Morris (1962) 'with the layout of material in the high speed store of Mercury. For the present purpose we just have to accept it as an instance of the many awkward features that are likely to occur in practical autocodes'. It would be better now to say that this was the sort of thing that was always happening, in every language, in the late 1950's, but cannot be tolerated today.

It will also be seen that subscripts are single; that is, the array $a(1,1) \ldots a(3,3)$ must be treated as the vector $a(1) \ldots a(9)$, and $a(r,s)$ referenced by precomputing $m = 3(r-1)+s$. In Fortran II, in contrast, one, two or three subscripts were allowed, and up to seven in IBM Fortran IV. Subscripts to subscripts were still in the future.

9.5 Autocode and Fortran II compared

Both Autocode and Fortran II provided conditional jumps but not conditional expressions. The format was rather different. In Autocode the simple 'JUMP⟨label⟩' was extended to

$$JUMP\langle label\rangle,\langle arith\ exp\rangle\langle relational\ op\rangle\langle arith\ exp\rangle$$

and in Fortran the unconditional 'GOTO⟨label⟩' was replaced by

$$IF(\langle arith\ exp\rangle),\langle label\rangle,\langle label\rangle,\langle label\rangle$$

all three labels being mandatory and being selected according as the arithmetic expression was less than, equal to or greater than zero. Fortran IV incorporates instructions of the 'IF (⟨boolean⟩)⟨statement⟩' type. Both languages, incidentally, use integer labels.

Again, both languages provided for a compact syntax for the writing of loops. In Autocode the simple assignment of a value to an i-letter could be expanded to the form

$$\langle i\text{-letter}\rangle = \langle int.value\rangle(\langle int.value\rangle)\langle int.value\rangle$$

and complemented by a statement 'REPEAT' lower down. The i-letter was then assigned the first of the integral values and the program executed as far as the REPEAT; the program then repeated this block of instructions as often as necessary with the i-letter increased each time by the second value until it executed it with the i-letter equal to the last value, when it ignored the REPEAT and continued. In Fortran the corresponding statement was

$$DO\langle label\rangle\langle int.var\rangle = \langle int.exp\rangle,\langle int.exp\rangle,\langle int.exp\rangle$$

with the increment in the *third* place on the right, and the label identifying the last instruction before the return point, which could be a dummy 'CONTINUE' whenever it was inconvenient to label an executive statement for the purpose. The i-letter in such a syntactical construct is known as the *controlled variable*. The precise syntax adopted is relatively uninteresting, but the semantics holds the possibility of all sorts of traps. What happens if the controlled variable is altered within the block that is being repeated — is the change accepted at the next incrementation, or nullified, or is such a manoeuvre illegal? How is the final test made? In Autocode the second variable could be positive or negative, but the final test was on equality, and a loop such as $i = 1(2)6$ would loop for ever with $i = 1, 3, 5, 7...$ In Fortran the test was a 'greater than', avoiding this trap, but all three values had to be positive. What is the value of the controlled variable on exit — the last accepted value or the first rejected one? The answers to these questions can take much space and are only of historical interest now; what is significant is that their importance has now been recognized, and the answers are a part of the specification of any language proposed today, and not, as in those days, the result of the way the first compiler was written.

Both languages made provision for the natural handling of subroutines and functions, the parameters being evaluated down to the state of a machine address if possible, or to a single value in the case of an expression, before entry to the routine; this is effectively what has since been described as call by simple name. (see Section 11.2.)

Whenever subscripted variables are involved it is necessary to give the machine some indication of the amount of storage required by specifying the number of components to which each subscripted variable can run. In Autocode this was done by directives of the form $a \rightarrow 20$, implying that in addition to the simple variables a and a', storage for a vector a with suffixes running from 0 to 20 is needed. A series of such directives caused consecutive allocation of storage, so that if this was followed by $c \rightarrow 5$, then a call for a_{22} would yield c_1. This would normally be the result of erroneous programming but was occasionally exploited. The corresponding facility in Fortran was the 'DIMENSION statement', and one such as

DIMENSION A(2,3)

provided the information that A was the name, *not of a simple variable* (contrast this with Autocode) *nor of a function but of an array* whose suffixes run from $1(sic)$ to 2 and from 1 to 3. Going out of bounds was monitored in the course of finding a required address.

Finally, because the high-speed store of Mercury was small, an Autocode program had to be written in terms of a number of 'chapters' each limited in size to what the high speed store would hold. (In case of chapter overflow the monitor referred the program back to its writer for revision). Each chapter had its own labels, and special arrangements were provided for going 'across' or 'down' into other chapters ('down' implying a return 'up' later). Chapter 0 was always the last in a program and was the signal for entry into the execution phase. A Fortran program was organized in terms of named subroutines and an unnamed main routine; 'CALL ⟨subroutine⟩' arranged the transfer into a subroutine and 'RETURN' the exit back to the calling routine. It was always a claim of Fortran devotees that while compilation might sometimes be slow, no routine need be compiled more than once, since a complete program could be assembled with some parts in Fortran and some already compiled into machine code. Provision was made for a declaration 'COMMON' to indicate that the variables so declared were not local to the routine but global. To this concept was added another declaration 'EQUIVA-LENCE' which permitted the same storage area to be called by different names within a routine. Unfortunately different interpretations of the interaction between these two declarations resulted in an incompatibility between Fortran II and Fortran IV, so that programs in the former could not always be compiled as though in a subset of the latter.

As a result of this difficulty and of a growing number of local variations, a committee was set up in 1962, and in 1964 a draft standard specification was published (Heising, 1965) for two languages to be known as Fortran and Basic Fortran. These were as compatible as possible with the various existing versions of Fortran IV and Fortran II respectively, and Basic Fortran was defined as a strict subset of Fortran. The Fortran specification was a document of some 16,000 words and that for Basic Fortran was a duplicate with some omissions and some consequent modifications. (The number of words in this book is about 90,000.) Since then, developments in computer technology have provided even minicomputers with sufficient storage to handle a compiler of reasonable size, and the emphasis on Basic Fortran has diminished.

Fortran is still the most popular language. Its selling points have been (1) the wide availability of its compilers, (2) the sheer quantity of work written in it that can be 'begged, borrowed or stolen', (3) the emphasis on efficient runtime code which often gives it an edge in production work, and (4) the efforts made on behalf of users to maintain continuity with former versions. Thus it is the most conservative of languages in both the best and the worst senses. At the time of writing (1976) the current standard is one known as ANSI Fortran.

9.6 Jovial

In 1958 the committee who were working on Algol produced an interim report which proved, in retrospect, to have two main results. By introducing CBNF to the world it inspired the earliest work on syntax directed compilers. And it inspired a team under Jules Schwartz at System Development Corporation to improve on its linguistic proposals and develop Jovial (Shaw 1963; the name is an acronym of 'Jules' Own Version of Algol'). This language resembles the music of Bach, which one critic has described as 'a hundred years behind its times and a hundred years in advance of every other time'; which is regarded with suspicion by the world at large and with devotion by everyone who has taken the trouble to understand it. Lacking some features which appeared in Algol 60, it pioneered many others (such as the ability to modify itself to suit an individual programmer's notational preferences) which are desirable when programming (a) *very* large systems, in which (b) a number of programs operate independently on a common data pool, and (c) operator communication in English is desirable; its largest area of application has been the writing of programs for the American Air Defence System.

10

COBOL

The main drive for the development of Cobol (a COmmon Business Oriented Language) came from the United States Department of Defense. It is very difficult to have a truly objective opinion about it, since in some directions it has set its sights extraordinarily high and in others its attitude is almost cringing. Its distinguishing features, which it shared with a number of short-lived, industrially sponsored languages such as the Honeywell 'Fact', the N.C.R. Language H, and the I.C.T. 'Nebula' were:

1. to attempt to be a subset of English, and as such readable (though not writeable) by the uninitiated,
2. to cater for data structures of the sort found in typical office records, whether personnel, stores, financial, or a combination of these,
3. to aim at a realistic approach to the attainment of complete compatibility.

As regards the first of these, it is only fair to say that it was not taken seriously for very long, although it has left a permanent mark on the appearance of the language. We discuss subsets of English later, and it will suffice here to recall (with approval) one sarcastic comment about the assumption that there are people for whom it is necessary to make allowances, who can understand the meaning *and implications of*

MOVE X TO Y.
ADD BALANCE TO OLDTOTAL GIVING NEWTOTAL

but are unable to do the same for

$$Y = X; \text{ NEWTOTAL} = \text{OLDTOTAL} + \text{BALANCE}$$

The strength of Cobol lies in (2) and (3) above. A Cobol program is punched to a quite rigid format and a lot can turn on whether eight or nine blanks occur before the first visible character in a line. Its designers did not envisage load-and-go operation. The compiler produces two things, a program in machine language punched in a form suitable for feeding into a machine for immediate obedience, and a printed copy of the original Cobol edited in certain respects

96

(i.e. a documentation to accompany the punched output). In the simplest case the editing may be no more than the insertion of the date of compilation for reference. At the other extreme, an I.C.T. Rapidwrite compiler produces a text in true Cobol although the input is in a subset of Cobol so simplified by various conventional abbreviations that purists refuse to allow it to be called a form of Cobol at all.

In one matter arising out of (2) and (3) it is possibly still unique. A compiled Cobol program relies more heavily on subroutine calls than do programs written in most other languages. At first sight this is inefficient, but it is claimed that the identical compiled Cobol program using different local subroutines in different environments achieves a greater overall efficiency than other methods of approach would do. This is a difficult matter to discuss unless one is prepared to go into the various requirements of different environments ranging from the small privately owned machine up to the very big service-bureau machine.

The original Cobol report appeared in April 1960, and a revised specification appeared in June 1961. This contains 'required' and 'elective elements. Strictly speaking this distinction is not part of the language but of the examination syllabus in the language. A compiler 'passes' if it translates correctly all required elements, and passes 'with honours' if it correctly translates the elective features as well. In November 1963, E.C.M.A., the European Computer Manufacturer's Association, produced proposals for 'Compact Cobol', in which the boundary between 'required' and 'elective' is shifted in the direction of requiring less, with the object of assisting small machines.

10.1 Program structure

A Cobol program is in four parts known as divisions. These are the Identification, Environment, Data and Procedure divisions. The last of these contains the program proper, but this is meaningless (or at best incomplete) without the pre-supposition of a data structure to work upon defined in the third division. The environment and data divisions are further divided into sections, the former into configuration and input-output sections and the latter into file, working-storage and constant sections. A division or section is headed by its name, followed by a full stop, on a line to itself. The contents of a section or division consists of sentences grouped into named paragraphs.

The identification division is small and relatively fixed in format. For example

```
000100  IDENTIFICATION DIVISION.
000200  PROGRAM-ID.  PAYROLL.
000400  AUTHOR.  JOHN DOE.
```

```
000450   DATE-WRITTEN.   APRIL 5TH
000460      1960.
000500   SECURITY.
000600   INSTALLATION.
000700   DATE-COMPILED. TODAY
000800   REMARKS.
```

The card numbering system has been explained in Section 6.1. Any or all of the paragraphs after the second may be omitted; their names are fixed. The program name must be a proper Cobol word, in effect a sequence of not more than 30 characters constructed from the numerals, the letters and the hyphen (used internally). This division is copied on to the listed output, replacement of the contents of DATE-COMPILED by the actual date being an elective feature; nothing else is done with it.

10.2 The environment division

The Environment division is supposed to contain all that information which is needed to solve compatibility problems, although not necessarily explicitly. This consists of a description of the computer on which the translation is to be done, a similar description of the computer on which the compiled program is intended to be run (not necessarily the same machine), an indication of any cross-referencing of names which may be necessary when referring to peripherals and so on.

In practice, the valuable information which can be conveyed in this division lies at a lower level than its wording might suggest. A Cobol compiler is a big enough program in any case, without trying to give it a multi-lingual output, in terms of the machine order-codes it can use. And one might also very reasonably suppose that the only purpose the SOURCE-COMPUTER paragraph could possibly serve would be a similar one to the DATE-COMPILED paragraph — viz., that on the listed output the computer actually used would sign its own name. But commercial computers are sold in varying 'configurations'; that is, a machine may be advertised as fitted with a minimum of two, maximum of eight, tape units, and your installation may have six. So although it is quite possible, by compiling first into an intermediate language (probably of some sort of macrogenerator type) to write a compiler with a multilingual output, it is of greater practical advantage to write a compiler which can automatically adapt the efficiency of the object program to the configuration of the machine on which it is to be run. And this applies even to the name of the source computer, since although the compiler must be written for the machine on which it is to be run, it can be made self-adapting to the configuration, again with possible implications on the efficiency of the object program, and even adapt itself in emergency to a configuration which has been temporarily reduced by a peripheral breakdown.

A typical example of the Environment Division might begin thus:

```
001101   ENVIRONMENT DIVISION.
001201   CONFIGURATION SECTION.
001302   SOURCE-COMPUTER. COPY ME.
001402   OBJECT-COMPUTER. BIG-BROTHER.
001412   6 TAPE-UNITS.
001503   SPECIAL-NAME. TYPEWRITER IS TELEPRINTER.
001601   INPUT-OUTPUT SECTION.
```

and continue with I-O section material. In this example we have used the final digit of the card sequence number for reference purposes. Thus those that end in '1' are absolutely fixed in format, apart from the general rule which allows the separator between the words to consist of any number of spaces. In the computer names, reference 2, two formats are allowed, of which both are shown. COPY can be followed by any Cobol name which has been used to identify a suitable description which is kept stored in a part of the computer memory called the Cobol library. Alternatively a detailed description (in general more complicated than the example) can be given, and the manner in which this should be done is not laid down in Cobol itself, but is left to the compiler writer to lay down. In this way the writer of a compiler for a bizarre installation — e.g. one containing a microphone/loudspeaker for in/output — would not be impossibly constrained by rules which had not foreseen it. The paragraph SPECIAL-NAME, reference 3, is more straightforward; it means that (1) the procedure division, possibly originally written with some other installation in mind, refers to a teleprinter, (2) there is on the object computer a peripheral which the compiler writer always calls the typewriter, and (3) this is what is to be used when the procedure division asks for the teleprinter. The name of this paragraph is permitted to be in the plural, and the paragraph to contain as many such sentences as are required (the rest of the paragraph being indented four spaces, like the '1960' in the identification division).

The INPUT-OUTPUT SECTION is concerned with similar correspondences of names between data-files and the hardware items on which they are to be read or written — these are in a paragraph with the fixed name FILE-CONTROL — and also optionally with certain RERUN facilities — these are in a paragraph with the fixed name I-O-CONTROL.

10.3 Further details

The grammar of Cobol is not written in CBNF but in a less general notation peculiar to it and a few languages which resemble it fairly closely. The sentences in a FILE-CONTROL paragraph will serve to illustrate it; they must conform to the following format:

SELECT[OPTIONAL] file-name-1 [RENAMING file-name-2]

ASSIGN TO [integer-1] hardware-name-1 [, hardware-name-2]

[FOR MULTIPLE REEL] [, RESERVE $\begin{Bmatrix} \text{integer-2} \\ NO \end{Bmatrix}$

ALTERNATE $\begin{Bmatrix} \text{AREAS} \\ \text{AREA} \end{Bmatrix}$] [SELECT . . .].

In this schema, words in lower case are type names such as would be in metalinguistic brackets in CBNF, but the '-1' and '-2' are explicit signs of what is tacit in CBNF, namely, that the replacements are independent. (Cf. Section 7.4.1.) Words in capitals appear literally; those not *italicised* are 'noise words', allowed but unnecessary and contributing nothing. No other noise words are permitted. Braces show alternatives, and square brackets mean that their contents may be omitted or included according to the meaning required. The simplest FILE-CONTROL paragraph would therefore be something like:

```
001704   FILE-CONTROL. SELECT CONTROL-SEQUENCE
001800      ASSIGN PAPER-READER.
```

but in addition to the possibility of a whole series of SELECTs, any individual one can expand thus

```
001704 FILE-CONTROL. SELECT OPTIONAL SUPPLEMEN
001800 - TARIES RENAMING MASTER ASSIGN TO 1
001900 TAPE-UNIT FOR MULTIPLE REEL, RESERVE
002000 1 ALTERNATE AREA
```

Here CONTROL-SEQUENCE, SUPPLEMENTARIES and MASTER are the names of files; PAPER-READER is the name used in this installation for a paper tape reader. OPTIONAL means that the program is not to mind if this file is absent during a run which does not take a course that requires it. FOR MULTIPLE REEL is concerned with files that take more than one reel and therefore require action of an unusual sort when the file is half read, and RENAMING is rather a misnomer (STRUCTURED ON would be better) since it means that file-name-1 has not been described in the Data division because it is exactly like file-name-2. ALTERNATE, of course, does not mean 'alternate', but 'alternative'.

RESERVE raises a point which deserves a slightly longer look. Computers cannot look at information on magnetic tape just as and when they like, so they have to take a copy of a part of it and refer to their copy, which is usually known as a buffer. Since a program which has finished with what is in its buffer will be held up until the next bit of tape has been copied, it may pay off in speed to be extravagant in storage demands by using two (or more) buffer areas, used alternately (or cyclically), so that one is being copied into while another is being worked upon. This is the function of the RESERVE clause. The reason we note it specially here is that it is concerned with communication of an unusual type of information — effectively a policy preference in the manner of compilation — a type which most programming languages do not cater for at all.

We presume that only middle-sized machines take any notice of RESERVE; the small ones have to say, 'Sorry, but we just haven't the extra space available', and the large ones say, 'Look, chum, if it's any use to you on this time-sharing system by which you don't pay if you are forced to wait, we give it to you without your asking for it'. This is rather like air-mail stickers which are a waste of time (a) on journeys too short for air, but also (b) for destinations to which the post office uses the currently quickest route irrespective. Be this as it may, we do call attention to the fact that Cobol finds it desirable to communicate not only instructions as to how the data reduction is to be carried out, but also advice as to the preferred method of organizing data queues.

To summarize, any nasty taste (and there usually is one) which a study of the Environment division leaves on people more familiar with other languages should not be blamed on Cobol as a language, but on the nastiness of the compatibility situation which it tries to face more honestly and completely than more mathematical languages have to do, or than industrially sponsored languages (which often have a minor aim of selling a particular group of machines) always wish to do.

10.4 The Data division

The DATA DIVISION is based on the concept of a FILE and consists of a series of file-descriptions together with a small amount of material (working space and constants) which does not fit into a file-structure. A file consists of an indefinite number of RECORDS all of which conform to one or other of a small number of structure patterns contained in the Data division, and it is presumed that when a file is READ, it is the next record that is read, and that when the name of a file is used in the Procedure division it is the last-read record from that file that is meant. Thus unless provision is made to preserve data in working space, successive records are dealt with independently. The implication is that each file referred to by an ASSIGN in the Environment division will be given a buffer area adequate to hold one record of the (maximum) size shown by its description in the Data division to be necessary. However, although this is the basic theory, a record may be an inconveniently small unit for the mechanism of the magnetic tape, and the concept of a BLOCK of records is introduced to get around this. In its physical form as a magnetic tape, a file may well begin with a title or LABEL; such material can be of two sorts, the first in a form laid down by the person in charge of the installation, to ensure that tapes do not get mixed up or otherwise wrongly used, and the second in a form desired by the programmer. Concerning the former nothing can be said and it is laid down that the latter must be regarded as an alternative form of record. Provision is therefore made to describe LABELS simply as STANDARD or OMITTED. (Oddly, in view of the wish to attain as high a degree of compatibility as possible, the alternative FOREIGN is not provided, though if it were, it would be necessary to have a universally accepted standard method for recognizing the *end* of the label.)

The remaining part of the description of a file consists of a description of the records it may contain. This is best detailed by an example. The 'F' of 'FD' stands in Col. 8, and the three hyphens in Col. 7.

```
 FD COSTS-FILE; BLOCK CONTAINS 10 RECORDS; LABEL
    RECORDS ARE STANDARD; VALUE OF IDENTIFICA
-   TION IS 'COSTS'; DATA RECORDS ARE WAGE-ITEM,
    PURCHASE-ITEM, DEPENDING ON ITEM.
 01  WAGE-ITEM.
    02  ITEM; SIZE IS 1 AN.
    88  WAGE-TYPE; VALUE IS 'W'.
    02  EMPLOYEE-DATA.
       03  EMPLOYEE-NO; SIZE IS 6 NUMERIC DISPLAY.
       03  SALARY; SIZE IS 4 COMPUTATIONAL
       03  BONUS-CODE; SIZE IS 3 AN.
    02  ITEM-DATA.
       03  PROJECT-NO; PICTURE IS 999999X.
       03  NORMAL-TIME; SIZE IS 3 COMPUTATION
-         AL; POINT LEFT 1.
       03  OVERTIME; SIZE IS 3 COMPUTATIONAL;
          POINT LEFT 1.
 01  PURCHASE-ITEM.
    02  ITEM; SIZE IS 1 AN.
    88  PURCHASE-TYPE; VALUE IS 'P'.
    02  INVOICE-NO; PICTURE IS AAX99999.
    02  DEBIT-VALUE; SIZE IS 8; USAGE IS COMPUTA
-      TIONAL; POINT LOCATION IS LEFT 3 PLACES.
    02  PROJECT-NO; PICTURE IS 999999X.
```

So far as the FD portion is concerned, note, in addition to what has already been said, that 'VALUE OF . . .' means that the standard label of the correct file will include the word 'COSTS' as a check that the file is the right one, and that 'DEPENDING ON . . .' is a Honeywell idiom meaning that, the records being of two types, the type to which a given record belongs can be determined immediately by inspection of the field 'ITEM'. Thus the two '01' portions are alternative possibilities. Two records from this file might read

W1428571950NIL004321 217000   PJJ-0021400063550004321

which we interpret initially by dividing them thus

W/142857/1950/NIL/004321 /217/000/
P/JJ-00214/00063550/004321 /

in accordance with the data descriptions. In both types, that is, the first 'element' is a single alphanumeric character (1 AN). If this is 'W', it is followed by (i) the employee number, consisting of six numerical characters, (ii) his salary, a four decimal-digit number already in the most convenient form for computation (probably binary), (iii) a bonus-code symbol of three alphanumeric characters, (iv) the project number, of six decimal digits and a general character (in this office either space or asterisk and in this example a space), (v) the normal time, which in this example was *21.7 hrs*, and so on.

The indentations, after the first, are optional; it is the level-numbers which define the tree-structure. The term 'data-item' is used to cover 'elements', complete 'records', and also intermediate items such as EMPLOYEE-DATA. Thus because this term is used in the syntactical description of MOVE, it is possible to say

MOVE EMPLOYEE-DATA IN COSTS-FILE TO EMPLOYEE-
    DATA IN REPORT-FILE

(this is a copying process, but the word COPY is reserved for copying *from the library*). Levels may go up to the generous limit of 49, with 66, 77, 88 serving special purposes. 88 introduces a 'condition name' and as used in our example it enables one to write

READ COSTS-FILE. IF WAGE-TYPE THEN . . .

(instead of IF ITEM EQUAL TO 'W' . . .). When a structure shows a repetitive pattern, it may be described once with 'OCCURS integer-1 TIMES', and the item so described must then be subscripted when used in the Procedure division. If a part of a record is irrelevant to the program, it may be referred to by the name FILLER in the Data division.

Files belong essentially to the external world and must be brought in and out, one record at a time, by READ and WRITE. In addition to the FILE SECTION there are similarly organized WORKING-STORAGE and CONSTANT SECTIONs, with level 77 available for items that do not fit into a structure. These sections are for material which never gets outside the machine. VALUE may be used to initialize such material. In Compact Cobol the CONSTANT section is merged into the WORKING-STORAGE section and 01 is used instead of 77.

10.5 The procedure division

Concerning the PROCEDURE DIVISION, a colleague once remarked to me that 'Cobol ceases to be interesting once you understand it', and there is some truth in this. If we allow that IF means EVALUATE THE BOOLEAN AND THEN . . . , then every statement begins with an imperative verb, and the grammar is simply a list of the structures permitted after each verb — all different, since even ADD. . . TO and MULTIPLY . . . BY have different prepositions. The problem in Cobol has been the semantics, in many fields, but particularly where editing is required. And there has been the sorry story (not unknown in other languages, but aggravated by pressure from the Department of Defense) of competing implementers producing different interpretations of intricate cases, often with the result that the intricate case has been declared illegal in the language. For example, it is possible to write, for a sum of less than £100 to the nearest 2/-, PICTURE IS 99V9, PICTURE IS 99·9 or USAGE IS COMPUTATIONAL POINT 1 LEFT. £6.10s would then be stored as the characters 065, the characters 06.5, or the number 65 in binary, respectively. In MOVing this value, the editing required is obvious, and will be done. But arithmetic is banned on the second, though not between items in the first and third styles. It has also been necessary to say that 'it is illegal to MOVE a group item whose format is such that editing would be required on the elements in separate operations'. All this was the result of a struggle between the linguistic requirements and the state of the art several years before, in which the latter won, thereby stamping Cobol as a language of the early sixties.

In one respect, Cobol appears to be a non-pure-procedural language. Given a paragraph which consists of a single statement 'GO TO . . .', one can write elsewhere 'ALTER paragraph TO PROCEED TO . . .'. This oddity is more apparent than real, as it is no more than a means of expressing a switch, or (an initialized) variable of type label. Cobol also has the switch, since it can say 'GO TO label-1, label-2 . . . DEPENDING ON integer-variable'.

In most languages a subroutine is either open or closed. That is, if it is required more than once it is either repeated at both places (open) or it is completely detached, given a name, and called by this name at both places. Cobol does not make this distinction. Sentences are grouped into paragraphs with names, and paragraphs may be further grouped into sections if desired. The verb PERFORM, followed by any paragraph or section name, calls in that paragraph or section as a subroutine, but if the same paragraph is entered in sequence it is left in sequence. The standard form of the exit is the sequential one; it is modified by the PERFORM before the entry, and resets itself after use. (This description defines what happens when it is jumped to in the middle.) This verb is a complicated one; in Compact Cobol its only other syntax is the addition of 'THRU paragraph-name-2', which causes the execution of paragraph-name-1 to paragraph-name-2 (inclusive), but standard Cobol uses it also to provide compact coding of loops by providing for '*n* times', 'until. . .', and 'varying . . . by . . .' with nesting of up to three controlled variables. Cobol does not provide for subroutines with parameters in the usual sense; a library subroutine can be introduced by 'COPY routine-name [USING variable-name-1 . . .]' but if it is required with different parameters in different places then distinct copies are created.

In addition to the usual 'IF . . .', Cobol has another form of conditional dictated by the file concept but adapted also to deal with the trap on numerical overflow. The syntax of a READ statement is

READ file-name RECORD [*INTO* data-name] [AT *END* imperative statement]

and the third portion of this is equivalent to 'if the result is not another record but an end-of-file indicator then. . .'. A similar phrase 'ON SIZE ERROR . . .' deals with overflow in arithmetic processes.

One problem which has to be faced by all languages modelled on a natural language is whether and to what extent words can be reserved. The Compact Cobol report lists 226 words which are part of the Cobol system and should be avoided — and does not include SORT among them, although a 'sorting' verb has been the subject of much study (Paterson [1963]). There is no reason why use of the word OMITTED as the name of a file should ever cause ambiguity, but one is told that it is unsafe to try to do so. The real problem in a situation like this is that, if words are reserved wholesale (i.e. not just the inevitables, whatever they may be) then all the words of the *extended* language must be reserved to the *minimum* one.

The above description and comment has concentrated on those features of Cobol which distinguish it from other languages, and in particular those arising from problems which languages in other classes do not have to meet. In other respects it is of its time — e.g. it allows for subscripting, but not being recursive, up to three subscripts only, and no subscripts to subscripts. Nested calls of subroutines are possible subject to elaborate rules which, among other things, rule out all recursive calls. Subroutines cannot raise their own storage and the division between data and procedure divisions is absolute. Working storage must be anticipated by providing it in the Data division under level 77. The Environment division is something new. It is therefore interesting to see that in Algol subscripting is completely free, subroutines can be freely called without checking whether the context permits it, they may be called with parameters and may raise their own storage. But there is no environment division in Algol 60, and only a rudimentary one when the in/output proposals are added, though there are proposals within the maintenance organization for a radically new approach to environment problems (see Section 15.2.1). The reserved word problem has been shelved for as long as we wish by printing reserved words, used in their technical capacity, in black type.

11

ALGOL 60

The appearance of the 'Report on the Algorithmic Language ALGOL 60' (Naur, 1960) marked a very great step forward in the subject of programming languages. The major characteristics of this language, which should be taken into account when describing any language as Algol-like, are

(a) Use of CBNF to define syntax, with semantics in English
(b) Acceptance of as much of current mathematical notation as could be proved workable, with elimination of all arbitrary restrictions whose origin lay in compiler design.
(c) A clear distinction in symbolism between the imperative (assignment) equals and the predicative (relational) equals.
(d) Use of English words in a distinct font (e.g. black type or underlined) to supply such new symbols as it required.
(e) Page lay-out completely at the service of legibility to human readers. (Not even a single space has any semantic significance, which may have been going too far.)

Its deficiencies would appear all to have been due to its authors' awareness that they were making a big step forward and their determination not to overstep their abilities in the circumstances (which included the usual need to work to some sort of target date). In fact, a few slips were made, the more obvious of which were cleared up in a revised report in 1962. Maintenance of Algol 60 is now in the hands of IFIP (the International Federation for Information Processing); IFIP runs an Algol Bulletin which serves as a forum for this purpose and also for the discussion of related languages including Algol 68.

In the syntax, integral and real numbers are first built up from the numerals, the plus and minus signs, the decimal point and the symbol $_{10}$. (Thus $3{\cdot}5_{10}+6$ means $3{\cdot}5 \times 10^{+6}$.) Names, referred to as 'identifiers', are built up by

⟨identifier⟩ ::= ⟨letter⟩|⟨identifier⟩⟨letter⟩|⟨identifier⟩⟨numeral⟩

that is, as any sequence of letters or numerals beginning with a letter. No identifier may be used without a 'declaration' of the type of object it names, except for labels, whose very use defines them. ⟨Simple arithmetic expression⟩s are built up as in Language 3 of

Section 7.2. This corresponds to normal practice except that it would leave *a*/*bc* meaning (*a*/*b*)*c* etc. But this particular case does not arise in quite this blatant form, because owing to the use of multi-letter identifiers, the multiplication sign must never be suppressed. Special notation for exponentiation and suffixing enable the input string to be kept strictly linear; x^y becomes $x \uparrow y$, where y may be a name (simple or suffixed identifier), an unsigned number, or any expression in brackets, and $x_{y,z}$ becomes $x[y,z]$, where y and z may themselves be expressions which may be or contain subscripted variables. The notation $f(x)$ for the function f of x is available, and is used for all more complicated purposes: thus

$$\sum_{x=m}^{n} p_x \text{ becomes sigma(p[x],x,m,n).}$$

But subject to these notational hurdles, if an expression is meaningful and valid in algebra, however involved it may be, it is valid in Algol with the same meaning. A similar development from the values **true** and **false**, the relational operators between numbers ('=', '>', etc), and the boolean operators embeds boolean algebra into the language in the same way. Conditional expressions are built up by the productions

⟨simple expression⟩ ::= ... |(⟨cond.exp⟩)
⟨cond.exp⟩ ::= **if** ⟨boolean exp⟩ **then** ⟨simple expression⟩
        else ⟨expression⟩

The range of structures which this grammar permitted was not in itself enough to force compiler writers to abandon non-recursive techniques, but was a strong pointer in this direction.

Algol 60 is a procedural language, programs being built up from units (called 'statements') each containing its own imperative(s). The elementary unit takes one of three forms:

(1) X := Y   (2) **go to** Z   (3) a name

where X is a simple name or a subscripted name, Y an expression, and Z a label-name or a designational expression (a conditional label-name or a switch (see below) or combination of these). In the third form the name is a procedure name (see next Section). Such elementary units are separated by semicolons, as are the compound units formed by surrounding a sequence of units by **begin** ... **end**. Statements as well as expressions may be conditional, and the inclusion of the option by which

if B **then** Z;   is equivalent to   **if** B **then** Z **else**;

(i.e. to 'Z if B, dummy if not B') while a very natural mode of expression, has been a fruitful source of unexpected ambiguities.

A program is a single self-contained statement, that is to say it is a message in the form **begin** ... **end** which uses no names whose meaning it does not define (or which are not system defined). Declarations must be made immediately after a **begin** and are valid up to the *corresponding* **end**; this makes them effectively imperatives for the creation of the objects they refer to before value-assigning imperatives are reached, and allows such creation to be temporary if there is any point in arranging it this way. The permitted types are 'real', 'integer', 'boolean' and arrays of these; thus '**begin real** x, y;...' means 'start this phase by assigning further storage for two real numbers to be called x and y; throughout this phase x and y refer to these numbers whatever may be the case elsewhere'. However, the further types 'string', 'label' and 'procedure' are permitted to *bound* variables, as we shall see, and an object of type 'switch' permits indirect reference to labels; this is an array of labels or expressions of type label that is embedded in the message and not in created storage.

11.1 The development of the procedure

Although the fully recursive nature of the syntax of expressions may have suggested recursive methods in implementation, it is in fact possible to implement by non-recursive methods any program in which the degree of nesting can be determined explicitly by a preliminary scan. However Algol permits routines to be written in which the depth of recursion cannot be determined until run time. Mostly this is due to the development, out of the subroutine, of the procedure. The following account of how this happened may not be strictly historical but cannot be far off being so.

In the notation of algebra, we can express the fact that the H.C.F. of three numbers is that of any two with the third thus

$$HCF(a, b, c) = hcf(hcf(a, b), c)$$

In Algol, a sequence for reducing both of two numbers to their h.c.f. might be written

> A: **if** x = y **then go to** Z;
>   **if** x > y **then** x := x—y **else** y := y—x;
>   **go to** A;
> Z:

and (without bothering to improve on this) we consider the problem of using it to find the h.c.f. of three numbers, a, b and c given on an input tape. We assume that the system specifies that the name *next* always refers to the next value in the input tape, and that *print* (x) similarly provides us with an output facility. At a level of programming which is very close to machine-practice language, we should have to see that x and y are started with the correct contents and that proper return information ('link') is organized. A complete program along these lines would be

109

```
begin integer a, b, c, n, x, y; comment see text;
        a := next;   b := next;   c := next;
        x := a;   y := b;   n := 1;   comment setting operands
            and link for first use of subroutine;
A:   if x = y then go to Z;
        if x>y then x := x−y else y := y−x;
        go to A;
Z:   if n = 1 then go to B else if n = 2 then go to C;
B:   y := c;   n := 2;   go to A;   comment second setting,
        but x already contains the appropriate value;
C:   print(x)   end.
```

This is over-elementary and can be simplified. (1) Only three of
a, b, c, x, y are really necessary. (2) One can use a switch by replacing
the first **comment** by 'switch S := B, C;' and line *Z* by 'go to S[n];'.
But the *link* planting is clumsy and could be eliminated if one could
do something like

```
begin integer a, b, c, x, y;
        a := next;   b := next;   c := next;   x := a;   y := b;
H:    begin A: if x = y then go to Z;
                    if x>y then x := x−y else y := y−x;
                    go to A;   Z: end;
        y := c;   perform H;   print(x) end.
```

as indeed one can in Cobol, although the *parameter* planting is now
looking clumsy. There is some evidence (the **do** of the 1958 report)
that this direction of development was considered, but if so, then it
was seen to be outclassed by the following alternative:

```
begin integer a, b, c, x, y;
    procedure H;   begin A: if x = y then go to Z;
                                if x>y then x := x−y else y := y−x;
                                go to A;   Z: end;
        a := next;   b := next;   c := next;
        x := a;   y := b;   H;
        y := c;   H;   print(x) end.
```

For now it becomes possible to deal with the parameters in a way
that matches conventional mathematical practice. We write

```
begin integer a, b, c;
    procedure H(x,y); comment 1;
        begin A: if x = y then go to Z;
                    if x>y then x := x−y else y := y−x;
                    go to A;   Z: end;
        a := next;   b := next;   c := next;
        H(a, b);   H(a, c);   print(a) end.
```

110

At **comment** 1, it is permissible to assist the compiler by inserting 'integer x, y;', thus indicating that x and y are intended to be replaced by other variables of type integer, and many compilers demand this assistance. Such information on bound variables is called 'specification' as opposed to the 'declaration' of free variables; it is not a storage-raising imperative in the sense in which a declaration is (but see Section 5.1 above, and **value** below). The statement $H(a, b)$ means 'carry on as though you had here a copy of the "body" of the definition of H with a and b taking the place of x and y respectively, each time they occur'. Thus $H(a,b)$ reduces both a and b to their h.c.f., and $H(a,c)$ reduces the reduced a and c to *their* h.c.f.

This last feature is something which does not arise in the static conditions of algebra. In many circumstances it is just what we want; in others it is most inconvenient. To avoid it, a variation is provided in which we would write the procedure declaration thus:

```
procedure H(x,y,z);   value x,y;
  begin A: if x = y then go to Z;
          if x>y then x := x−y else y := y−x;
          go to A;   Z:z := x end;
```

The **value** specification requires the procedure to start by making local copies of the values of x and y and to do all further work on these copies. It now becomes necessary to find a way of getting the answer out of the procedure; this is the purpose of z which is not given a value specification. The main program would read

```
... integer a, b, c, d; ...
    H(a,b,d);   H(d,c,d);   print(d) end
```

But in all this we are still one step short of the algebraic notation by which $hcf(a,b)$ is not 'how to get' the h.c.f., but is its actual value. A name cannot be both of these at once, and it has been made possible to define it either way. The new form of definition is known as a 'type procedure'; it begins '**integer procedure**...', to show that it stands for an integer type value, and it 'gets the value out' by an assignment to the name. The effect on the main program is rather breathtaking, as it *can* be written thus:

```
begin integer procedure hcf (x,y);   value x,y;
      begin A: if x = y then go to Z;
              if x>y then x := x−y else y := y−x;
              go to A;   Z:hcf := x end;
  print(hcf(hcf(next, next), next)) end.
```

A more cautious programmer would retain a, b and c; nevertheless, on account of the value specification, each 'next' is only called once, and also in this problem the order of calling does not matter, with

111

the result that certain possible traps do not materialize. When Algol is written in this style the result is very close to a function language.

Overt recursion is explicitly permitted in Algol; that is, the following formulation, however inefficient, is valid:

> **integer procedure** hcf(x,y); **value** x,y;
> hcf := **if** x = y **then** x **else if** x>y **then**
> hcf (x−y,y) **else** hcf(x,y−x);

Implicit recursion also occurs in an expression like *hcf(hcf(a,b),c)* since (even on a call by value) the parameters are not evaluated before entering a routine but while in it, so that the evaluation of the inner *hcf* takes place *during* the evaluation of the outer one.

11.2 Calling styles

A parameter of a procedure that is not called by value is said to be called *by name*. The principle of call by name is the Markovian one of interpretation by implicit textual substitution. Precautions are necessary whenever independent but identically spelt identifiers may thus be brought into confusing proximity (e.g. replacement of every *jones* by *jones the block*, or *jones the program*, or *jones the squareroot*, as appropriate), and type procedures lead to syntactic structures not available to the programmer (but see **valof**, in Section 13.1.3). The principle was criticized by Strachey and Wilkes (1961) who proposed a 'call by simple name', later renamed 'call by reference', more like the Fortran method of calling a simple variable (Section 9.5; some implementations of Fortran are very clear that X is a variable but (X) is an expression, so that F((X)) has the effect of a call by value). The distinction between these three parameter styles may perhaps be best seen from the following very artificial example, which is written in Algol 60 extended to admit all three types of call.

> **begin integer** i, **array** A[1:3]; comment this means that A has components A[1] .. A[3];
> **procedure** report(x,y,z); **value** x; **ref** y; **name** z;
> **begin** i := 3;   A[1] := 5;   print(x,y,z) **end**
> i := 1;   A[1] := 2;   A[3] := 4;
> report(A[i], A[i], A[i]) **end**

The result of this program will be to print the numbers 2, 5, 4. In printing *x* the procedure has noted that *x* is *A[i]*, which had the value 2, and since *x* is called by value, this is what *x* means, since no assignments in the form '*x* := . . .' occur. In printing *y*, the process is stopped after determining the *location* referred to, and since *A[1]* is assigned the new value 5 before printing is called for, 5 is what is printed as the value of y. Finally, *z* remains *A[i]* up to the last moment, and therefore when it comes to printing it, it is interpreted as *A[3]*, which has the value 4. To avoid misunderstanding, we repeat

112

that this example is in an extended Algol 60; in true Algol 60 the first effect is obtained by writing the **value** specification, the third by refraining from writing this, and the second is not available.

Call by name is essential to the correct interpretation of the function $sigma(p(x),x,a,b)$ which we introduced earlier. The declaration of this function might be

```
real procedure sigma(p,q,r,s); value s;
    begin real S;
        S := 0;   q := r;
Y:      if q>s then go to Z;
        S := S+p;   q := q+1;   go to Y;
Z:      sigma := S end
```

We give s a value specification to avoid evaluating it (in case it is an expression) repeatedly at the statement Y. But p must be called by name or it will not vary as q is changed. This trick of making parameters functionally dependent on one another is known as the Jensen device. (Note that the two uses of p are completely independent, and do not lead to any clash.)

A fourth calling style, known as call by (value and) result, has been adopted in some implementations of (variants of or sucessors to) Algol 60. This is a call by value in which the final value of the local copy is assigned to the actual parameter during exit. In the example

```
begin integer i;
    procedure inc(x,y); comment result x,y;
        begin x := x+1;   y := y+1 end
    i := 1;   inc(i, i) end
```

it will be seen that it is not always as satisfactory as one might wish.

11.3 Higher level facilities

Like its immediate predecessors, Algol 60 has a higher-level format for direct writing of loops. The following statement incorporates all the possibilities in a *for-statement*:

$$\text{for } i := a \text{ step } b \text{ until } c, d, e \text{ while } f \text{ do } X$$

There is a single controlled variable of numerical type, which is assigned values from a list separated by commas; these may be single values like d, or sequences like $a, a+b, a+2b \ldots$, or a single value such as e which is repeated until some condition occurs. However, this 'single' value need not be a 'constant' value, it can be a variable or an expression. We defer further discussion to Section 13.5, where it can be seen alongside later developments.

Another feature of Algol 60 which has proved more complex in elaborate situations than was originally envisaged is the declarator

113

own. This can be applied to any local variable of a block and strictly speaking is not high-level since its effect cannot be reproduced in simpler Algol. Normally storage for local variables is raised on entry to the block (which may be a procedure body, of course) and relinquished on leaving it, but **own** preserves it until the next call. The effect of this is the same as declaring it globally except that (1) it cannot be referred to outside the block, and (2) there is no need to check that it is notationally different from other global identifiers; complementary to (2) is that in the case of library routines its declaration is inside them and one does not have to remember to add it, An example of its use would be a pseudo-random number generator. in which the result of the current call must be retained as the starting value for the next call. The usefulness of **own** in Algol 60 is greatly diminished by the lack of any method in the language for initializing variables, so that one always has to take care that a first application of the routine does not call for an **own** variable while it is still void. More serious are the difficulties which arise in two less simple circumstances, (1) when the routine is called recursively, and (2) in the case known as 'dynamic **own** arrays'. An example of the latter is the declaration '**own real array** A[n, n+3]'; suppose this to be called under circumstances in which n is alternately 0 and 1 — are the values of A[0] and A[4] to be lost or to be kept in cold storage when out of bounds?

Landin (1965) has some remarks on the semantics of **own** which suggest that it would be sounder if the storage for an own variable 'sat' on a level with the declaration of the block, i.e. that in

begin ... **begin real** x; **procedure** P; **begin own real** y ...

y should not exist globally, but come and go with x. More recently (Higman 1976a) it has been realized that the simple **own** technique can involve keeping two or more copies of a complete routine for the sake of the distinct copies of the own variable they provide (e.g. if two independent pseudo-random number series are called for by a problem) and that an own variable should be regarded as a frozen parameter — frozen to a local generator (Sections 13.15. and 13.3.3) suitably initialized at the moment of freezing.

114

12

LIST PROCESSING LANGUAGES

List processing languages arise (a) when the data structure is elaborate and has to be taken into account, but more importantly, (b) when this structure has to be operated upon as well as the values contained in it. (Were (a) the only reason, Cobol-type resources might well suffice.) The first work in this field began with Newell, Shaw and Simon in 1954 onwards, culminating in the 'Information Processing Language 5', or IPL-V, the manual for which appeared in 1961 (Newell, 1961). This work was directed towards simulating the 'more intelligent' types of computation, such as proving geometrical theorems in the Euclidean manner, or cybernetic simulation, and this aspect has all along proved a strong motivation for this type of language. IPL-V is a procedure language practically at the machine code level. In contrast, Lisp (McCarthy, 1960) is a function language. About the same time, Gelernter, Hansen and Gerberich (1960) published an extension of Fortran to accommodate lists, and Alp, a similar extension of Mercury Autocode, was announced two years later (Cooper and Whitfield, 1962). Slip (Weizenbaum, 1963) aimed at being embeddable in any existing procedural language, but was initially embedded in Fortran. Most recent is Wisp (Wilkes, 1964) — 'an experiment in a self-compiling compiler'; this is a system based initially on a simple but self-extending language, which is perhaps more comprehensible to conventional programmers than most of its predecessors. This brief history (written in 1967) fails to do justice to a lot of work on list structure and list processing which did not result in a language whose name became known.

When computers first appeared, the owner of one was often asked 'but can your machine solve an equation *algebraically*?' The honest answer at that time was 'Yes, of course, if I could only think how to write the program'. It was list processing techniques which first showed how to program a computer so that it could, for example, input a character string such as '$ax+b = cx+d$' and manipulate it so that it can be output in the rearranged form '$x = (d-b)/(a-c)$'.

In a list processing context as initially conceived, the external world to which a message refers is organized into *list-structures*, that is, lists of objects which can themselves be lists. This is done by making each object in it consist of two parts (i) an intrinsic part and

115

(ii) a pointer to the next object in the list, or, in the case of the last member of a list, a conventional termination. The intrinsic part can be either the value or the name of an object which represents the value. In the first case storage is saved but it also becomes inevitable that reference to any object can also be interpreted as reference to the list which it heads (which is only the same thing for the last member of a list).

12.1 The list processing primitives

New types of object are bound to introduce new functional concepts, and, just as introduction of complex numbers forces one to augment the standard arithmetical functions with new ones such as 'real part', etc, so the introduction of lists forces the introduction of five or so new concepts and several other more convenient but less basic ones. The basic ones are usually referred to in the notation used in Lisp, and they are

A. Three functions of a single variable:
  1. $atom(x)$, a boolean function which is false if the value of x is a list, true otherwise;
  2. $car(x)$, which is what we have called the intrinsic part of x;
  3. $cdr(x)$, which is what we have called the pointer part of x;
B. Two functions of two variables
  4. $eq(x,y)$, a boolean which is true if x and y are the same atom, false if they are different atoms, and undefined if either of them is a list;
  5. $cons(x,y)$, which is the list z such that $car(z) = x$ and $cdr(z) = y$.

A notation is also required for conditionals (see Section 12.4). The origins of car and cdr are inconsequential; McCarthy partitioned a machine word which represented an object in the same way as it would have been partitioned had it been an instruction in machine code, and he used the same abbreviations (for 'content of address (or decrement) register') as were meaningful in the latter case. This is rather as though, because one originally had a machine designed to work in sterling, one always, when referring to the date, called months 'the shillings part of the date', but these names have caught on, and no rivals (such as head and tail, for example) would appear to have much chance against them. The concept of an atom is perhaps as relative as it is in physics; like the Algol black-type symbols, car, cdr, cons, etc, are atoms, but when it comes to numbers of more than one digit the choice is more open. Because arithmetic on numbers in pure list form is so inefficient, some compromise is necessary. Conversely, even the basic function names must be non-atomic to input/output routines.

12.2 Procedural list processing languages

When thinking procedurally about list processing, the functions of the previous section will be used in the way *sin*, *cos* and *log* are used in numerically oriented procedural languages. Certain other functions and objects are also so often used as to have acquired fairly universally used names. Storage which is not actually in use is kept on a 'free list', which we may call F. The following table takes the functions which Alp adds to Autocode and translates them into a form of Wisp. A few comments appear to be all that is necessary to clarify what must be, for some readers, a translation from one unfamiliar language into another unfamiliar one!

ALP	WISP	Comments
TO LIST(L,x)	CAR(L) = x	The first object in L is given the value x, overwriting previous contents.
FROM LIST(L,x)	x = CAR(L)	Converse of above (but see following text)
PUSHDOWN(L,x)	Z = F F = CDR(F) CDR(Z) = L CAR(Z) = x L = Z	A temporary name Z is needed. The first object in F is detached from it, given the value x, and then put on the front of L.
POP UP(L,x)	x = CAR(L) Z = L L = CDR(L) CDR(Z) = F F = Z	Converse of above. The Wisp translation omits a branch on IF CDR(L) = O, in case L is already the last object.
INSERT AFTER(L,x)	Z = F F = CDR(F) CDR(Z) = CDR(L) CDR(L) = Z CAR(Z) = x	The first object in F is detached and inserted into the second place of L and then given the value x.
LINK(L,M,R)	TO R IF CDR(L) = O M = CDR(L)	M now names the tail of L; if L has no tail, control is transferred to R.
SETLINK(L,M)	CDR(L) = M	I.e. L = CONS(CAR(L),M)
NEWCELL(L)	L = F F = CDR(F)	The first object on F is removed and called L.
ERASE(L)	Z = L R: TO S IF CDR(Z) = O Z = CDR(Z) TO R S: CDR(Z) = F F = L	Simplified by assuming that L is unbranched. Returns the whole of L to F. (See note below on labels)
FIND(L,M,R,x)	M = L S: TO T IF CAR(M) = x TO R IF CDR(M) = O M = CDR(M) TO S T:	Finds first object on L which refers to x, leaving its name in M; in case of none, leaves name of last object of L in M and transfers control to R.
ADDSPACE(a,b)	(None)	Concerned with setting up a free list when first going from Autocode to list working.

117

In this table both languages have been adapted slightly to each other both in notation and semantics. In Wisp, for example, the arguments of *car* and *cdr* are written without brackets, and labels are integers on a line to themselves, not alphanumeric with a colon. Considerable liberty has been taken with the variable x; in Alp x is a complex of three 'fields' whose interpretation is dependent on the usual Autocode conventions in integer and real variables, etc, while in Wisp it does not really exist at all. This is because Wisp was designed as a compiler writing aid, and admits only single characters or lists as values; hence the true Wisp equivalent to the first Alp instruction is one of the three forms

CAR L = M   The value of the first object in L is made equal to the name of the list M

CAR L = M: The value of the first object in L is made equal to the character 'M'

CAR L = CAR M   The value of the first object in L is made equal to the value of the first object in M

and the second Alp instruction is now already covered by the last of these three. In Alp the pre-existence of the Autocode variables is assumed, and they play the part for which we shall see that 'data-terms' are introduced into IPL-V. The data-terms of Wisp are all single characters, and the more economic storage scheme is practicable.

12.3 IPL-V

IPL-V is the assembly code of a hypothetical machine, and, like most list processing languages in the current state of the art, it is interpreted, not translated. The store of this hypothetical machine is, of course, the store of the actual machine less that part taken up by the interpretive system, and at the start of a program it is arranged to suit the problem by setting aside certain locations as named list-heads, and putting the remainder on to a free-list. (Contrast the more limited facilities of Wisp which has single letters only as list-head names and therefore no need for preliminary setting.) Such a list-head name is known as a *regional symbol*, and consists outside the machine of a letter (or punctuation mark) followed by an integer. All symbols with the same letter are said to belong to the same region, and the setting up is done by means of directives which state the maximum integer used in each region, and possibly its starting point in the store. Synonyms can be arranged by making the regions overlap. Regions *H*, *J* and *W* have preset size and purposes which will appear. Besides regional symbols there are also *local symbols*, of the form 9-⟨integer⟩ (e.g. '9–12'), which retain a fixed meaning only within a given list-structure starting at a regionally defined head. Internally, all symbols are machine addresses, combined with a prefix to distinguish regional, local and anonymous symbols (the last derived usually by transfers from the free list).

Being at the assembly code level, a program consists of a series of 'lines' equivalent either to a machine word plus a label, or to a directive. We can expand this to

$$\langle\text{line}\rangle ::= \langle\text{preamble}\rangle\langle\text{machine word}\rangle$$
$$\langle\text{preamble}\rangle ::= \langle\text{type}\rangle\langle\text{label}\rangle\langle\text{sign}\rangle$$
$$\langle\text{machine word}\rangle ::= \langle P\rangle\langle Q\rangle\langle\text{car}\rangle\langle\text{cdr}\rangle|\langle P\rangle\langle Q\rangle\langle\text{value}\rangle$$

where

$\langle\text{type}\rangle$ is an octal digit, zero or blank except in directives. We shall denote a line whose type is n by $\langle\text{n-line}\rangle$.

$\langle\text{sign}\rangle$ is blank except on numerical values, or as a means of distinguishing data items in instruction lists.

$\langle P\rangle$ and $\langle Q\rangle$ are octal digits known as the prefix.

Since the system was designed for card input, on which syntactical units occupy fixed columns, blank causes no trouble. The units $\langle\text{label}\rangle$, $\langle\text{car}\rangle$ and $\langle\text{cdr}\rangle$ are all symbols or blank; in the case of $\langle\text{label}\rangle$ a blank implies that the symbol is an address removed from the free list during input, in the other two cases a blank implies the label of the next line.

A complete program has the structure

$$\langle\text{program}\rangle ::= \langle\text{controls}\rangle\langle\text{mainpart}\rangle\langle\text{endline}\rangle$$
$$\langle\text{controls}\rangle ::= \langle\text{9-line}\rangle|\langle\text{controls}\rangle\langle\text{region control line}\rangle$$
$$\langle\text{endline}\rangle ::= \langle\text{5-line blank except for the label of the entry}$$
$$\text{point in } \langle\text{symbol}\rangle\rangle$$
$$\langle\text{mainpart}\rangle ::= \langle\text{block}\rangle|\langle\text{block}\rangle\langle\text{mainpart}\rangle$$
$$\langle\text{block}\rangle ::= \langle\text{5-line}\rangle\langle\text{list sequence}\rangle$$

On the whole, data and instructions are kept in separate blocks, being distinguished by $\langle Q\rangle = 1$ or 0 respectively in the 5-line of the block. The structure $\langle P\rangle\langle Q\rangle\langle\text{car}\rangle\langle\text{cdr}\rangle$ is known as a list-cell and the structure $\langle P\rangle\langle Q\rangle\langle\text{value}\rangle$ as a data-term. The latter obtains (a) when $\langle Q\rangle$ has the value '1' and the item occurs within a data block, or (b) when the $\langle\text{sign}\rangle$ is not blank; values $0 \ldots 3$ of $\langle P\rangle$ then cause it to be interpreted as decimal integer, floating point number, alphanumeric or octal quantity, respectively. Case (b) will apply to 'program constants' and the item will need a local symbol to be referenced by. In case (a) it must have a regional symbol as its label, thus appearing under the guise of a single membered list. True lists in data blocks have a label, followed on the *next* and succeeding lines by '$\langle Q\rangle = 0$' lines whose *car*'s are either the names of data terms or the names of other lists. (In many applications of IPL-V it is assumed that the list is a list of objects, and that the *car* of the

119

initial line is the name of a list of properties associated with the objects.) The last line in any list has a zero *cdr*. IPL-V imposes certain restrictions on the input of data lists which, for example, bar circular lists. Some of these restrictions can be overridden during the subsequent operation of the program.

In instruction lists, each word is an instruction unless a sign has been punched, ⟨P⟩ being the function, ⟨Q⟩⟨car⟩ the operand (denoted by '*S*') and ⟨cdr⟩ the 'next instruction source'. The ⟨Q⟩ part of the operand determines whether the ⟨car⟩ part is to be taken literally, its value to be used, or (when its value is in turn a symbol) the value of its value. The eight codes for ⟨P⟩ are

0   'Execute' or 'obey'. *S* must be the label either of a subroutine or of one of the nearly two hundred machine order sequences in region J.
1   Pushdown(HO, S)
2   Pop up(HO.S)
3   Pop up(S, S)   i.e. destroying top contents
4   Pushdown(S, S)   i.e. duplicating top contents
5   To list(HO, S)
6   From list(HO, S)
7   Branch to S if H5 holds '−'

The head cell of list HO is known as the 'communication cell' and plays a ubiquitous role resembling that of the accumulator of an ordinary machine, but being the head of a push-down list it can hold an indefinite amount of information, and parameters of routines, irrespective of their numbers, are handed over in it. Thus the nearest simple equivalent to Alp's FIND would be a sequence to find the first list cell (other than the head) in *L2* (say) which has *X3* as its *car*, leaving its name in *MO* or, if there is none, leaving the name of the last cell in *MO* and jumping to *R1*. Routine *J62* is defined thus:

A search of list with name (1) is made, testing each symbol against (0) (starting with the cell after cell (1)). If (0) is found, the output (0) is the name of the cell containing it and *H5* is set +. . . . If (0) is not found, the output (0) is the name of the last cell on the list, and *H5* is set -.

Here (0), (1) . . . refer to the top, next . . . cells in *HO*. So the coding is

P	Q	car	cdr	Comments
1	0	L2		Push name of *L2* into *H0*
1	0	X3		And name of X3
0	0	J62		Obey *J62*
2	0	MO		Pop up *H0* to *M0*
7	0	R1		Branch on content of *H5*.

ERASE(L) can be treated similarly using *J71*, which erases the list named in (0), or *J72*, which erases the list structure, i.e. the list and all its *locally defined* sub-lists.

It will be clear that at this point there is a barrier to any further discussion of this language unless we are prepared to reprint the complete specifications of all the routines in the *J* region. A facsimile of a one-page summary of the J-routines will be found in Sammet (1969).

12.4 Lisp

Lisp is probably the most widely used pure list-processing language. A difficulty in describing it briefly lies in the fact that it can be written in two notations, the one used in implementations being the more difficult to follow. In the easier, or 'M' form, it is only data that is in list form, ordinary mathematical notation being used for function definition, though subject to slight changes to avoid confusion with data. A data-, or S-expression is defined by the extremely simple grammar

$$\langle\text{S-exp}\rangle ::= (\langle\text{S-exp}\rangle.\langle\text{S-exp}\rangle)|\langle\text{atom}\rangle$$
$$\langle\text{atom}\rangle ::= \langle\text{string of numerals or capital letters}\rangle$$

or by this grammar augmented for convenience to

$$\langle\text{S-exp}\rangle ::= (\langle\text{S-exp}\rangle\langle\text{tail}\rangle)|\langle\text{atom}\rangle$$
$$\langle\text{tail}\rangle ::= .\langle\text{S-exp}\rangle|\langle\text{separator}\rangle\langle\text{S-exp}\rangle\langle\text{tail}\rangle|\langle\text{empty}\rangle$$

If the augmented notation is used, the ⟨separator⟩ is often no more than one or more spaces, though a comma may be included. An empty ⟨tail⟩ is synonymous with a '.NIL', where NIL is a special reserved atom, and

(A   B   C)   is synonymous with   (A.(B.(C.NIL))).

It is sometimes convenient to restrict the term 'list' to S-expressions which terminate in NIL in this way. All S-expressions are actual values, i.e. constants. Variables, which can *take* a value, are represented by small letters, as are function names. Because round brackets and commas are preempted for value denotations, square brackets and semicolons are used for function notation, thus *cons*[x; S] is a new S-expression whose *car* is the current value of x and whose *cdr* is the atom S. Boolean functions yield one of the atoms T or F, and for

if a **then** b **else if** c **then** d **else** e

either of the notations

$$a \rightarrow b; \ c \rightarrow d; \ T \rightarrow e \quad \text{or} \quad \text{cond}[[a;b];[c;d];[T;e]]$$

may be used. (In some implementations NIL is used for F, and any other value behaves like T.) The first of these two notations has been

121

adopted in CPL and BCPL (Section 13.4). A very important feature of this notation is that the booleans are evaluated in order until one evaluates to **true**, then *its* result; anything skipped or not reached by this process may legitimately be uncomputable — i.e. lead, in the circumstances, to an infinite loop (Sections 7.7.1 and 13.4).

Being a function language, Lisp gets by with the basic functions, though it finds certain abbreviations helpful, like *caar*[x] for *car*[*car* [x]]. As the M form is not the implementation form, we can write the definition of a function in either of the alternative notations

f[x;y] = cons[car[x]; cdr[y]]

or

    f = lambda[[x;y]; cons[car[x]; cdr[y]]]

and for recursive functions the operator $Y\lambda$ of Section 2.5.1 appears under the guise of 'label'; thus the first atom in a list structure is given by the function

first[x] = [atom[car[x]] → car[x]; T → first[car[x]]

or equivalently

    first = label[p; lambda[[x]; [atom[car[x]] → car[x]; T → p[car[x]]]

For implementation purposes, one feeds an interpreter with S-expressions which are alternately a function and an argument-list to which the function is to be applied. This means that an S equivalent to the M language has to be used. Brackets become round, semicolons become commas, and all function names go inside the bracket (this is the reason for the *cond* notation); letters which were small become large, and expressions already in S form (except T, F and NIL) are quoted — i.e. a constant like S becomes (QUOTE S).

The worst implications of this approach are obviated by a facility to predefine the functions (auxiliary and/or main) required in a calculation. The function DEFINE takes one argument which is a list of definitions — thus DEFINE (((A B) (C D) . .)) defines A as B, C as D etc. (DEFINE is the function, the outer brackets hold its arguments (only one for DEFINE), the middle brackets are those of the list (of definitions), and the inner ones hold the separate definitions.) What happens when this is seriously applied on even a small scale can be seen from

```
DEFINE (((REV (LAMBDA (A) (REV1 A NIL)))
        (REV1 (LAMBDA (A B) (COND ((NULL A) B)
                            (T (REV1 (CDR A)
                            (CONS (CAR A) B )))))
        (MEMBER (LAMBDA (OBJ SET) (COND ((NULL SET) NIL)
                            ((EQ OBJ (CAR SET)) T)
                            ( T (MEMBER OBJ (CDR SET))))))
        ))
MEMBER (A (A B C))
REV (A (B C) D)
```

This program comes up with the answers that A *is* a member of (A B C), and that (A (B C) D) reversed is (D (B C) A).

Other complications have been obviated by incorporating a sequential programming feature, but this contains no features of importance here, other than to emphasize that no extreme in style is likely to be the final word. A plain man's guide to Lisp has been published by Woodward and Jenkins (1961).

12.5 Envoi

The grammar of S-expressions relates very directly to the form of internal storage, the two S-expressions separated by a dot corresponding to the intrinsic and the pointer parts in the internal form. A feature of both Lisp and its internal representation is that it is easy to pass down a list but very difficult to pass up it. An immediate reaction was the emergence of systems (possibly languages) containing additional pointers, the structures being referred to as 'knotted lists', 'threaded lists', etc. It was soon realized that a more liberal basic structure was needed, and that these new features then become programming techniques rather than language features.

For example, if one writes in Algol 68,

mode node = **struc(item** car, cdr)
mode item = **union(ref string, ref node)**
proc cons = **(item** head, tail)**ref node** : **(heap node**
                                      n := (head,tail); n)

then one has provided for objects of the sort assumed in Lisp, and for their creation in a manner (use of the generator **heap node**) equivalent to setting up an initial free list. More general structures including additional fields can provide the facilities required for knotting or threading. This paragraph may be held to be an amplification of the statement in the first edition that the day of (pure) list processing languages would seem to be over; they served their purpose in isolating for study the features required for facile handling of lists, and these are now being included in general purpose languages, not as added grafts, but as an integral part of the language from the moment of its inception.

Nevertheless, one language had just appeared with a radically different approach, namely L[6] (or L-six). L-six stands for the six L's which constitute a sort of acronym of 'Bell Telephones Low Level List processing Language'. Because of the implications of 'low level' we defer a more detailed account to Section 13.2.1.

13

THE LAST TEN YEARS

In 1967, this chapter was concerned with two languages that had recently appeared, CPL and PL/I. Each was introduced by an excellent article in advance of the issue of manuals (Barron *et al*, 1963; Radin and Rogoway 1965). The reader is referred to these for the material on which a lengthy comparison of objectives, in the first edition but omitted here, was based.

CPL (Combined Programming Language) had been developed in England by workers in the universities of Cambridge and London. Its fortunes were closely linked with those of the Atlas computer, and it did not survive the demise of the latter except in an offshoot called BCPL (Basic CPL), which exploited much of the syntactic felicity of CPL while belonging to a new class of languages described in the next section.

PL/I (Programming Language 1) was developed by a team set up by the Share organization of IBM Fortran users. It has been adopted by a number of large corporations, but elsewhere it has rather fallen between two stools, having neither weaned the large body of users with vested interests in Fortran from that language, nor persuaded the more progressive users that it was a satisfactory successor to Algol 60.

Various groups of Algol 60 users were pressing at that time for different extensions to the language, the main desiderata being **complex**, list processing, string and character handling, the ability to handle records, and a standardized input/output. Despite the object lesson from dynamic own arrays, they each wanted their own additions without considering how these might interact. In January 1968, 'MR93', a draft Algol 68 report, was circulated; the world considered that because the report was difficult reading, the language must be difficult both to use and to compile, and it held up its hands in horror. In this situation the author got involved in consideration of an interim measure. It quickly became clear that a superset of Algol 60 was out of the question, as the declaration structure had to be rationalized (Section 13.3). The Cobol record structure had to be incorporated, and list processing requirements made it necessary to include pointers as possible structure components. Complex is simply a structure of two reals, but as it must be useable with

124

infixed operators, definition of infixed operators between structures was unavoidable. It was necessary to divorce the Cobol record structure from input/output and make it an extension of type; thus a concept best described as 'Cobol on the stack' seemed indicated. But this analysis suggested that there was very little that could be dropped from the proposals in MR93 without producing a very ragged and half-hearted extension of Algol 60 (trimmed slices was an obvious possibility) and then the first Algol 68 compiler appeared with a rapidity that surprised even the writers of the MR series of reports (Currie *et al*, 1971).

The month of October 1965 had been a crucial one for the IFIP Working Group 2.1, charged with the production of a successor to Algol 60. Meeting at St. Pierre de Chartreuse in the mountains north of Grenoble, it had before it three designs for an Algol X, two based on BNF (by Wirth (1965) of Zurich and by Seegmüller (1965) of Munich) and one (by van Wijngaarden of Amsterdam) based on new syntactic techniques. A committee hitherto working harmoniously and successfully at formulating the surface structures needed to accommodate new computational techniques suddenly found itself deeply divided on a matter of deep structure. The ultimate outcome was that Wirth developed his ideas into Algol W and Pascal, while a series of reports emanated from the Mathematical Centre at Amsterdam, culminating in one (MR101) which was submitted in February 1969 for official adoption as Algol 68. An informal introduction was prepared by Lindsey and van Meulen (1971), and the user's guide to the first implementation (Woodward and Currie 1972) proved an excellent introduction for users who like their theory well diluted with examples. After several years of experience on this basis, a final and definitive report was issued in March 1974, an accompanying revision of Lindsey's work being promised.

Meanwhile, other languages were developed, and though none received general acceptance, experience from them also contributed, since many were widely used in specific contexts. Algol W, for example, was implemented on the 360 series against a system background tuned to the running of large numbers of student exercises, and the satisfaction it has given to a large number of users of this type should not go unrecorded. Most of these languages show a greater or lesser reaction to the introduction of interactive terminals. One effect of this development was an increase in the number of computer users who, though not programmers, yet do their own programming. For these, Basic has proved a natural mode of expression. Its main interest in a comparative study is its replacement of 'x := 3' or (in Fortran) 'x = 3' by 'LET X = 3'; by this means the compiler is simplified since it allows every statement to be typed by its first word. Initially, at least, it was not interactive in the full sense.

The first moves towards truly interactive use had been systems like Joss, which allowed the computer to function as an on-line calculating machine for the evaluation of typed-in expressions. Pop-2 retained this aspect while aspiring also to provide the level of sophistication to be expected of a successor to Algol 60. As each line of source text is completed, it is executed and destroyed, but of course execution of declarations leads to retention in memory of named working space, and compiled forms of procedures. For further details see Section 13.1.6. Other languages in this sphere of development are Coral and RTL2; their significance is primarily political. Interactive compilers are very extravagant and some workers doubt their value; Wirth (1976) claims that Pascal has achieved, among its design objectives, that its compiler is sufficiently efficient that recompilation is preferable even to the retention of relocatable binary, whence the corollary follows that editing of the complete source text is the natural mode of program development.

Acceptance of Algol 68 by the educated has had two hurdles to face. The earlier reports are masterpieces of gobbledygook, a fault which the final version makes a conscious but only partially successful attempt to rectify. And each new report has combined important but small improvements in the language with much greater developments in the use of the new syntactic techniques. Acceptance of any language by less sophisticated users tends always to turn on implementations, including matters like diagnostics which are extraneous to the language itself.

Algol 68 is less a revolutionary language than it is an evolutionary language bearing revolutionary ideas. If it seems to claim an unjustified prominence in this chapter, this may be put down in part to the author's bias in its favour, but more to his decision that the only alternative to a completely new book was to convert this chapter into a history of the ideas that programming languages are being called upon to express, rather than of the languages themselves. Because Algol 68, whether right or wrong, is usually the furthest ahead in such matters, it inevitably becomes the final stage in each section. The maintenance of continuity with the first edition which this decision has facilitated has probably been at its most unfair with PL/I, by resulting in over-concentration on the development process rather than the finished product.

13.1 Concepts in development

The traditions set by Fortran and Algol 60 were strong enough that despite their attempts to set the standard for a new generation, CPL gave the impression of being a new Algol with acknowledgements to the necessity for lists, and PL/I of being a new Fortran with acknowledgements to Cobol. One reason for this superficial impression was the character sets used; it is unfortunate that neither team looked ahead sufficiently to employ the standard I.S.O. character set. Another was the syntactical form adopted for statement brackets. Whereas in Algol **begin** and **end** are *symbols* with the properties of brackets, in Fortran the corresponding objects are *statements*, and this divergence of usage persists. Both sides can claim precedents in natural languages; compare

1. According to his letter 'violence may be necessary'.
2. According to his letter, and I quote, violence may be necessary. (Quote ends.)

The Algol usage is simpler and more natural in a language *per se*, but the compiler writer finds that a bracket often involves action to implement it and to him it takes on the character of a statement. Preference here is probably personal, but there can be no doubt that the occurrence of words like PROCEDURE and DO followed immediately by a semicolon is a deep-rooted source of the superficial impression.

What is more important is that CPL and PL/I both incorporated a number of ideas that were tentatively being explored in the mid-1960s.

13.1.1 Modes of evaluation

One of these was the concept of a 'mode of evaluation'. In a statement such as $A[i] := A[j]$, the left hand side must be evaluated as far as the *address* of $A[i]$, the right hand side must be evaluated to the *contents* of $A[j]$. These were known in CPL as left-hand and right-hand modes of evaluation, leading to left and right hand values.

The idea is far from trivial. Consider that in a byte-addressable decimal machine, reading from or writing to the hundreds digit of a number without disturbing the others could take precisely this form (a machine order reading or writing to the hundreds digit), whereas given binary-stored values, small subroutines or procedures would be necessary. Such a pair of procedures was known as a load-update pair, or LUP, and a theoretical superstructure can be built on the assumption that *every* declared variable needs a load-update pair implicitly, even if simpler processes exist in some cases. Altering the nth decimal digit upsets all the octal digits; it is as though a radix of notation defines an orthogonal coordinate system for expressing the state of the store, oblique to that defined by some other radix. But why stop at detached integers, why not consider the whole store as a phase space, in which the current state is represented by a particular point, and the course of a computation as a trajectory, and the addressing system as but one of many possible coordinate systems? Such flights of fancy apart, two things emerge (1) modes of evaluation as an alternative to Algol 68's concept of the dereferencing coercion, and (2) the idea that a declaration may involve the creation of subroutines (for examples of which see Section 13.1.6, and 'field definition' in Section 13.2.1).

13.1.2 Attributes

Another concept, exploited particularly by PL/I, was the liberal use of 'attributes'. (Natural linguists were already making play with this concept to secure agreement in gender, etc., in transformational grammars.) Apart from boolean (which it called LOGICAL and which we discuss in Section 13.4), PL/I set out to provide eight scalar types — FIXED (point), FLOAT(ing point), COMPLEX, CHAR(acter string), BIT (string), LABEL, PROCEDURE VARI- ABLE and FILE VARIABLE, the last three being known as 'address types'. However, it also provided that the first three may have a *precision attribute* specified after them in brackets, a system precision being assumed only by default; the string types *must* have *lengths* specified in the same way (or, in the case of CHAR by a picture), though (*) can indicate that the specification has been made elsewhere when the variable is EXTERNAL (see later), and VARIABLE means that the length specified is only a maximum. Later it was arranged that numerical types could be specified independently as fixed/float, binary/decimal and real/complex — eight variations of 'numerical' in all. Note that FIXED is not INTEGER; a precision (3.2) means three significant figures, two after the decimal point.

Declarations in PL/I count as statements (but cannot be jumped to and should not be labelled unless for purposes of reference within comment). They take the form

DECLARE⟨variable list⟩⟨attribute list⟩

where the variable list is either a single identifier or a series of identifiers separated by commas and enclosed in brackets, and the attribute list is a series of words, describing the variables being declared. Thus the Algol 60

integer a, b; **real** x, y; **value** a, b, x;

becomes (keeping the Algol words for the moment)

DECLARE (A, B) INTEGER VALUE;
DECLARE X REAL VALUE;
DECLARE Y REAL NAME;

and one is also allowed to 'factor' the first two thus

DECLARE ((A, B) INTEGER, X REAL) VALUE;

This inversion is a lucidly simplifying stroke for which there is some precedent in Cobol; it transforms the 'properties tree' into the form in which it is usually required, and unifies the syntax with that of

128

statements in general. As well as the type attribute, which we have already discussed, there are others. A variable may be either IN-TERNAL (= local) or EXTERNAL (= global); this is necessary because a variable used in several modules must be declared in each. Formal parameters are assumed to be INTERNAL, and the earlier proposals also allowed the attribute (by) NAME or (by) VALUE, with the former going by default and no provision for 'simple name'. The final specification reverted to the Fortran system of determining the style from the syntax of each individual call. Variables other than formal parameters can be initialized by the attribute INITIAL ($\langle$value$\rangle$).

A PL/I declaration is not a simple store-raising imperative. The raising of storage is dependent on another attribute which may have one of the three values STATIC, AUTOMATIC or CONTROLLED. (The attribute DEFINED, described later, is effectively a fourth value here.) An EXTERNAL variable is STATIC by default; this means that the name is associated with a single location when the various modules are first brought together. An INTERNAL variable is AUTOMATIC by default; this means that the name is associated with a push-down list to which a new location is added each time the procedure is entered and from which one is removed each time it is quitted by RETURN. The declaration INTERNAL STATIC is roughly equivalent to the Algol 60 **own**. A CONTROLLED variable is given an empty push-down list on to which a location is added by the command ALLOCATE, or which is popped up by the command FREE (the imperative being followed by the name of the variable); this permits the control of storage to be kept distinct from the block structure of the program when need arises.

A formal parameter is, by its nature, redefined in use by the actual parameter of the call. In the case of a variable which is not a formal parameter, an attribute DEFINED is available which allows the same stored quantity to be referred to in different ways. Originally a way of tidying up the untidy EQUIVALENCE-COMMON feature of Fortran, this opened the way to greater possibilities than could be handled without compromising efficiency. A useful application was seen in

DECLARE 1 A DEFINED X, 2 B CHAR(3), 2 C CHAR(4).

Here the initial integers are level-numbers (as in Cobol), and A is said to be declared as a STRUCTURE. Without 'DEFINED X' it declares A to consist of two fields, B of three characters and C of four. As printed it assumes the existence of a previously defined X, possibly a seven character string on which, by referring to it as A, we can impose the 3+4 structure. As in Cobol, the first three characters may be referred to as B if this uniquely describes it,

129

otherwise it must be referred to as A.B (where Cobol would have B IN A). Another possibility was

DECLARE X (210) FLOAT;
DECLARE A (20, 20) DEFINED X ((1SUB*(1SUB−1)/2)) +2SUB)

as being a method of mapping a triangular array on to a vector, but efficiency considerations ultimately restricted this technique to examples linear in the subscripts. A third possibility,

DECLARE X DEFINED DYNAMICALLY;
    :
    DEFINE X AS Y;
LOOP: FREE X;

would provide means for exploring a push-down list headed by a CONTROLLED Y without losing the head, but this possibility was not even considered.

When one PL/I module calls another, the *name* of the called module must be *declared* in the calling module by the statement

DECLARE⟨name⟩PROCEDURE⟨attributes1⟩

The called module will begin with a statement in the form

⟨label⟩: PROCEDURE ⟨formal parameter list⟩⟨attributes2⟩

(the formal parameter list in brackets or empty) and it will conclude with a statement *END*; (or, cf. Section 13.2.2, *END⟨label⟩*;). This syntax is identical to that of an embedded procedure definition. The label is mandatory in the opening statement since it is the name of the procedure for calling purposes. Otherwise the similarity in structure shown by these statements and the variable-declaration statement exemplifies the unified syntax, compared with earlier languages, which the designers of PL/I strove to achieve.

The attributes are those useful in compiling the module they occur in. Those in ⟨attributes1⟩ refer largely to properties that could be ascertained by inspection of the procedure body, were it available. BUILTIN allows declaration of a system-defined procedure even though its name has become inaccessible in the ordinary way because it has been used for some other purpose. SETS(⟨list⟩), where the list items are integers (*n* implying *parameter-n*) or names of external variables or * (meaning all external variables), implies that the variables referred to may have their values set (i.e. assigned) by the procedure, and USES(⟨list⟩) similarly indicates what external variables may be read. These assist in optimizing safely. ABNORMAL is a less precise attribute which can be used as a general warner-off; it must also be applied to ordinary variables if, for example, they can become involved in asynchronous processes which might cause their values to change at unpredictable times. INDEFINITE is used if the variable is a formal parameter whose attributes may vary from call to call. The properties in ⟨attributes2⟩ are those necessary or at least useful in compiling the definition. They include MAIN for the main program module, REENTRANT for a module that, in a multiprogramming situation, can be simultaneously in use by more than one branch, RECURSIVE for modules that call them-selves, any implementation-dependent attributes that the local system may need, and the attributes of the results of a function.

A procedure is invoked as a subroutine by the statement

CALL⟨procedure label⟩⟨actual parameter list⟩;

and the return is made by a statement *RETURN*;, which is either explicit or else implicit in the final *END*; of the definition. There is no formal distinction between 'routines' and 'functions'; a procedure intended to be used as a function designator must use a statement in the form *RETURN(X)*; to return, where X is an expression whose value is the value required, and there will also be implications on the attribute lists.

Although a procedure name is syntactically a label, a distinction has to be drawn between procedure names and other labels, and a parameter with a procedure name quality is given the attribute ENTRY, not LABEL. Procedures being briefings and not imme-diate imperatives, *GO TO X;* where X has an ENTRY attribute, if it means anything at all, would seem to mean either 'make sure you have not forgotten what X means' or 'go to the point lexicogra-phically following the *END X;*' — since that is the first overt imperative after the label. The word ENTRY is also used as a verb inside a procedure; it does not have the property of bracketting with an *END*;, but its label may be used in a CALL statement to provide alternative entry points, and in this respect it is syntactically and semantically exactly like PROCEDURE. A very interesting de-velopment is the GENERIC function. This has numerous entries with inconsistent parameter attributes, and (were ABS not built-in) could be used thus:

```
DECLARE ABS GENERIC (ABS1 ENTRY (FIXED), ABS2
   ENTRY (FLOAT REAL), ABS3 ENTRY (COMPLEX));
ABS1: ABS2: PROCEDURE (X); DECLARE Y;
   Y = X; IF Y LT 0 THEN Y = −Y; RETURN(Y);
ABS3: ENTRY (X);
RETURN (SORT (REAL(X)**2+IMAG(X)**2));
   END ABS1;
```

When the program encounters *ABS(Z)* it scans ABS1, ABS2 . . . for an entry where the attributes match those of *Z*. Many of the built-in routines are generic. Note that in the absence of an explicit declaration of attributes for Y, $Y = X$ declares them 'contextually' to be the same as those of X.

We may note, in anticipation of later discussion, that Algol 68 permits operators to be generic; a new declaration is required for each pair of operand types and does not 'cover up' previous declarations unless they refer to the same types. Procedures, on the other hand, achieve the same effect by parameters of UNITED mode; an actual parameter being in a strong position will undergo the uniting coercion on entry, and the different cases must then be sorted out inside the procedure body by a 'conformity case clause'.

The precision attribute, referred to briefly earlier, raises some difficult questions. Whenever control of precision is provided, default precision is likely to be that of a machine word, since for most users the disadvantage of machine dependence will be outweighed by the advantage of efficiency. However there are certain situations in which *relatively* greater precision is required in *some variables* on theoretical grounds. A simple example is the variable in which the expression

$$(\textstyle\sum x)^2 - N\sum (x^2)$$

is accumulated in statistics, and there are others in numerical analysis such as the ill-conditioned matrices required in the computation of Chebychev coefficients. If default is used to get efficiency in such cases then PL/I provides no means of asking for double precision where it is required, other than knowing the precision of the system at single length. CPL took the alternative view that precision is an inescapable function of the system, and provided means of asking for multi-length working. Algol 68 has also followed this line, but provides information as to what the single precision happens to be through the medium of an environmental enquiry (see Section 13.1.4). It still does not provide the 'conditional mode declarations' that would be required to ask for a specific precision without lumbering the program with procedures and operators half of which it will not use. The real requirement here is a facility to make the environmental enquiry at compile time and to perform a conditional compilation (Section 15.2.4).

13.1.3 General Structure

The distinction which Algol 60 syntax made between expressions and statements was not altogether maintained in its semantics, since it was held that a type procedure could stand alone as a statement. CPL attempted to maintain the distinction rigorously, even to the point of trying to prohibit side effects in functions but to allow them in routines; this has its disadvantages since it prevents the programmer from inserting diagnostics into functions, and in any case it is probably unenforceable. PL/I respects this concept in its default allocations, but does not try to force it on the unwilling user.

But CPL coupled this distinction with a new construction permitting statements to occur within expressions. (This is only the extension of the notion of open and closed subroutines to functions.) As retained in BCPL it is that one can write, for example,

$$X := X + VALOF\langle command\rangle$$

provided that the ⟨command⟩, probably a compound one, contains the statement

RESULTIS⟨expression⟩

which is the exit cue.

Algol 68 has abolished this distinction completely; every construct has a value even if, as it were, its value is *void*, whether intrinsically or by coercion (Section 13.3.2). The value of an assignment, for example, is the address of the location into which the value of the right hand side has been written, but this is voided by a following semicolon. The build-up in Algol 68 is as follows (for an explanation of 'weak rowed', etc., see Sections 13.3.1 and 13.3.2).

Elements:
denoter	52, 7.5, **true**, "c"
identifier	*x*
format item	$ddd.d$
enclosed clause	(⟨serial clause⟩), ⟨conditional clause⟩, etc.

Other primaries:
slice	⟨weak rowed primary⟩[⟨indexer⟩]
call	⟨meek procedure⟩(⟨actual parameters⟩)
cast	⟨mode⟩⟨enclosed clause⟩

Secondaries: primaries and
generator	**loc real** (= new storage for a real) etc.
selection	⟨field⟩ **of** ⟨weak structured secondary⟩

Tertiaries: secondaries and
formula	secondaries linked by infixed operators
nihil	**nil**

Units: tertiaries and
assignation	destination := ⟨unit⟩
identity	a boolean relation between addresses (not contents)
routine text	(⟨parameters spec⟩)⟨yield mode⟩:(⟨body⟩)
jump	**goto** ⟨label⟩
skip	**skip** (N.b. ⟨empty⟩ is not allowed as a dummy)

Serial clause:
serial clause	units and declarations separated by semicolons

Four features here are worth special mention. (1) In Algol 60 a multiple assignment is ⟨left part list⟩⟨expression⟩, one value (from

133

the expression) being assigned to all the addresses in the left part list (which therefore must be all the same type); in Algol 68 it is a recursive structure, each level being a single assignment. Thus

begin ref int h, **int** i, j; h := i := j := 3; . . .

puts 3 into *j*, the contents of *j* (viz. 3) into *i*, and the address of *i* into *h*. (2) The semantics of a call, illustrated in more detail in Section 13.3.3, involves a simple modification to the routine text shown above, viz. to

(parameters declaration; ⟨yield mode⟩(⟨body⟩))

the last part of which, by dropping the colon, has become a cast, viz. an expression whose value is strongly coerced into the yield mode. (3) The usual rule that at any given level all declarations must precede all statements is relaxed in Algol 68 to one that all declarations must precede any labels. (4) Side effects are completely accepted, but attempts to use them in 'clever' ways are discouraged by the rule that items separated by commas may be assigned to parallel processors and thus evaluated in any order. This includes operands of infixed operators.

Pascal retains the distinction between expressions and statements in its formal grammar. Further details will be found in Section 13.1.7.

13.1.4 Environmental accommodation

As long ago as 1963, in the Algol 60 compiler for the GIER (a very small machine) provision was made to include, within comment, cues to the compiler as to which routines could be relegated to overlays (Naur 1964b). Since then many facilities for accommodating the compiled version of a program to the environment have been tried.

Thus Algol 68 has implemented what in 1967 were described as extensions by which programming languages as a whole might benefit. These include environmental enquiries (Naur 1964a), such as the maximum integer, or the minimum non-zero real, which the system will support. (They also include enquiries for information such as the current bounds of dynamic arrays, which hardly belong here.)

It has also made the GIER trick official. A variant form of comment, known as a pragmat, is reserved for conveying information which can assist, but is not necessary to, the program. Suggested uses are various directions to the system (e.g. overflow action) which the system may or may not be able to accept, certain compile time checks, and even suspension of certain rules of the language designed for safety but over-protective for the responsible and experienced programmer. An important use could be '**pr use** ⟨filename⟩

pr' for incorporation of independently compiled parts of a program. (See also Section 14.6.)

CPL introduced, and BCPL has retained (and other languages have adopted), the *manifest constant*. This is a value that can be computed at compile time and dealt with more efficiently in consequence, e.g. (if reals are allowed)

MANIFEST $(PI = 3.1415927; DEGREE = PI/180 $)

The most efficient way of handling integer constants is the PutN technique of Section 9.1. Next comes keeping the constant (whatever its type) in the part of the store containing the program. Keeping it among the outermost variables, the strictly local variables, and elsewhere, are three more possibilities each less efficient than the previous one, though the differences vary from one implementation to another. (Can the locations of outermost variables be fixed at compile time, for example?) Manifest constants can be dealt with in either of the first two ways.

They really come into their own in what may be termed 'application constants'. A large part of the BCPL compiler is written in BCPL. It needs 'constants' such as the number of bits in a machine word, constant not merely from one run to another but from one program to another, yet needing to be changed when applied to another machine. Most programmers, rather than change such a literal each time it occurs in a program, will assign it to a variable during the initializing stage; this also makes the program more readable, but may result in a loss of efficiency. Declaration as a manifest constant avoids this dilemma.

Macro facilities also come under this head but are dealt with in more detail later.

It was mentioned in Section 9.5 that Cobol has found the need to introduce AT END and ON SIZE ERROR as a conditional statement alternative to an IF statement. PL/I has developed this not only for traps but to handle the requirements of parallel processing. Anticipation of traps is provided for by the ON statement — ON ⟨emergency name⟩⟨emergency action⟩, which can provide general anticipation by standing in its own right, or provide specific anticipation at a particular point in the program by being appended to any other statement (as in Cobol). Names are provided for the commoner emergencies, and systems with special ones will provide names for them. A programmer can invent his own traps giving them his own names, and cause them to occur by the statement SIGNAL⟨name⟩. There is also a variant of the CALL statement which takes the form

CALL⟨proc name⟩⟨(arg list)⟩,COMPLETE(⟨log variable⟩)

(Syntactically very similar to an attribute, an addition to an executive

135

statement such as this is called an 'option'.) The CALL then sets the logical variable to 'false' and the RETURN sets it to 'true', and the calling and called procedures may be executed in parallel. This is complemented by a statement in the calling procedure WAIT(⟨list⟩), with an option WAIT(⟨list⟩), ANY(⟨expression⟩), where the list is of logical variables and the expression is numerical; this holds up the calling procedure until all the logical variables are 'true' or until the number which are 'true' exceeds the value of the expression. For dealing with peripherals the logical variables may be hardware states with system-defined names. These arrangements should be compared with the notion of a semaphore as outlined in Section 6.1.

13.1.5 The heap

Reference has already been made in Chapter 12 to extensions to older languages to accommodate list processing. As well as calling for additional operators or functions, these have always involved provision of a 'list processing area', possibly initialized to the form of a free list. The reason for this is that list processing often violates the principle of 'last in, first out' which underlies the stack manipulation on which block structure languages are based.

It then became apparent that the problem is a more general one. CPL contemplated the function-generating function. If we define

$$F = \lambda(a,b,c)[\lambda(x).(a+bx+cx^2)]$$

and then make the assignment $G := F(1,2,1)$, we have defined G as the function $G(x) = (1+x)^2$. The Landin approach regards such an action as all in the day's work. But it has its new problems. If G is declared in an outer block (without any initial assignment of value), and the assignment is made in an inner block using local variables as parameters, then the assignment must remain valid throughout the outer block. Compare

begin integer a; **begin integer** b; b := 1; a := b **end**; print(a) **end**

which gives no trouble at all.

Algol 68 faces the same problem. Also, having introduced **ref ref amode** variables, it has had to make the rule that a value assigned to such variable must be 'not newer' (not in a *new*er LAYER, see Section 13.6) than the variable itself, i.e., a program like

> **begin int** i := 4; **ref int** a;
> **begin int** j; **comment** loc int? **comment**;
> a := j := 9; print(sqrt(a));
> L: a := i **end**;
> print(sqrt(a)) **end**

is illegal; although this particular program is innocuous, it is the good sense of the programmer (at statement L) that has made it so, and Algol 68 is not prepared to rely on this. (This is one rule that might be open to suspension by a pragmat.)

The answer to these problems in Algol 68 is the *heap*, a term which it is convenient to use for all storage, whatever the language, which is not subject to the automatic relinquishment on block exit which is characteristic of the stack. In Algol 68 the declaration **int** n is equivalent to **ref int** $n =$ **loc int**, meaning that n is synonymous with a new address on the stack (i.e. 'local'), but **heap int** n makes n synonymous with a new address on the heap, and this remains available as long as means are retained to access it.

A heap always implies a garbage collector, but the nature of the garbage collector depends on the nature of the language. In Lisp, every cell on the heap is of the same size. Numerous objects are created as parameters of subsidiary functions only to be abandoned when the function has been evaluated. The garbage collector is invoked when free space runs short; it traces all lists from known heads, marking their components, and then regards unmarked cells as abandoned, collecting them up into a new free list. In L-six (Section 13.2.1), at the other extreme, cells are of varied size and there is no means of knowing which subfields hold pointers. So here the responsibility for freeing space that is no longer required rests firmly on the programmer. The function of the L-six garbage collector is not to find but to tidy up the free space; it is called when the supply of large blocks runs short, in the hope that freed blocks of smaller size can be reunited into ones of the required size. In Algol 68, objects vary in size, but there is very strict control of type. Provided that each block level on the stack holds a means of identifying the procedure it represents, it is possible to trace, by means of the stack structure, every heap object that has not been abandoned, and to collect up the rest. In Pop2 (see next section) the type of every object can be determined by inspection and the problem is different again.

13.1.6 Pop2

The definitive reference for Pop2 is Burstall *et al* (1968). Its outstanding feature is its combination of stack and heap manipulation at almost all levels; against later languages which seek to avoid heap overheads whenever possible, it can be argued that an interactive language must in any case keep all its facilities at least on call. Being a fully recursive language, it must have pushdown storage for return addressing during routine calls, but there is one special stack that plays an essential part in user understanding of the semantics. Objects on this stack are of fixed size, say two 24-bit words, and are of a form known as *items*. Within the compass of an item is a bit pattern that can be uniquely interpreted as one of the following

(1) some integer

(2) some real number

(3) one of the values **true, false, undefined** or **terminator**

(4) a pointer to a structure on the heap.

Items falling within (1)–(3) are called simple; items of the last sort are called compound, and the structure on the heap consists of a type indication and a value which is often one or more items, but may be packed and can be the 'value' of a function variable. To illustrate, a complex number can be put on the stack in the form of two items of type (2), but as a single item it must be of type (4) and the language provides a means (see below) to convert the former into the latter and vice versa.

A variable is a combination of an identifier and an item to hold its value. Precautions, not altogether adequate ones, are taken against clash of identifiers. (Cf. Section 11.2. These precautions are more difficult to apply interactively, when user forms must be recognized at run time.) Variables are created by execution of a declaration; they are not kept on 'the' stack. Pop2 has 18 'syntax' words and a number of system functions that are protected against redefinition Only one type font is used, but it is convenient for clarity to print the syntax words in heavy type.

In a way, Pop2 is the highpoint of the application of Landin's ideas. The notions of identifier and infixed operator are unified by the syntax

$$\langle \text{identifier} \rangle ::= \langle \text{sign} * \rangle | \langle \text{letter} \rangle \langle \text{alphanumeric} * ? \rangle$$

and separated again by the requirement to declare a priority for an infixed operator. Thus

vars p $+-+$ q **operation** 5 absdiff r;

declares five identifiers, restricting the type of the fourth (*absdiff*) to that of an infixed operator of priority 5. (Contrary to the usual conventions, highest precedence means weakest binding power. Restriction to function names is also possible but has no deep significance such as **operation** has.) Then

lambda x y; **if** x$>$y **then** x$-$y **else** y$-$x **close end** $\rightarrow$ absdiff

shows the assignment of a particular function to the identifier *absdiff*. (Note that **lambda** . . **end** and **if** . . **close** are bracket-like symbols.) And now,

2.6 absdiff 3.7 $\rightarrow$ $+-+$

has the effect of assigning the real number 1.1 to the variable $+-+$. This is a perverse illustration, of course, but the point is that, in true Landin style,

138

p absdiff q
nonop absdiff (p,q)
(p,q).**nonop** absdiff

are three ways of saying the same thing, the *second* being the definitive one. If there is no intention to use the first form, then '**operation
5**' can be omitted from the declaration and '**nonop**' from the second
and third forms. (The purpose of **nonop** is to prevent infix interpretation during syntactic analysis; it disappears from later stages of
interpretation.) The main purpose of the third form is to enable a
remote structural relationship, like $tl(hd(x))$, which is Lisp's $cdar(x)$,
to be written *x.hd.tl* analogously to L-six's XHT. The alternative
declaration syntax

function absdiff x y; **if** . . **close end**

is also available; prior declaration using **vars** is then optional.

The user stack enters explicitly into the semantics of the language.
Thus ' → a' is a syntactic unit meaning 'remove the top item from
the stack after copying it into the variable a', and the effect of an
expression is the creation of a new item on the stack containing the
result of evaluating it. For use on-line, the operator ⇒ prints the
complete contents of the stack (from bottom to top) and clears it.

The semantics of a function call is that its operands are evaluated
to a sequence of items on the stack — the number of these is not
necessarily the same as the original number of parameters (see
destplex, below), nor as the number of formal parameters. Next the
formal parameters are declared and assigned to form the stack
(restoring the stack to its previous state if the parameters produced
the correct number of items); the body of the procedure is then
entered. Some results may be put on the stack during the execution
of the body. On exit the declaration of the formals is cancelled.

A curious feature which may be traceable to the Alcor group of
German workers (who advocated a similar feature in Algol 60) is a
second mechanism for output. One may write

function a b ⇒ c d; **vars** e f . . .

and this makes c and d into 'output locals' of a. These are local
variables but their values are stacked during exit.

The treatment of structures is also oriented to a notion which
has been much used by Landin and other theoreticians, that of
explicit constructor and destructor functions. Structures are known
as records, and a system function *recordfns* is available to generate
the functions required for a given structure type (or 'record class').
To introduce complex numbers, for example, we have to write
something like

139

    vars consplex destplex re im z;
    recordfns (complex, n [0,0]) → im → re → destplex → consplex;
    consplex (1.0, 2.5) → z;

The identifiers are at the user's choice, of course. The parameters *n* and [0,0] are primarily concerned with efficiency, but the number of integers in the list in square brackets is the number of components, *c*, in the structure and a zero value means that the corresponding component is of a size that cannot be packed. (The second parameter, *n*, is a usage estimate). The effect of *recordfns* is to leave $c+2$ compound items on the stack, each pointing to an object created by *recordfns*; these objects are then given names by the assignments shown. As mentioned earlier, it is impossible to put a complex number on to the stack as one simple item, but one can put it there as two (real) items; this done, *consplex* is a function that converts these to a single compound item. Thus the third line above effectively assigns the complex number $1.0+2.5i$ to *z*. (Note that *consplex*() will use the top items already on the stack as parameters; *consplex* without brackets will stack the item which 'is' *consplex*. Note also that there is nothing that forces the components to be real numbers!)

destplex is a function that reverses the action of *consplex*. *re* and *im* are function pairs (the load-update pairs of Section 13.1.1, known in Pop2 as doublets) which provide read-write access to the real and imaginary parts respectively. A system function, *dataword*, is available which will yield the type word ('complex', as supplied to *recordfns*) when applied to *z*. The provision of infixed operators between complex numbers needs only the techniques already described. Because equality refers to the bit patterns of two items, and not the the values they point to, a function

    vars operation 7 eq;
    function eq x y; re(x) = re(y) and im(x) = im(y) **end**;

will be among those required.

Two more of Landin's ideas that found implementation in Pop2 are the closure and the stream. The object on the heap corresponding to a function includes access to the body for execution, of course, but by a process known as partial application, some or all of what were originally parameters can be 'frozen' to specific values which are included in a new object. This is done by the 'convenient' syntax

    oldfn (% ⟨the values⟩ %) → newfn

but this is defined, as always, as equivalent to the application of some function to some parameters, in this case the system function *partapply* to two parameters, the original function and the list (see below) of values to be frozen. This combination of access to instructions with values to be used conforms, in many cases, to Landin's definition of a closure. (Cf. also the function G in Section 13.1.5 and Section 13.7.)

A stream is a generalization of a list (a NIL-terminated S-expression as defined in Section 12.4; Pop2 uses the word 'list' for the generalized form). A record class called a *pair* (components *front* and *back*) provides an equivalent to the **node** of Section 12.5, any item which is not a pair counting as atomic. NIL is represented by the variable *nil* holding the word (see below) 'nil' as its value. A list can be constructed from pairs and terminated by NIL; the functions *hd* and *tl* are identical to *front* and *back* in this case. But *hd* and *tl* are written to recognize a second form of pair as potentially non-atomic; this has a function as its back and should have a boolean as its front. When a list terminates in storage with such a pair, then if the boolean is **true**, this is accepted as a representation of NIL, but if the boolean is **false**, then *hd* and *tl* regard it as an implicit list of the results obtained by repeated application of the function (e.g., (**false**,*random*) represents a list of random numbers); they automatically manipulate it so that the next item from the implicit list is made explicit (and if this is **terminator**, they set the boolean to **true**). Thus the list structure [0, [1−1,], 2, 3, 4...] appears on the stack as the item that heads the following structure ('@' stands for an address):

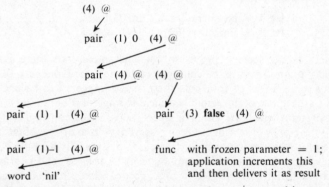

The form in square brackets would be used to represent this structure for input.

The single word **vars** contains no provision for declaring arrays, so these too are on the heap. When selection of a component is not by name but by number, a data structure is not a 'record' but a 'strip'. Whereas a record is 'constructed' by copying its component values from the stack to the heap, a strip is 'initiated', i.e. brought into existence with undefined components. All of these must have the same packing potential, so only one 'size' is required. The initiating function and the subscripting doublets are created by the

141

function *stripfns*. Thus the primitive way of declaring two arrays *vals5* (1:5) and *vals8* (1:8) is

> **vars** nthval makevals vals5 vals8
> stripfns (vals, n, 0) → nthval → makevals
> makevals(5) → vals5
> makevals(8) → vals8

Note that subject only to packing requirements, components of a strip need not be of the same type. This set-up does not allow us to write *vals5*[3] → *vals8*[1] but only *nthval*(3,*vals5*) → *nthval*(1,*vals8*). The more convenient (and usual) syntax, though with round brackets, is made available together with extra facilities (multiple subscripts, variable lower bounds, initialization) by embedding the above in two further system routines; these allow either of the forms exemplified in

newanyarray([%1, 5 %], **lambda** i; undef **end**, makevals, nthval)
→ vals5
newarray([% 1, 8 %], **lambda** i; undef **end**) → vals8.

The second of these is the first with the system initiator and doublet for non-packed components frozen in. In this example, the initializing function is a mere nuisance. CPL adopted a similar notation for declaring arrays, namely,

> **let** A = Newarray[**real**, (0,n)];
> **let** B = Formarry[**int**, (1,5)][2, 4, 6, 8, 10]

There is no specific provision for characters, but there is an implicit mapping of a 64-character set on to the integers 0. .63 during some forms of transput; these size 6 integers can be packed eight to the space of an item. Canonical storage of program text is as a list of items which are either integers, reals, string constants (input in quotes) or words (identifiers, reserved words or punctuation). The input channel is normally treated as a stream (whose function carries the analysis to this point but can be told to read character by character). A word is a special record class; its constructor, *consword*, takes an integer and that number of characters off the stack but surreptitiously precedes these by a component called *meaning* initialized to **undefined**. Its destructor, *destword*, yields all its components including *meaning*. It has one doublet for *meaning*, and another called *charword* that reverses the constructor when reading and ignores *meaning* when updating. The values of most words are held in a dictionary without duplication, so that value equality of two words can usually be recognized by testing item equality. (The exceptions are words that have been updated). As there is no limit to the complexity of the data structure that can be assigned to a meaning, the utility of this arrangement needs no demonstration.

Strings are handled as packed character strips. Owing to the nature of compound items, references are comparatively unnecessary, but there is a set of system routines for creating a reference to an item from the item, and for accessing and updating it. The language also has provision for macros, and for functions written in machine code.

Pop2 is extremely beloved by its fans and has much to recommend it. Conventional critics are aghast at a language with no loop control statement. Well-wishers find it a difficult language to acquire a smattering of; the reversal of right and left gives assignments an unfamiliar appearance, and system functions like *popmess* (which links a peripheral to a stream) or *recordfns* are obscure in action and repulsive in appearance. In fact, mnemonics to something one has not yet understood usually are repulsive, in any language. Another reason may be (as demonstrated in the above description of arrays) the problems of simultaneously following two different levels of generalization. But are these not the price of its successes? Storage management may have to come more to the surface in complex data processing, and are constructor and destructor functions any more obscure to the newcomer than Algol 68's generators, for example? In most languages interactive compilers are costly; the Pop2 compiler is geared to interactive working from the start. If importance derives from breadth of achievement, then there is one further system function to consider. This is *popval*, which, applied to a strip (which may have been constructed by an earlier phase of the computation), causes it to be obeyed as a piece of Pop2 text. In what other language can one do this?

13.1.7 *Pascal*

Despite the damage done by protagonists who regard the rivalry between Algol 60 and Fortran as an opportunity for political activity, there will be those that advocate Pascal simply as a stick to beat Algol 68 with. From the standpoint of this book, Pascal has certain unique features that provide it with a claim to individual treatment. One is that its grammar is published in the form of flow diagrams strictly analogous to those we have described for the parsing machine; another is its wholehearted incorporation of the notion of sets. Its declared aim is twofold, efficiency as measured by compilation and runtime speeds, and the encouragement, by its linguistic structure, of the writing of well structured programs in a wide variety of problem areas by students and professionals alike. It is maintained that over-powerful languages were paying a price in execution speed and that Pascal represents a turning point in this trend. (These aims may be compared with those of Omnibus (Section

13.7), which are efficiency as measured by minimum demands on material resources such as store size, and the encouragement, in a broad machine-independent way, of an understanding of what will be involved behind the scenes by what the programmer has written.)

Pascal was first described in Wirth(1971a), a description of its compiler appearing almost simultaneously (1971b); after some experience with its use a revised report was issued (Jensen and Wirth (1973)).

Although a successor to Algol 60, Pascal (like Pop2 and, indeed, some implementations of Algol 60) eschews the notion of heavy type. This involves (1) using spaces to separate words, (2) reserving some thirty-five words (which we print in heavy type solely for convenience in reading), and (3) extending the notion of an identifier to cover the names of modes, field selectors, etc., as well as the names of variables, routines and manifest constants. Labels are unsigned integers. A block is a fully recursive structure, but it does not occur as a production of ⟨statement⟩, only as the body of a program, or of a procedure or function declaration. It consists of a number of sections, each identified by its first word, and strictly in the following order

label followed by unsigned integers separated by commas;

const followed by declarations of manifest constants in the form '⟨identifier⟩ = ⟨constant expression⟩' and separated by semicolons;

type followed by mode declarations in the form '⟨identifier⟩ = ⟨type⟩' and separated by semicolons;

var followed by declarations of variables in the form '⟨identifiers separated by commas⟩ : ⟨type⟩' and separated by semicolons;

items in the form '{**procedure**|**function**}⟨identifier⟩⟨parameter list⟩{:⟨type⟩}ᵢf function; ⟨block⟩' separated by semicolons;

begin followed by statements separated by semicolons, and **end**.

Any section except the last may be omitted, and the last by itself *is* a production of ⟨statement⟩ as well as a possible routine body. Similar remarks apply to a statement; an initial numeral must indicate a label, the words

goto   with   for   repeat   while   case   if   begin

each indicate a specific sort of statement, and any other first word can be immediately typed as a procedure identifier (= call), a function identifier (yielding the destination for an assignment) or a variable (leading directly into an assignment). All labels and identifiers must be declared before they are used, except that use of ↑⟨type⟩ (equivalent to **ref amode**) may precede declaration of its ⟨type⟩. (When procedures are mutually recursive, the declaration of one may be split, declaring it first with *forward* as its body, then again later with a skeletal head and the complete body.) The effect of these provisions is that syntax analysis proceeds without back-tracking, and compilation in a single pass.

The set concept is made to underlie the type concept in the following way. The type *integer* is the set of all the integers that the implementation can handle. This can be written [− maxint .. maxint]. The type declaration

$$\text{month} = [1 .. 12]$$

signifies that the type *month* is the set of all integers in the subrange shown. The effect of the type declaration

$$\text{day} = (\text{mon, tues, wed, thurs, fri, sat, sun})$$

is to declare the seven identifiers to be the complete set of denotations for constants of type *day*, and to provide them with internal codes by mapping them on to [0 .. 6]. (It is worth noticing that *boolean*, *true* and *false* are *not* reserved words, but consequences of a declaration

$$\text{boolean} = (\text{false, true})$$

in the enclosing 'block'.) These covert subtypes of *integer*, together with the integers themselves and the reals, are called scalar types. The mapping comes to the surface in the sense that, if *day1* is a variable of type *day*, then one may write '**if** day1>fri', but not in any more general sense. Indeed, the actual internal representation of the nth day may be n, and packing possibilities exploited, or 2^n, if set manipulation is involved. The latter is invoked by the declaration

$$\text{days} = \textbf{set of} \text{ day},$$

and by assignments such as

    days1 := [mon, wed, fri]
    days1 := days1+[thurs]   (here '+' denotes set union)

and by the boolean infixed operator **in** for testing set membership. It is understood that to facilitate bitwise interpretation of a set, the number of items in a set may be restricted to the number of bits in a word, which was all very well in the original implementation (CDC 6000, 60-bit word) but hard on owners of minis. The range concept is also used in declaring arrays; not only V : **array**[1 .. 20]**of** *integer*, accessed e.g. by V[8], but also W : **array**[*days*]**of** *boolean*, accessed by W[*tues*].

Both set and array sizes are defined in terms of manifest constants, with the unfortunate result that there are no dynamic arrays. Structures and unions are combined under the type of *record*, as in

145

(type) date = **record** dayofweek : day;
dayofmonth, month, year : integer **end**

(Unions are considered further in Section 13.4.)

In procedure and function declarations, the ⟨parameter list⟩ mentioned earlier has the format {(group list with semicolons)}$_0^1$, where

⟨group⟩ ::= ⟨call style⟩⟨identifier list with commas⟩ : ⟨type identifier⟩
⟨call style⟩ ::= **var|function|procedure|**⟨empty⟩

Thus call by value is the default option; **var** leads to call by reference, while **function** and **procedure** postpone evaluation until call within the body. But there is no multiple dereferencing; use of a ↑⟨type⟩ type as an actual to replace a ⟨type⟩ formal must be explicitly dereferenced by writing ⟨identifier⟩ ↑. (The same applies to field selection, as in

familyfete := individual.father ↑ .birthday

where the individual's father-field is a pointer.) Wide coercion facilities are undoubtedly expensive; another feature of the same sort is that while there is an option to declare a structure **packed**, fields from a *packed* structure may not be quoted as actual parameters.

Habermann (1973) lists a number of criticisms of Pascal. (1) Lack of block structure. This is trivial; it is simply that every Algol 60 block must, in Pascal, be given a name and called a procedure. The compiler might well do this in Algol 60 anyway. (2) Omission of **own**. Algol 60 **own** was not satisfactory, and unless a language is prepared to offer a more satisfactory treatment of this concept, it is better advised to omit it. (3) Lack of conditional expressions. (4) After the 1973 revisions the distinction between functions and procedures is too marginal to be worth it. (5) Absence of multiple assignments. But multiple assignments as in Algol 60 or as in Algol 68? Taking the latter interpretation of (5), all of (3)–(5) are valid criticisms which would disappear if the distinction between expressions and statements were abolished, as it should be. (6) Inclusion of **goto**. This is a ridiculous criticism. The minimization of **goto**s is an excellent practical rule, but advocacy of their complete elimination is pure fetish. (7) The absence of dynamic ranges, including dynamic arrays. Habermann conjectures that the reason is the difficulty of treating variable ranges as types, but Wirth states quite clearly that the objective was that 'all variables within one data segment are to be allocatable by the compiler', i.e. that within the part of the stack devoted to the current block all displacements must be manifest constants. Here the boot is on the other foot; a valuable facility

146

is sacrificed to the fetish of manifest constants, since there is in fact no problem in implementing dynamically defined types (except perhaps as sets).

Pascal is an excellent language in its own eyes, i.e. judged by a measure of efficiency in which compile times, run times, program writing times, programmer education and other considerations are weighted according to its own design specifications. Slight changes in these weights are enough to suggest that some of the sacrifices made in tuning to this specification are too great.

13.2 Mixed Level Languages

Among the advantages of a high-level language are (1) the provision of a convenient syntax, (2) isolation from machine dependent features such as instruction formats and internal addresses, and (3) protection against treating a stored value in a manner inappropriate to its type. It is possible to want the first without the second, particularly when writing compilers. As for the third, it is a solemn thought that every load and go compiler contains at least one example of 'jumping into data' — so solemn that ICL, in the 2900 series, have taken steps to ensure that this can only be done by means of a system subroutine call. In this section we discuss a number of languages which break the association of these features in some way, whether or not compiler writing is their main objective. (N.B. The association can also be broken by providing 'high-level hardware' — e.g. automatic stacking of subroutine return addresses. For the sake of clarity we ignore this throughout.)

PL/360 is an example of this at the lowest level. It is the assembly language of the IBM 360 series with two added features of interest, an Algol-like syntax for the writing of loops, and the introduction of 'synonyms'. One of the problems of reading low-level programs is to know, particularly after a lengthy jump, what the accumulators, and possibly other temporary storage locations, contain. PL/360 allows a mnemonic symbol to be defined as a synonym of the name of such a register, even if it is an accumulator. This does not prevent mistakes, but it does make it easier to avoid them, and to correct those that do occur.

Without descending quite so low, it is possible to want *some* freedom from the strict type control of a high-level language without altogether relinquishing the protection it provides. The system described in Section 13.7 provides clues as to what it is reasonable to expect. There are two approaches to this. For the first, consider the following as a test case. The boolean 'much greater than' between two reals is most efficiently implemented by subtracting the exponents. This cannot be done without a knowledge of where to find them, but assuming this to be available, it is suggested that a notation such as

147

$$\textbf{mode quad} = \textbf{struc}(\textbf{int } a, b, c, d);$$
$$\textbf{proc } mgthan = (\textbf{quad}(\textbf{real } x, y))\textbf{bool} : (b-d>16)$$

might be suitable. It implies that two reals, x and y, as a structure, can be 'coerced' into being regarded as four integers, a, b, c and d. Note (1) that all six identifiers will be meaningful in the procedure body, and (2) that although the notation is that of a cast, it applies to *formal* parameters, and the coercion rules are different. E.g. **int** will not coerce into **real** because the lengths are different, but *anything* will coerce into the equivalent number of integers. Assuming that a compiler is to be written with a facility of this sort in mind, what checks are still desirable? Two would seem to be necessary to retain complete security, (1) that the lengths of (i.e. number of machine words in) the two structures are the same, and (2) that no word that is not an address is ever 'coerced' into being one. (The reverse of (2) is harmless, and is required for, e.g. diagnostic printouts.)

The above is an extension of the language allowing the programmer a new facility while maintaining full security checks. The alternative approach is to trade security for freedom. For this purpose we note that modes which describe objects of the same length and with addresses located in the same places form an equivalence class among modes. Description in terms of such equivalence classes loses some machine independence, but retains security and the full facility of garbage collection. We can abandon the address discipline in either direction or both, resulting in fewer but larger classes. Treating addresses as integers permits diagnostics but can interfere with garbage collection, while treating integers as addresses permits jumping into code we have written but involves abandonment of almost all security. Abandonment of length control may work with a values-only stack (cf. Pop2) but can easily lead to system crashes if, for example, it leads us to a wrong location for a stacked return address.

13.2.1 L-six (L^6)

The principle of L-six is as follows (Knowlton 1966). The programmer works with a predefined set of bases (called *bugs*) and with blocks of arbitrary size which he may get from or return to free store at any point in a program. A request for a block includes nomination of a bug (or other area) to receive the address of the block. He may also dynamically define (and redefine) an arbitrary 'subfield of a block'; such a definition creates a load-update pair of procedures. (In fact, a pair of closures (Section 13.7) is all that is implied.) Names are ⟨name of bug⟩ followed by zero or more ⟨name of subfield⟩s; such a name refers to the object accessed by starting from the pointer held in the bug and chaining through the

148

subfields, each of which (except the last) is assumed to hold a pointer to another block. (There is no check that a subfield does, or even can, hold an address, nor that a block is actually large enough to include a required subfield; results of violating these conditions are undefined.)

In practice, for implementation reasons, blocks are of 2^n machine words $(0 \leqslant n \leqslant 7)$, and bug and subfield names are confined to the thirty-six characters A .. Z, 0 .. 9. (No confusion is possible between use of the same symbol as a bug name and as a subfield name.) A name like SJ2X is loosely equivalent to Algol 68's

X of 2 of J of S

— very loosely, because (1) subfield names are global, not related to a specific structure, (2) subfield names may overlap, and (3) the Algol 68 could apply (according to the declarations) to nested as well as to chained structures. It is claimed that such a name has not only the advantage of brevity, but that in a particular program it acquires a user-semantics of its own, such as 'maternal great-uncle' might to an anthropologist studying a particular society (who would not mentally work out the implied sequence, but rather would associate the term directly with its legal and sociological implications).

The syntax is based on a format which is usually

$$\langle bracket \rangle ::= (\langle destination \rangle, \langle op\ code \rangle, \langle source \rangle)$$

with two classes of op-code, those that 'test' and those that 'do'. The most general form of a line is

$$\langle label1 \rangle \langle if\ form \rangle \langle test\text{-}brackets \rangle THEN \langle do\text{-}brackets \rangle \langle label2 \rangle$$

The first, 'defining', label may be omitted. The $\langle if\ form \rangle$ may be IFALL (or IF), IFANY, IFNONE (or NOT), or IFNALL; it and the test brackets, each of which yields a boolean, may be omitted, as may be either the do-brackets or the second, 'applied', label, but not both. (This second label foreshadows the Algol 68 decision that **goto** is redundant, the label itself, there syntactically a procedure call, being sufficient.)

The precise collection of $\langle op\ code \rangle$s available is of less interest than their format, which is usually two letters (the second sometimes missing), the first of which is the true function and the second defines the 'mode' of the $\langle source \rangle$ as a string, a decimal integer, an octal integer or a name. But there are exceptions, such as D for 'define': (3,DN,5,8), for example, defines field N as the 5th to the 8th bits inclusive of the 3rd word of the block. More typically we have E (copy) or S (subtract); (ZW, E, SJ2X) copies the contents of SJ2X into ZW, and (PX,SO,261) subtracts 261(octal) from the contents of PX.

This language is low-level in two senses. It operates on bit-patterns as told, making no checks on type but leaving all responsibility for correct interpretation to the programmer, and its order code resembles that of a multiaccumulator mini. In such a machine, however, the operators act between accumulators, and the sophisticated addressing available for the arguments in L-six is a high level feature. So, too, are the features which make it completely recursive. These are (1) the special form of the newblock request order (GT) to facilitate its operation as a pushdown operator, and (2) facilities to push down information not immediately available to the programmer. Whereas (W,GT,2) merely gets a new, empty, two-word block, putting its address in W, (W,GT,2,WA) puts the old contents of W into the new WA, converting the operation into a pushdown action, and (W,FR,WA) reverses this, returning the popped-up block to the free list. But the programmer has no immediate access to the numerical values he used in defining a sub-field, so if a subroutine wishes to redefine a subfield, the special operations (S,FD,f) and (R,FD,f) (for save/restore field definition of f) must be used. Subroutines are called by (DO,LABEL) or (FAILEXIT,DO,LABEL), return being by the special ⟨label2⟩, DONE (or, when appropriate, FAIL). The syntactic nature of a line is an interesting first step towards thinking of program structure by encouraging the grouping of machine instructions into compound operations. (This can be done in any assembly code that allows a semicolon, for example, to double as a new line semantically, but few programmers seem to have the motivation to exploit it; L-six encourages it.)

13.2.2 BCPL

CPL had a very rich syntax, most of which BCPL has taken over, but some of which was based on a luxurious character set derived from the Flexowriter set, including backspacing for underlining and for some other overprinting (e.g. ≠ from = and /); BCPL has forgone the latter in the interests of transferability between machines. In the following account we use BCPL notation. To some extent this syntactic richness is an application of the process of natural development described in Section 2.1, since it means incorporating so many of those things one does with Algol when merely scribbling first drafts — **unless** and **until**, for example, as alternatives to **if** and **while** to save a **not**(. . .), and the use of more compact brackets, '$(' and '$)', in place of '**begin**' and '**end**'. In principle, any variation which is natural and unambiguous goes — in practice, provided enough people find it natural to make it worth forcing the compiler to recognize it, of course — so that the following are all equivalent, the differences serving to cater for personal preference or for one's feeling for the English language:

150

```
TEST B THEN APPLY OR CONVERT
TEST B THEN DO APPLICATION OR CONVERSION
TEST B DO APPLICATION OR CONVERSION
IF B THEN APPLY;   UNLESS B DO CONVERT
```

But **if** and **test** are not equivalent; the ambiguity problems into which Algol 60 ran are eliminated by distinguishing in this way whether one or both alternatives are explicit. For a fuller account of conditionals see Section 13.4.

A second feature taken over almost intact is the philosophy of its loop statement. BCPL has

```
WHILE⟨expression⟩DO⟨command⟩
UNTIL⟨expression⟩DO⟨command⟩
⟨command⟩REPEAT
⟨command⟩REPEATWHILE⟨expression⟩
⟨command⟩REPEATUNTIL⟨expression⟩
FOR⟨var⟩ = ⟨exp⟩TO⟨exp⟩BY⟨const⟩DO⟨command⟩
FOR⟨var⟩ = ⟨exp⟩TO⟨exp⟩DO⟨command⟩
```

having dropped one or two variations of the for-statement that were available in CPL. For the semantics of this statement see Section 13.5.

Another feature is the tagging of statement brackets to allow implicit closing (which PL/I also allows by a different technique). In Algol 60 one can find oneself writing sequences like

A: **begin** ... B: **begin** ... C: **begin** ... **end** C **end** B **end** A;

but the C, B and A following the **ends** rank as comment. Such comments help one to count up the number of statement brackets which need closing. It is clear that under these circumstances the compiler can do the counting, so that '... **end** A;' should make it redundant (though not wrong) to write the inner **end**s. PL/I adopts almost exactly this technique, while CPL and BCPL, instead of using labels for the purpose, allows 'section and subsection type' numbering of statement brackets, thus

$$(4.2 ... \$(4.2.1 ... \$)4.2$$

where \$)4.2 implies a preceding \$)4.2.1 if an explicit one has not already occurred.

Since the omission of a closing bracket is a fairly common error, it is worth noting that even if a language does not possess the feature just described, it is still possible, if it includes brackets of varying 'strength' — e.g. **begin** ... **end** and (...) — for the computer to apply the principle to faulty programs. The implicit insertion of a missing 'weak' bracket at the closing of a 'strong' one will often restore sanity to the parsing process in a way that makes further error detection more meaningful. (See also Section 13.4.)

In its declarations, BCPL follows CPL syntactically but shows its true nature semantically: 'the basic data object is a [machine] word with no particular disposition as to type. A word may be treated as a bit-pattern, a number, a subroutine entry or a label. Neither the compiler nor the runtime system makes any attempt to enforce type restrictions. In this respect BCPL has both the flexibility and the pitfalls of machine language' (Richards 1973). The resemblance to L-six is obvious. In addition to (1) the MANIFEST declaration already discussed in Section 13.1.4, other forms are (2)

GLOBAL $(⟨identifier⟩ : ⟨manifest expression⟩)$)

The expression evaluating to n, the identifier refers to (is made synonymous with the address of) the nth word of a global vector; this is the equivalent of Fortran's COMMON and is the sole means of communication between independently compiled parts of the program (not excluding certain system routines; the lower values of n are preempted for these). (3)

STATIC $(⟨identifier⟩ : ⟨manifest expression⟩$)

The identifier is associated with a single location, initialized to the expression, outside the block structure, rather like Algol 60's **own**. Both of these forms allow several declarations, separated by semicolons, within the brackets. (4)

LET⟨identifier list⟩ = ⟨expression list⟩

The identifiers, initialized to the current values of the expressions, are variable identifiers associated with locations claimed on entry to the block in which the declaration occurs and relinquished on leaving it. (The list items are separated by commas.) (5)

LET⟨identifier⟩(⟨parameter list⟩) = ⟨expression⟩
LET⟨identifier⟩(⟨parameter list⟩) BE ⟨statement⟩

The identifier is that of a function or a routine, and is associated with a location holding the entry address of the code for the expression or statement. The parameters are identifiers, effectively declared by their occurrence in this list, and the brackets are essential even if the list is empty (if they are absent the identifier becomes a variable, and the expression is evaluated at once). It is permitted that the identifier has already been declared as part of the global vector, otherwise the location is a new one. Because ⟨expression⟩ includes the VALOF option (Section 13.1.3), the function declaration has the full generality of a type procedure. (6)

LET⟨identifier⟩ = VEC⟨manifest expression⟩

The expression evaluating to n, the identifier is associated with a location that contains the address of the first of a set of $n+1$ contiguous words (associated with the identifier by subscripts $0 \ldots n$).

In Algol 60 it was the rule that the scope of an identifier (i.e. the part of the text throughout which it is valid) is the whole of the block in which the declaration stands, including inner blocks unless these redefine it. In CPL the scope normally began only as the declaration was complete, but could include its own definition provided this was annotated **rec**; thus in

> **let** sqrt(**real** x, **label** L) = **result of** § **if** x$<$0 **goto** L;
>
> **result is** sqrt(x)§;
>
> **let rec** fact(**integer** x) = (n$=$0 $\rightarrow$ 1, n*fact(n$-$1));

both declarations are valid but the *sqrt* inside the first is the library routine, whereas the second is recursive. Another feature of CPL, retained in BCPL by the syntax

> $\langle$local definition$\rangle$ $::=$ LET$\langle$compound definition$\rangle$
>
> $\langle$compound definition$\rangle$ $::=$ $\langle$definition$\rangle$AND$\langle$compound definition$\rangle$$|$$\langle$definition$\rangle$,

allows several definitions to be grouped into one for mutual recursion. But BCPL omits any equivalent of **rec**, taking the recursive interpretation for granted. The 'cumulative declaration' principle facilitates one pass compilation.

Little else in BCPL calls for comment except for the operators that distinguish it from other languages, including CPL, less concerned with what actually happens in the machine. As well as machine level operators like left and right shift, these include ! and @, for which the significant synonyms RV and LV may be used (right and left hand value — see Section 13.1.1). The first of these forces an extra 'contents of' into the interpretation, the second suppresses one (and is thus invalid on the LHS of an assignment statement where there is none to suppress). E1!E2 is subscript notation. According to the description above, if E1 is the identifier of a vector, then the LV of E1 is the address of a single cell, the RV of E1 is its contents, identical with the LV of E1!0, while the LV of E1!E2 is E1$+$E2 (interpreted in the normal way, i.e. as the sum of two RV's).

Thus these operators perform explicitly what type-checking languages do by coercion. In procedure calls the parameters are called by (R-)value, but the equivalent of an Algol 68 call, $f(p, r, q)$ in the context of

> **begin int** p, q, **ref int** r;
>
> **proc** f = (**int** i, j, **ref int** k)**void** : ($\langle$body$\rangle$);

would be the call F(P, !R, @Q) in the context of

```
        LET P, Q, R = 0, 0, 0;
        LET F(I, J, K) BE ⟨statement⟩;
```

13.3 Algol 68 Concepts

From the first, Algol 68 was defined as a new language, not as a revision of Algol 60; it also makes an explicit claim that advancement of the art of language description is among its aims. Nevertheless, it is recognizably a successor to Algol 60. It fulfils all our requirements for an Algol-like language in spirit, and all but one of them to the letter (it uses an *extension* of CBNF). At the most elementary level it differs from Algol 60 only in its use of **int** and **bool** for **integer** and **boolean**, and in the **fi** which must balance every **if**.

The syntactic developments introduced by the report have already been described in principle in Section 7.4.1, and a background provided for its technique of semantic description in Section 7.7. The following sections deal with the new features of the language itself and give an actual example of the semantic technique.

13.3.1 Types and modes

In Section 2.7 a distinction was drawn between objects *internal* to a piece of language text and their referends in an *external* world; it was implied that this external world might be a computer store. The Algol 68 report also makes the distinction but reverses the terminology by taking a hypothetical computer, instead of the language, as its basis.

Section 2.7:

An object *internal* to the *refers to* an object in the *external* language (identifier, number, world; if this is the computer etc.) is, in ordinary English, a store, the object has an *ad-* *name* *dress* and *possesses* a value

Numbers, being literal, re- (which may be an address).
fer to themselves, but an
identifier . . . .

Algol 68 report:

An object *external* to the *possesses* an object *internal* to the com-
computer (an identifier) . . . . puter; this has a *name* which
refers to an *instance* of a
value (which may be a name)

Numbers, etc., are also in-
stances of values, known as
denotations (which may not
be names).

154

Objects within the computer are usually patterns of bits; objects within the language are strings of characters. The three basic types of Algol 60 (**integer, real** and **boolean**) distinguish inside the computer different *interpretations* of bit patterns and in the language texts *mutually exclusive sets* of value denotations.

Granted (1) that the Algol 68 name is more than an address — more like a codeword — and (2) that it is quite possible to find 'Santa Maria' and 'No.56' as neighbouring houses, yet it must go on record that wanton violation of normal English usage (such as 'name' where most English speakers would say 'address') has been a most unnecessary cause of psychological resistance to Algol 68. On the other hand, it does emphasize (as is also emphasized in the design of Pascal) that integer arithmetic on addresses has no place in the language.

In addition to **int, real** and **bool**, Algol 68 has admitted two other basic types, **char** (for *character*) and **format** (though see 'simplification (5)', below). The former is a necessary extension to shake off the over-mathematical viewpoint of Algol 60; the latter is merely a special name for a string in an input-output-describing sublanguage.

Algol 60 also has arrays (of basic types only), procedures and switches. Algol 68 is unrestricted in the way combinations of basic types may be built up, and as **goto** ⟨label⟩ is regarded as a procedure denotation, the 'switch' can disappear into an 'array of procedures'. Better still, **goto** *switch* [*subscript*] can be replaced by an integer case clause as in Section 13.4. But structures and unions are provided. Whereas an array is an ordered set of like objects separately identified by subscripts, a structure is a (for most purposes) unordered set of (possibly) unlike objects, separately identified by field-selectors, similar to a Cobol record. The generalization of type to which this leads is covered by the word 'mode'. Differently structured objects, even like-structured objects with different field-selectors, belong to different modes, as do procedures whose parameters- or results-structures are different. A united mode is one in which the true mode can vary, within a defined list of non-united modes, during the program. The full range of modes available is given by the totality of productions from the upper level non-terminal MODE according to a grammar of which the following is a somewhat simplified version.

MODE:: SIMPLE; union of MOODS mode.
MOODS:: MOOD; MOODS MOOD.
MOOD:: SIMPLE; void.
SIMPLE:: LONGSETY integral; LONGSETY real; boolean; character; reference to MODE; PROCEDURE; structured with FIELDS; row of MODE.
LONGSETY:: long LONGSETY; EMPTY.

PROCEDURE:: procedure PARAMETY yielding MOID.
MOID:: MODE; void.
PARAMETY :: with PARAMETERS; EMPTY.
PARAMETERS:: MODE parameter; MODE parameter and
    PARAMETERS.
FIELDS:: MODE field TAG; MODE field TAG and FIELDS.
TAG:: LETTER; TAG LETTER; TAG DIGIT.
LETTER:: letter a; letter b; . . letter z.
DIGIT:: digit zero; digit one; . . digit nine.

The simplifications consist in the following omissions

(1) Explicit names for sub-classes — e.g. PLAIN and STOWED for the first and third lines of SIMPLE, UNITED for 'union of MOODS mode',

(2) 'transient reference to' which is used to prevent long-term use of pointers to substructures of movable objects (flexible sized objects on the heap),

(3) features designed to ensure semantic equivalence of, for example, **union(int, real)** and **union(real, int)**,

(4) features designed to prevent the writing of modes which, though conceivable, give rise to difficulties elsewhere. The definition **mode bad** = **struc(int** i, **bad** b) gives rise to an object of unbounded size, though **mode good** = **struc(int** i, **ref good** g) is all right. The mode **union(real, ref real)** presents no problems in itself, but is illegal on account of the ambiguities it gives rise to in situations where the dereferencing coercion (see next section) is possible before assignment to it.

(5) '**format**', which was a simple mode in earlier drafts, is a structured mode in the final report, defined in the standard prelude.

The reader should observe how field-selecting 'identifiers' do, but formal parameter identifiers do not, enter into the definition of a particular mode.

One of the bitterest criticisms of Algol 68 has been that high level languages aim to 'conceal the machinery' and that by introducing **ref** modes it is reneging on this. This criticism fails to distinguish between the machinery of the computer, which must be concealed, and that of the calculation, which is a different matter. The latter is concealed at the highest level of a well structured program by being buried in procedure bodies, or it is disciplined but not concealed in loop statements, but it is never banished from the language. If a hand calculation, in which values are written in columns headed by names of variables, is best performed by admitting a column into which the name of some other variable is written, then the mechanism of the calculation requires a reference variable whose name heads that column. No good language does entirely without the notion. It underlies the call by value or simple name concept, and lack of it caused the difficulties behind the value-name distinction in Algol 60; it is the right and left evaluation modes of CPL and BCPL, and the ↑ concept in Pascal. Most languages require it for handling lists, and even Pop2, which handles lists without it, includes it as a possibility for occasional use. But two comments are necessary to insure against misunderstanding. (1) It is not exactly the 'variable — manifest constant' distinction. In terms of this distinction the Algol 68 non-ref identifier is perhaps a 'locally manifest constant' — not manifest at compile time, but manifest at block or procedure entry time and unchanged throughout its existence. (2) Many mixed level languages admit integer arithmetic on 'pointers'. This is where the rot sets in (i.e. the high level language begins to decay into a mixed level one). The contents of a truly reference variable is a pointer to a specific object whose relation to objects in its neighbourhood is never considered; in other words store address machinery is still completely concealed.

13.3.2 Coercion

The issue of the intrusion of semantic considerations into syntax has been considered in Chapter 7, where it was shown that it makes sense to write a context-free grammar and admit that grammatically correct nonsense can be written, but that once the context-free barrier is broken (as it must be to secure 'agreement' in natural languages) then it becomes very difficult to know where to draw the line. We saw the fumbling way in which Algol 60 tried to deal (in its grammar) with the need for type agreement between the two sides of an assignment.

It is simple enough to secure exact agreement. One needs a hyper-rule of the form

> MODE assignment: MODE destination, colonequals,
>   MODE source.

(the second and third occurrences of MODE securing the agreement, and the first defining the mode of the resulting value — cf. Section 13.1.3). But this is too restrictive, it permits only one — depending on how 'destination' and 'source' are developed — of the two forms of assignment in

> **begin integer** i; **real** y, z; y := 2.0; z := y **end**

because the left-hand sides (y and z) are of the same mode (**ref real**) but the right-hand sides (2.0 and y) are of different modes (2.0 is **real**). The necessary relaxation to permit both forms of expression is secured by a rule which makes immediate provision for the first form but includes, *in its syntax*, a mechanism for the second form by which the *name* 'y' is permitted provided that it is coerced into yielding the *value* to which it refers. (The process is more easily understood if the complementary relation between the words 'relaxation' and 'coerced' is noticed.) The hyper-rule is therefore recast into

reference to MODE assignment: soft reference
to MODE tertiary, colonequals, strong MODE unit.

with rules for eliminating 'strong' and 'soft'. The process is at its clearest in the notation of MR 101, where the rules eliminating 'strong' read, in effect,

strong MODE: MODE; strongly dereferenced to MODE;
strongly widened to MODE; etc.
strongly dereferenced to MODE: reference to MODE.
strongly widened to LONGSETY real: LONGSETY integral;
strongly dereferenced to LONGSETY integral.

It will be seen that these rules also provide for $z := 2$, and for the use of two coercions in sequence as is required for $z := i$.

In its application of these principles, Algol 68 has defined five sorts of position and eight forms of coercion, two of the latter having been abandoned in the final report.

In *soft* positions, mostly left-hand sides, the result may be
deprocedured, i.e. the occurrence of a procedure may imply the result of applying that procedure. For this purpose, **if** b **then** x **else** y **fi** is a procedure denotation.
In *weak* positions, mostly the names of arrays or structures from which a part is being selected,
dereferencing is also allowed, if there is more than one 'reference to' in the mode. (Consider

ref . . **ref** [] **real** A, [] **real** B; A := . . . := B; . . .;
A[m] := A[n]; . . .

The last statement must be coerced into $B[m] := B[n]$. Although the real $B[n]$ could be obtained from a row-of-real B, the ref-real $B[m]$ can only be obtained from a ref-row-of-real B; thus although superfluous *refs* can (indeed, must) be removed, it is fatal to remove the *last* one until after subscripting has been completed.)
In *meek* positions full dereferencing is allowed since the above complication does not arise. Meek positions include the names of procedures being called with parameters; some are positions not requiring any better facilities (one can never widen to boolean or integer, for example) and some result from the problems of applying coercions in sequence.

In *firm* positions, mainly operands, all the above are allowed, and also

uniting, which is e.g. conversion of a value of mode **int** into one of mode **union(int, real)**.

proceduring is the conversion of an expression into a procedure for evaluating that expression. It is the coercion required to allow F(1) when the specification of F calls for a **proc int** parameter. This is Algol 60's call by name. To remove ambiguities it has been disallowed in the final version of Algol 68, and F(**int**:(1)) must be written to show the parameter explicitly as a procedure. (For a vestigial survival see Section 14.5.)

In *strong* positions, which include parameters of procedure calls and right-hand sides of assignments, the above may be supplemented by

widening — converting integers to reals, thence to complex if necessary (also some unpacking processes). In general, treating a member of a subclass as though it had been pre-sented in a form appropriate to a member of a wider class (a description that shows why the converse coercion is not available). But note that there is no lengthening in this (or any other) coercion in Algol 68. One must write **long real** $x :=$ **long** 1 because **long real** $x := 1$ leaves open whether x is floated or lengthened first

rowing — converting a value into a one-membered array. Converting a character into a string of length 1 is the com-monest case of this.

hipping was providing a mode for a dummy value for form's sake, but rewriting the grammar has eliminated the need for this.

voiding — conversion to **void** by throwing away an unwanted value.

The main difficulty in using this concept in Algol 68 appears to have been the control of several coercions in sequence to prevent resultant ambiguity.

It would appear that this development has important applications to the theory of language in general, and not only of programming languages. It can be used, for example, to show how the normal rules of grammar can be relaxed to permit a figure of speech such as personification to be maintained. Details vary from language to language but consider in English

The sun, which had just risen, was hot and its rays were warming.

Poetically, but not otherwise, 'its' may be replaced by 'his', but it is doubtful whether 'which' can ever be replaced by 'who'. This suggests a 'depersonification' coercion, with the position of a coordinated pronoun being 'stronger' than that of a subordinated one.

13.3.3 Declarations

The weakness in Algol 60 which most effectively prevented its incorporation as a subset of any improved version, was the diversity of its declaration structures. Thus while **integer array** A [1:3] defines locations for three integer variables without being able to assign initial values to them, **switch** S := P, Q, R defines an array of three labels whose contents are initialized and unalterable. Procedure declarations have a complicated syntax entirely their own. Such syntactic variations inhibited any generalization of the concept. In Algol 68, declarations either conform to a standard pattern or are definable as abbreviations for something that itself conforms to that pattern. The pattern can be represented by

CLASS demonstrator, CLASS definiens, equals symbol,
　　CLASS value.,

in the context of an upper level

CLASS : : mode; MODE identity; priority; MODE operation; etc.

(although these are not verbatim quotes from the grammar — compare COMMON in Section 13.6). The first two of these CLASSes develop further by

mode demonstrator: mode symbol.
mode definiens: new black type word.
mode value: MODE declarer.

MODE identity demonstrator: MODE declarer.
MODE identity definiens: identifier.
MODE identity value: strong MODE unit; MODE transformat.

The mode declaration allows the user to introduce a new black type word as a synonym for a more spelled out version of a mode declarer, e.g.

mode vector = **struc**(**real** xpart, ypart, zpart).

(The relation of this representation to the formal 'structured with real field letter x letter p . . .' of Section 13.3.1 should not need spelling out in detail.) In the same way a MODE identity declaration allows an identifier to be defined as synonymous with something spelled out in more detail, but in this area there are more options, as we proceed to show.

　　Ignoring, initially, the possibility of coercion, we can have

> **real** pi = 3.14159
> **ref real** z = y
> **proc(ref int)int** inc = (**ref int** i)**int** : (i := i+1)
> **ref real** q = **loc int**

In the scope of these declarations, $pi := 3$ is synonymous with $3.14159 := 3$ (and illegal, of course); $z := pi$ is synonymous with $y := pi$; the 'procedure name, inc' is synonymous with the procedure denotation shown, just as the 'real name' pi' is synonymous with the real denotation 3.14159. In the fourth, **loc real** is a 'generator'; the meaning of this declaration is that q is synonymous with the address of some currently unused location in local working space suitable for the storage of a real, and it is exactly this that is meant by Algol 60

> **real** q;

— a form which Algol 68 also allows as alternative to the longer one.

But to understand this from the reports, one has to learn to say 'identifier' when one means 'name', 'name' when one means 'address', and 'possesses' when one means 'is synonymous with'. Another source of mental confusion for those familiar with machine level coding can lie in the fact that at machine level a literal such as 3.14159 must have an address somewhere; perhaps the shortest cut to clarity here is to regard it as sited within the body of the pure procedure, and thus no more alterable than the machine orders contained therein.

When the significance of 'strong' in the development of the right hand side is realized, we can add, to those given above, further examples such as

> **ref real** A2 = A[2];
> **real** e = (**int** x := 1, y := 1, k := 1;
>   **while** maxint/k>x **do**
>   x := k*x+1; y := k*y; k := k+1 **od**;
>   x/y)

in which the identifier is made synonymous with that value of the appropriate mode into which the right hand side can be coerced. Thus $A2$ is synonymous with the address of the second element of A, and e with the real number which is the result of carrying out the process shown.

The procedure inc, which in Algol 60 would have read

> **integer procedure** inc(i); **integer** i; **begin** i := i+1; inc := i **end**

conforms in Algol 68 with the implications of Church's lambda concept, in that the formal parameter list is a part of the definition, not of the definiens. The semantics of a call, such as $inc(j)$, assumes that it is replaced by a copy of the body prefaced by a declaration of the form 'MODE formal = actual' — in this case

> **ref int** i = j

161

In the light of this interpretation, the whole concept of calling styles, and the associated debate, fades away. The program in Section 11.2 becomes

```
begin int i; [1:3] int A;
      proc report = (int x, ref int y, proc int z)void : (⟨body⟩);
      i := 1;   A[1] := 2;   A[3] := 4;
      report(A[i], A[i], int:(A[i])) end
```

(Note two things here, the permitted abbreviation of the declaration by omitting the duplicated mode details from the left hand side, and the need, consequent on the removal of proceduring from the available coercions, for the explicit proceduring in the third actual parameter.)

The Algol 60 report suggested that certain identifiers, such as *sqrt*, should be available without declaration; it soon began to be said that every program was implicitly enclosed in an outer block in which these procedures were declared. Because Algol 68 allows declaration of new modes, many features which would have been extensions in Algol 60 can be dealt with in this way in Algol 68. Some are, in a very large *standard prelude*, and particular groups of users may add others in a *library prelude*. The provision of complex numbers is an instructive example; they are introduced by the declaration **mode compl** = **struct**(**real** *re*, *im*) in the standard prelude. This makes declarations **compl** $z1$, $z2$ available to the user, and *re* **of** $z1$, *im* **of** $z2$, etc., as **ref real** expressions for access to their component parts. But to make this really useful we now need to be able to define infixed operators on, or yielding, complex numbers, and this is where the 'priority' and 'operation' members of CLASS come in. As well as defining the ordinary arithmetic operators between complex numbers, the standard prelude defines the operator **i** of priority nine (higher even than 'to the power') between two reals, such that the value of $r1$ **i** $r2$ is the complex number whose real part is equal to $r1$ and its imaginary part equal to $r2$. It also defines unary operators **re** and **im** (not to be confused with the field selectors *re* and *im*) which yield the reals (not the ref-reals) that one might expect, as well as the unary operators **conj** and **abs**. Unary (or 'monadic') operators in Algol 68 all have priority 10, higher than any dyadic operator, a decision that has been criticized because it is not the natural way to interpret $-p \uparrow q$. All these features employ techniques that are generally available within the language; they could be introduced in a user program if they were not there in the standard prelude already, and can be overridden by alternative declarations within the user program.

13.4 Conditionals

Translation from high level to reverse Polish represents the compiler's effort to arrange the things that have to be done into a linear performance order. There are three situations in which a strictly linear progression is inappropriate; each can be written without labels at high level but involves two jumps at machine level (including any form of Polish). These are

1. The procedure, requiring an initial subroutine jump which saves a return address, and a final return jump which is a variable destination jump.
2. The conditional, requiring an initial 'jump if false' and a later unconditional jump, both forward. A choice between more than two alternatives can be done in several ways, including reduction to a series of conditionals.
3. The loop, which is similar to the conditional except that the second jump is a backward one to a point behind the first. The most logical form of this would seem to be

loop⟨initialize⟩**while**⟨condition⟩**do**⟨body⟩   **pool**

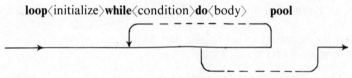

e.g.

> **loop int** i := 2 **while** i⩽30 **do** ...; i := i+4 **pool**

which has (apart from the local scope of i) the same effect as Algol 60's

> **for** i := 2 **step** 4 **until** 30 **do** ... ;

but no language seems to have gone for precisely this structure.

Notice that **pool** implies at least the low level sequence

> jump to **while**

> false jump from do: exit from block (i.e. cancel declarations at **loop**)

The expression

> **if B then** sqrt(x) **else** sqrt(−x)

serves as an object lesson in the handling of all similar expressions. If any attempt is made to choose between alternative *values*, this will *always* fail on one side or the other; the choice *must* be between alternative *processes*. The conclusion generalizes to a warning against *any* premature or unnecessary evaluations, and efficiency arguments support this view. We have already seen (in Section 12.4) how carefully McCarthy avoids this trap in Lisp. But it requires closer examination.

At one stage in its development, PL/I proposed the abolition of booleans, substituting the use of integers 1 and 0 for **true** and **false**, and treating the above expression as

$$B * \text{sqrt}(x) + (1-B) * \text{sqrt}(-x).$$

Now the usual Polish reduction of $a*b+c*d$ is $ab*cd*+$; that is, the second factor is evaluated before the multiplication sign reveals its purpose. There is a conflict here between two quite deep-rooted principles. The only valid Polish string would seem to be

$$a \zeta b * c \zeta d * +$$

where ζ is a 'jump if zero' operator. Although we have already seen that a 'jump if false' is necessary to Polish, and this is almost the same operator, one wonders whether its introduction into every multiplication sequence is altogether desirable. And although this system works at machine level for opting between two machine addresses, its application to multi-word values leads to difficulties, and the propriety of its application to any non-numerical types at high level is very questionable.

The ambiguity in the statement

$$; \textbf{if } B1 \textbf{ then if } B2 \textbf{ then } X \textbf{ else } Y;$$
$$\alpha \qquad \beta \qquad \gamma$$

was realized from 1960 onwards but proved hydra-headed enough to give rise to a long story of heart searching. Algol 60 required **then** to be followed by an unconditional statement; thus a **begin** was required at α, and the ambiguity was resolved by the position of the matching **end**, which would be at either β or γ. But in 1962 it was necessary to treat for-statements (for this purpose) as conditional, to kill another form of the same trouble.

The origin of this ambiguity is the option to omit **else** $\langle dummy \rangle$; it does not arise in expressions, where the dummy is not an option. In CPL and BCPL the reaction has been to adapt McCarthy's (arrow) notation for expressions (as in Section 12.4, but omitting 'T→' with interesting syntactic consequences), and in statements to restrict **if** and **unless** to forms that omit **else**, using **test** . . **then** . . **or** when both alternatives are present. An example which includes most of the possibilities (and complicated enough to be difficult reading in any language) is

if $a > b \to B1$, B2 **then do test** B3 **then do** X **or do** p := B4 $\to$ 1, B5 $\to$ 2, 3

The **or** must belong to the **test** and not to the **if**. The Algol equivalent to this makes easier reading with a few redundant brackets, but without them it is

if if a>b **then** B1 **else** B2 **then begin if** B3 **then** X
else p := **if** B4 **then** 1 **else if** B5 **then** 2 **else** 3 **end**

The PL/I solution (in the 48-character set) would seem to be

IF (A GT B)*B1+(A LE B)*B2 THEN IF B3 THEN CALL X;
ELSE P = B4+(NOT B4)*(2*B5+3*(NOT B5));

in which the final expression might, on the 1,0 convention, be optimized to $P = 3 - 2*B4 - B5 + B4*B5$. It depends on (a) the rule that an ELSE always pairs with the nearest unpaired IF, and (b) the quaint consequences of the syntax of complex statements and the use of statements as statement brackets. The semicolon ends a simple statement, rather than, as in some languages, separating statements. The complex statement-forms end with simple statements and thus end with semicolons, but not in their own right. In Report 2 an attempt was made to get rid of THEN, which was possible because of the limited meaning of the space. If this was an attempt to get closer to English usage, it was a mistake, because although many English if-sentences omit 'then', the majority of those that do have a comma where it would have been, and the effect of the omission on clarity was deplorable. It led to strings like *IF B X = Y*, for *IF B THEN X = Y* (or *IF B, X = Y*). Even as it is, we are saddled with curiosities like

IF A THEN IF B THEN X = Y; ELSE; ELSE X = 0;

Here the final semicolon is part of 'X = 0;', and the middle one is a dummy statement, the alternative to 'X = Y;' for use when B has the value **false** (=0). The sequence

IF A THEN DO; IF B THEN X = Y; END; ELSE X = 0;

is equivalent, both make X = 0 the 'A is false' branch. But

IF A THEN IF B THEN X = Y; ELSE X = 0;

is different, since the ELSE attaches itself to the most recent unmatched IF, so that this is a dummy when A is false. In all three statements X = Y results when both A and B are true.

Pascal admits the ambiguous construction, analysis by the Parsing Machine leading to pairing an **else** with the *nearest* **if** not yet paired.

In Algol 68 the solution has been to make **if** a form of opening bracket, requiring a **fi** as the corresponding closer; in terms of the original example of this ambiguity, the **if** at α implies the **begin** but a **fi** is required at either β or γ (as well as a final one to match the *initial* **if**). But this is not the whole story. The structure

$$(\ldots \textbf{then} \ldots \textbf{else} (\ldots \textbf{then} \ldots \textbf{else} \ldots))$$

raises all sorts of questions when set alongside (1) the McCarthy notation, (2) the notation which had been proposed in many quarters for

$$\textbf{if } n = 1 \textbf{ then } X1$$
$$\textbf{else if } n = 2 \textbf{ then } X2$$
$$\textbf{else etc.,}$$

namely,

$$\textbf{case } n \textbf{ in } X1, X2 \ldots ;,$$

(3) the fact that the notation remains perfectly clear if | replaces *both* **then** and **else**, and (4) a curious suggestion that round brackets be 'strong brackets' and '?' a 'weak opener', so that in

$$(\text{Bool1}|X1|? \text{ Bool2}|X2|? \text{ Bool3}|X3)$$

the final strong closer implicitly closes the weaker brackets nested in it. (Compare the remarks on bracket tagging in Section 13.2.2.) Without attempting to reconstruct the interplay of these ideas, we proceed directly to the Algol 68 solution. This is epitomized in

$$(\text{Choice1}|\text{In1}|: \text{Choice2}|\text{In2} \ldots |\text{Out})$$

or in more detail by

CHOICE:: boolean; integer; UNITED.

MOID using CHOICE clause: CHOICE start symbol, MOID using CHOICE chooser, CHOICE finish symbol.

MOID using CHOICE chooser: CHOICE enquiry, CHOICE in symbol, MOID using CHOICE in part, MOID using CHOICE out part.

MOID using boolean in part: MOID serial clause.

MOID using integer in part: list of MOID units.

MOID using UNITED in part: list of MOID procedures from UNITED

MOID1 procedure from UNITED: procedure with parameter MOID2 yielding MOID1, where MOID2 is contained in UNITED.

MOID using CHOICE out part: CHOICE again symbol, MOID
        using CHOICE chooser;
        CHOICE out symbol, MOID
        serial clause;
        EMPTY.

with the table of symbols

	start	in	again	out	finish
brief CHOICE	(	|	|:	|	)
bold boolean	**if**	**then**	**elif**	**else**	**fi**
bold integer bold UNITED	**case**	**in**	**ouse**	**out**	**esac**

166

Note that 'again' cannot vary the CHOICE (as we have set it out, not even between different UNITEDs but Algol 68 avoids this). An enquiry is a serial clause without labels. (If an enquiry contains declarations, their scope includes both the in- and out-parts, and it must not be possible to jump back into the enquiry. But of course to exploit this scope it is important *not* to enclose the enquiry in additional brackets.) By the full grammar, the 'brief' and 'bold' representations cannot be mixed at the same level, but the illustrative example given earlier can be written

if (a>b|B1|B2) **then** (B3|X|p := (B4|1|: B5|2|3)) **fi**

An illustration of the scope rule would be

j := **if int** i = p+q; i>0 **then** i **else** 0 **fi**

otherwise the boolean choice clause needs no further discussion. The 'lists' in the other choices are separated by commas. If an integer enquiry clause evaluates to n, then the nth member of the list is chosen, or the out-part if n is out of range.

The third form of choice (using UNITED) is the outcome of considerable experimentation. Consider

mode double = **union(int, bool)**;
double p; **int** j; **bool** c;
:
(p|(**int** i):(j := i), (**bool** b):(c := b))   (A)

The reports asserts clearly that there are no values of mode **double**; possible values of p are either integer or boolean. Internally to the computer things are less simple. If (improbably) values are stored as the character strings which constitute their denotations, then their types can be inferred, but more usually bit patterns capable of alternative interpretations will be used and then the values which p can take must belong to a sort of special mode, **struc** (**mode** type, **bits** value). Either way, the interpretation of a unit such as (A) is that that member of the list is chosen whose parameter conforms in type to that of the current value of p, the procedure being called with its actual parameter taking this value; in the case of (A), this reduces to 'if the value of p is integral then assign it to j else if it is boolean then assign it to c'.

This 'conformity case clause' replaced earlier syntactic structures $x :: y$ and $x ::= y$. In both of these y could be of UNITED mode and x non-united; in such circumstances $x := y$ would be illegal. Both were boolean expressions testing the mode equality of the values of x and y, the latter also performing (as a side effect) the otherwise inexpressible assignment if and only if the result was **true**. No such provision is necessary in Pop2 where, it will be remembered, *dataword* (x) allows the type of x to be read as a value of type *word*,

167

thus *dataword* (x) = *dataword* (y) performs the function of $x :: y$. And as $y \rightarrow x$ is legal whatever the current types of x and y, no equivalent for $x ::= y$ is required.

In Pascal, (A) appears as

type pset = (int, boo)
      double = **record case** which : pset **of**
                         int: (i : integer);
                         boo: (b : boolean) **end**;
var p : double;
     j : integer;
     c : boolean;
  :

      case p.which **of**   or   **with** p **do case** which **of**
      int: j := p.i   int: j := i
      boo: c := p.b **end**;   boo: c := b **end**

The case construction is used in the declaration as well as in the statement. In the factored form using **with**, the parallelism is clearer. But why the proliferation of identifiers represented by *which*, *int* and *boo*, especially as in Algol 68 the last line could be written

$$(p|(\textbf{int } p):(j := p), (\textbf{bool } p):(c := p)) \qquad (A')$$

in view of the fact that i and b are formal parameters? Pascal's exposure of the type discriminating mechanism makes criticism of Algol 68's exposure of the **ref** mechanism a case of the pot calling the kettle black. (Even so, it is always a defence against libel to show *both* that the statement is true *and* its publication in the public interest!) The notational simplification suggested by (A') cannot be maintained when p in (A) is an expression, nor can the Pascal form be simplified without jeopardizing other uses of the case clause and the set concept. Algol 68 cannot bunch its cases, as Pascal does in

        case day1 **of**
          mon, tues, wed, thurs, fri: work;
          sat: play; sun: rest **end**

and Pascal, keeping expressions and statements separate, cannot apply the case construction to values. Oddly, Pascal only allows one explicit union in a structure, and it must come last; this is a syntactical restriction, as earlier fields may be described by a type identifier which has already been declared to be a union.

It is essential to ensure that the results derived from the alternative paths through a choice are compatible when the convergence point is reached. This is known as balancing. In a SORT (:: strong; weak; firm; soft) situation involving balancing, one side must stay SORT, but the other is strong to enable it to be adapted, and there is no constraint on which side is which. (The writer has met one Algol 60 compiler in which the result of

integer h, i; **integer procedure** p . . . ;
   h := **if false then** i **else** p;

was to assign to *h* the first instruction in the code for *p*. The compiler was apparently unaware of the need for balancing in this context, although in other contexts both $h := i$ and $h := p$ were correctly interpreted.)

13.5 Loop facilities

Loop facilities were originally introduced as a convenience. With the rise of the concept of structured programming (Dahl, Dijkstra and Hoare, 1972), they have acquired greater significance as the natural way of writing iterative processes without using **goto**.

We have already discussed the Fortran and Autocode constructs in Section 9.5, and the syntax of the Algol 60 for-statement in Section 11.3. The three types provided by the latter may be thought of as realizing (and generalizing) the three varieties of the one mathematical notation

$$\sum_{a,b,c} \qquad \sum_{r=1}^{n} \qquad \sum_{1}^{\infty}$$

Unfortunately the Algol 60 report is not precise about the semantics of

    for i := a **step** b **until** c, d, e **while** f **do** X

in circumstances when the calling style of some of the parameters is important. The expansion of the above statement in terms of simpler Algol is, according to the best authorities (Randell 1963)

```
begin real j, k;   procedure Y; X;
    i := j := a; k := b;
L: if sign(k)*(c−j)⩾0 then begin
        Y; k := b; comment b may have been changed by Y;
        i := j := i+k; goto L end;
        i := d; Y;
    M: i := e;
      if f then begin Y; goto M end
end
```

In performing the expansion, all expressions are replaced by name. Y replaces X because in practice X may be very elaborate. The statement $i := j := i+k$ means that both *i* and *j* are to be set equal to $i+k$; in obeying this the order of evaluation is (1) address of *i*, (ii) address of *j*, (iii) address-thence-value of *i*, (iv) address-thence-value of *k*, (v) value of $i+k$, and finally both assignments. The strictness and the inefficiency (in finding the address of *i* twice over) of this arises from the remote possibility that *i* might be a suffixed variable, whose suffix was defined by a subroutine which altered some of the values in *i* or elsewhere! It would normally be very bad programming technique if this occurred, but there are milder implications of call by name which must be allowed for, and the basic semantics of a language must give a definite ruling on the most outrageous things which it is possible to write. The above expansion does do this, and though it takes a clever compiler to know when it is safe to take a short cut, there are compilers which succeed in doing so.

Quite apart from questions of efficiency, when the 'parameters' involve *i* explicitly some surprises could await the naïve programmer faced with a naïve implementation. What, for example, might the effect be, of the following

for i := 5 **step** 10 until 30, i+1 **while** i ≠ 50 **do** print(i)

Note how the above expansion starts the second series at 36, whereas putting both '*i* := *j*'s immediately after L would start it at 26.

As experience accumulated, considerable dissatisfaction was expressed with the Algol 60 for-statement, but the reasons varied. The absence of a plain **while** led one user to begin every program with '**integer** *dummy*;' so that, without further thought, he could always write '**for** *dummy* := 0 **while** ..' when necessary! For-statements are so often used for counting, with indexing on the count, that other users called for the greater efficiency that could be obtained by implementing them in index registers, and indeed there is room for a maxim that 'what is easy for the programmer should be easy for the computer' — otherwise the language tempts the programmer into inefficiency.

So it is that whereas in Algol 60, **begin .. end** surrounds a block if declarations follow the **begin** but a compound statement if they do not, in PL/I a block is surrounded by BEGIN; ... END; and a 'group' by DO; ... END;, and the DO may be expanded in one of two ways

DO WHILE⟨logical expression⟩
DO⟨variable⟩ = ⟨iteration list⟩

the second of these providing a similar facility to the Algol 60 for-statement, and the former the plain **while** that was unaccountably absent from the Algol 60 for-repertoire. Each item in the iteration list is of the form

⟨expression⟩BY⟨expression⟩TO⟨expression⟩WHILE⟨expression⟩

in which 'WHILE TRUE' or 'BY 1' may be omitted, BY and TO may be interchanged, TO⟨expression⟩ may be omitted, or the first expression may stand alone or with only the while-clause. The controlled variable is called by simple name, the while-expression by name and the other expressions by value. Commas separate the items.

CPL provided a luxurious variety of syntactic forms, those that have survived in BCPL have already been listed in Section 13.2.2. The Algol 60 name calls were replaced by value calls, and the initial assignment replaced by a new initialized integer declaration, so that whereas Algol 60

> v := 5;
> **for** v := 1 **step** v **until** 12 **do begin** X; v := v+1 **end**;

leads to doing X with $v = 1, 4, 10$ and exits with v undefined, the CPL

> v := 5;
> **for** v = **step** 1, v, 12 **do** § X; v := v+1 §

led to doing X with $v = 1, 6, 11$ and v still 5 on exit. By writing '**for ext** v = ...' one could call the controlled variable by (simple) name, but this would not affect the increment. Thus the CPL semantics were nearer to those of PL/I but not quite identical with them.

Pascal omits the **by** (or **step**) element altogether, but provides the alternatives TO and DOWNTO — i.e. implicit ± 1 for the step size. This is presumably taking the efficiency argument to its logical conclusion, since all loops can then be implemented by ISZ or DSZ orders (if your machine has them). But these orders are an interesting example of how 'time makes ancient good uncouth'. Originally designed to make looping efficient, thus

```
      SET COUNT
M: . . . .
      . . . .
      DSZ COUNT        (decrement, and skip if result is zero)
      JMP M
      CONTINUE,
```

they now encourage bad techniques. If computer designers really understood programming, these orders would long since have been replaced by 'increment/decrement and skip, unless already zero', for two reasons. The first is that

```
      SET COUNT
M: DSUZ COUNT
      JMP N
      . . . .
      . . . .
      JMP M
N: . . . .
```

is better practice, since it allows zero performances of the loop. The second is that

> DSUZ SEMA
> JMP *—1   or JSR (subroutine call) SUSPEND ME

satisfies the necessary conditions for implementing the P function on a semaphore (see Section 6.1), namely (1) that decrementing and testing are both done in a single instruction, and (2) that failure leaves the semaphore at zero.

Algol 68 has distilled this experience into

> **for** i **from** u1 **by** u2 **to** u3 **while** B **do** C **od**

in which **while true, from** 1, **by** 1 and **to**⟨infinity⟩ may be omitted, and also **for** *i* if *i* can stay anonymous (no other reference to it occurring later). There is only one sequencing element. Thus **to 6 do C od** does C six times, and **do C od** is CPL's C **repeat**. There is **while B do C od**, but the equivalent of C **while** B is missing (and clumsy to manufacture), as is the list aspect of the Algol 60 form.

The semantics of the clause quoted above is defined at some length in the Report; subject to the assumption that $u3$ can take the value *undefined* by default it can be written more concisely as

> **begin int** f := u1, **int** b = u2, t = u3;
>   L: **if** (t = undefined|**true**: b>0|t⩾f|: b<0|t⩽f|**true**)
>   **then int** i = f; (B|C; f **plus** b; **goto** L)**fi end**

Certain implications should be noted; *i* is **int**, not **ref int**, and by the scope rules for conditionals it can be referred to (but not assigned to) in B and C. Likewise the scope of variables defined in B includes C. If t is undefined (or $b=0$) then comparison of t and f is never required. Note that f **plus** b is a way of writing $f := f+b$ that avoids recomputing the address of f.

The **od** fulfils the same function as **fi**; its syntactic strength defines the level of development possible within a for-statement. In fact, *i* is an identifier, the *u*'s are meek integral units, B is a boolean enquiry and C a serial clause. The for-clause itself is void; one cannot, for example, replace

> **for** i **to** 6 **do** A[i] := i **od**

by the pseudo structure-display

> A := (**for** i **to** 6 **do** i **od**)

13.6 Formal semantics in Algol 68

The Report describes the semantics of Algol 68 in terms of a process described as 'the elaboration of the program (text)', a phrase clearly related to the approach followed in Section 7.7. It is, however, one of the alternatives considered at the end of that section that is used. A computer capable of storing and working on the original text is assumed (i.e. no compiler) and in the process of working it creates new addressable store as required. An action by the computer, in elaboration of the program, may be associated with any phase in its syntactic decomposition. Such an action may result in a value, known as its *yield*.

We consider an example which draws on the following meta-rules:

NEST:: LAYER; NEST LAYER.
LAYER:: new DECSETY LABSETY.
PROPSETY:: PROPS; EMPTY. ⎫ and likewise for LABS,
PROPS:: PROP; PROPS PROP. ⎭ DECSETY, etc.
PROP:: DEC; LAB; FIELD.
DEC:: MODE TAG; MOID TALLY bold TAG; etc.
LAB:: label TAG.
COMMON:: MODE identity; REF MODE variable; routine identity; mode; etc.
REF:: reference to.

In quoting rules from the Report (v. Wijngaarden 1974) we take one justifiable liberty; a rule involving PROPS, say, will be quoted as though it read DECS, say, if this subset is all we are interested in and the clarity of the argument is improved thereby. The terminal productions from TAG are identifiers. The productions from MODE are given in Section 13.3.1. The example is the *real closed clause*

(**real** x, y := 1.5, **int** i; **ref real** A2 = A[2]; . . .; p)

which starts from the rule (Report 3.1.1.a, omitting SORT and developing PACK)

real NEST closed clause:
1. brief begin symbol, real NEST serial clause defining LAYER, brief end symbol.

This rule has no associated elaboration, and therefore (2.1.4.1.c) the yield of a closed clause is that of its serial clause. Further rules (3.2.1.ab) develop the serial clause

real NEST serial clause defining new PROPSETY:
2. real NEST new PROPSETY series with PROPSETY.
real NEST series with PROPSETY:
3. where PROPSETY is EMPTY, real NEST unit;
4. where PROPSETY is DECS PROPSETY1, NEST declaration of DECS, semicolon symbol, real NEST series with PROPSETY1.

Note the use of predicates as explained at the end of Section 7.4.1. Also that when rule 3 or rule 4 is applied, its NEST has grown from that of rule 2 by acquiring an additional LAYER, the *new* PROP-SETY of the right hand side of rule 2. Thus the NEST, when expanded, contains the identifiers (mode indicators, etc.) of this and all enclosing closed clauses, spelt out, with *new* separating each layer from the next. Rule 3 is included to indicate the derivation of the final p; that this production includes the word NEST allows the elaboration to include a test that p is in the nest and to fail if it is not.

We now consider rule 4. Since that which occurs before a semi-colon is elaborated before that which follows it (3.2.2.c), we develop the first item in this rule (by 4.1.1.a)

NEST declaration of DECS:
5. where DECS is DECS1 DECS2, NEST COMMON declaration of DECS1, comma symbol, NEST declaration of DECS2;
6. NEST COMMON declaration of DECS.

The elaboration of a *declaration* (4.1.2.a) consists of the collateral elaboration of its *COMMON declaration* and of its *declaration* if any. Thus all the *COMMON declarations* separated by commas are elaborated collaterally.

The various alternatives under COMMON lead to different structures which, however, share the syntax of a 'COMMON joined definition'. This is (4.1.1.bc)

NEST COMMON joined definition of DECSETY DEC:
7. where DECSETY is EMPTY, NEST COMMON definition of DEC;
8. unless DECSETY is empty, NEST COMMON joined definition of DECSETY, comma symbol, NEST COMMON definition of DEC.

The elaboration of a *COMMON joined definition of DECS* (4.1.2.b) consists of the collateral elaboration of its *COMMON joined definitions*.

The alternative that leads to the first declaration in our example is (4.4.1.e, 5.2.3.b, 4.4.1.f)

NEST REF MODE variable declaration of DECS:
9a. REF MODE NEST sample generator, NEST REF MODE variable joined definition of DECS.
REF MODE NEST sample generator:
10. actual MODE NEST declarer.
NEST REF MODE variable definition of REF MODE TAG:
11a. REF MODE NEST defining identifier with TAG, colonequals, MODE NEST source.
12. REF MODE NEST defining identifier with TAG.

After (5) we use (9a); the first part is then dealt with by (10) and the second by (8), followed by (12a), then (7) and (11a). We are left with the need to apply (6), (9a), (10) and (12). The alternative leading to the final declaration is (4.4.1.a, 4.6.1.b, 4.4.1.c)

NEST MODE identity definition of DECS:
9b.   formal MODE NEST declarer, NEST MODE identity joined definition of DECS.
NEST MODE identity definition of MODE TAG:
11b. MODE NEST defining identifier with TAG, equals symbol, MODE NEST source.

Taking these now in reverse order, an identity declaration is elaborated as follows (4.4.2). The constituent sources are elaborated collaterally. For each constituent identity definition the yield of its source is ascribed (see below) to its defining identifier. We omit details of how sources, being strong, have their yields coerced into forms acceptable to the MODE. In this case, A[2], being a subscripted name, yields 'one of the subnames with which A is endowed' (5.3.2.2).

We touch solid ground with a rule (4.8.1.a) that can be condensed to

MODE NEST defining identifier with TAG:
   TAG symbol.

Thus at last we have the identifier pinned down. But the full form is

MODE NEST new PROPSETY1 MODE TAG PROPSETY2
   defining identifier with TAG:
   where MODE TAG independent of PROPSETY1, TAG token.

This (1) splits off from NEST that part which belongs to the current LAYER and ensures that the new identifier is not among those already declared in this LAYER, and (2) by its use of 'token', permits a comment to precede the identifier. Note that it is the whole identifier that is a symbol. The associated semantics (4.8.2) is combined with that of *MODE NEST applied identifier* (*p* in our example); it details the ascription process (see above) thus: when a value is ascribed to a real defining identifier with TAG in an environ E, then the real identifier is made to access that value within the locale of that environ. (An environ is a locale, effectively the collective local storage, together with accessible non-local storage which constitutes a smaller environ.)

Further rules convert actual and formal declarers into the familiar symbols (with and without accompanying bounds). The elaboration of an actual declarer is said to yield an arbitrary value of the correct mode, and that of a sample generator to yield a newly created name which is made to refer to the yield of the actual declarer. (This seems to be a long-winded way of acknowledging that if a new storage cell is reserved, it is bound to have *some* contents. Or does

175

it imply that if a whole word is reserved for a boolean, then it must be initialized to either **true** or **false**?)

A variable declaration is elaborated as follows. The *sample generator* and all the *sources*, if any, are elaborated collaterally. For each variable definition, let N be a newly created name 'equivalent' to the yield of the sample generator. N is ascribed to the defining identifier and made to refer to the yield of the source, if any (i.e. the yield of the source is assigned to N). Two 'equivalent' names have different addresses but their other properties, such as mode and scope, are the same.

13.7 Omnibus

The difficulty of bridging the gap between formal semantics and actual implementation suggests a compromise in which the stack operations become the basis for the definition of the semantics of a language. This has been done in a machine independent way in an unpublished language called Omnibus (Higman 1976*b*).

In this language, every basic type has an internal representation whose length (in store) is known to the compiler but not necessarily to the user. (A given implementation may 'reveal' the lengths it uses, to assist diagnostics in octal, but is not bound to do so.) The internal form of a structure is that of its components placed on the stack in the sequence in which they occur in the definition of the mode of the structure. A procedure denotation is Algol68-like —

$$(\langle \text{param.specs} \rangle)\langle \text{result type} \rangle : (\langle \text{body} \rangle)$$

and the specification part constitutes the definition of an anonymous mode. In a procedure call, $f(exp1, exp2, \ldots)$, the expressions are evaluated in turn on top of the stack. Each expression is coerced after evaluation as may be necessary to ensure that the actual parameter list thus stacked has the structure expected by f. (Note, a structure can always be built up in this way from $(exp1, exp2, ..)$, but no coercion will take place unless it is either an actual parameter list or a cast, **amode**$(exp1, exp2, \ldots)$.) There are two calling mechanisms (roughly, that for an operator is simpler than that for a procedure) but in either case the overall effect is to replace the parameters by the result. For a procedure, the call is implemented by raising the stack pointer, SP, in such a way as to create the following structure

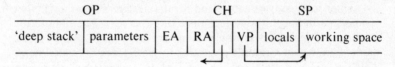

where OP is the original position of the stack pointer before the assembly of the actual parameters began, EA is the code entry

176

address (see below), RA is the return address, VP is the pointer shown, and CH is the 'chain pointer'. This last serves two purposes. (1) All the information required by the procedure is located at known displacements from the address contained in CH (known to the compiler, that is). (2) CH heads a pushdown list which is popped up on return to the calling procedure, SP being restored to OP (before copying down any results if the procedure is non-void).

The size of the space labelled 'locals' is determined at compile time, each identifier declared in the procedure body being allotted space according to its type. In the case of dynamic arrays this is simply space for a descriptor (dope vector) and VP is subsequently raised to create the storage for the elements. (Actually, *all* arrays are dealt with in this way, and so are procedures — see below.) Within the procedure body, statements (units) are separated by semicolons, and a semicolon is always implemented (at least implicitly) by $SP := VP$ (hence the name, void pointer, of which VP is a contraction). No procedure ever operates directly on any location below OP, though when its parameter list includes reference variables it may do so indirectly through them. In particular, CH is not used to access globals *via* the chain, although this could be done; such variables are converted by the compiler into additional parameters and passed as references or descriptors.

This basic scheme leaves a lot of detail to be filled in, and considerable room for variations in high level design, and the author has found it a very satisfactory basis for a final year course in which compilers are taught with special emphasis on the correct realization of semantically difficult situations. Procedures, like arrays, are given space for a descriptor, in this case a **struc(address** p, **union(int, address)**q). For each *procedure declaration* in a block, a 'closure' is constructed after entry to the block; firstly pointers to the variables constituting the environment are stacked and then the entry address to the code; finally the descriptor is made to contain the address and length of the new structure, and VP is raised to give its elements the same protection (against destruction when voiding) as is enjoyed by other declared variables. At a call, after the actual parameters have been stacked, the calling mechanism copies the closure above them, so that the *parameters* of the diagram consists of the actual parameters *and* the environmental items. (This mechanism is also the source of EA, the presence of which incidentally allows access to information stored in the neighbourhood of the entry address which may be useful for diagnostic, garbage collecting, and other purposes.) For each *label* in a block, if it is the destination of a jump from an inner block, a descriptor of the two-address type is constructed as part of the environment of the latter; it consists of the address represented by the label and the current value of CH. The calling mechanism discriminates on the type of the q part of the

177

structure, so that when a parameter of type **proc** is called, the actual parameter (a descriptor) may be either a true procedure or a **goto** ⟨label⟩.

Because the original motivations for Omnibus included a desire to integrate linguistic ability into general programming in an efficient way, the Parsing machine will be built into the syntax of Omnibus. A possible scheme is

> parse statement: woru, condition, goto symbol, branch.
> woru: when symbol; unless symbol.
> condition: is symbol, meek string unit;
>   is symbol, character denotation;
>   in symbol, meek string unit;
>   in symbol, strong range unit;
>   subroutine symbol, label identifier.
> branch: label identifier; boolean denotation.
> **mode range** = **struc(char** first, last)

One can then write, for example,

> **proc** read pos int = (**ref string** text)**int**:
>   (**int** i := −1 **c** negative result implies failure **c**;
>   **range** digit = ('0', '9');
>   **string** layouts = (space, newline, tab, newpage);
>   **parse** text **by** (K: **when in** layouts **goto** K;
>   **unless is** '+' **goto** L;
>   L: **unless in** digit **goto false**;
>   i := index − 1 **c** index is int in standard
>   prelude **c**;
>   M: **unless in** digit **goto true**;
>   i := i * 10+index−1;
>   **goto** M);
>   i).

14

INPUT AND OUTPUT

Input and output routines have much in common while differing in one fundamental respect; output routines are in control of what happens, while input routines must, within reason, accept what they are given. In particular, output routines create a layout; input routines find one and, apart from using what they find for interpretive purposes, throw it away. For this reason it is usual to make output the prime consideration, and then to adapt the conventions decided upon into a corresponding input system. The story is an evolutionary one. Simple provisions came first and only as refinements were attempted was the full complexity of the problem realized. The next four sections (including that on PL/I) have been reprinted with only minor changes from the first edition, to show the historical build-up.

14.1 Early languages
The problems which have to be overcome in any completely adequate output scheme fall into a number of categories which interweave in a most perplexing manner:
1. There are three levels of format control
   (a) Overall matters such as page size (margins both at the sides and top and bottom of pages, etc) and inclusion or exclusion of line numbers, page headings, etc,
   (b) Inter-item formats — broadly speaking, deciding where on the page the next item begins, and
   (c) Intra-item formats, concerning the way in which the value of a given variable is reproduced graphically quite apart from its position on the page.
2. All output is, in the last resort, output of character strings, at any rate while we remain within the definitions of Section 1.2. A well-defined set of transfer functions from all other types to this one is therefore a first requisite — but these must be flexible (e.g. it must be possible to output to a lesser precision than is used for the computation).
3. But, for the automation of office work, a backing store is equivalent in many ways to hard copy (e.g. it can constitute the archives). To put it mildly, this qualifies conclusions based on (1) and (2).

179

4. There are two respects in which the distinction between 'command' and 'briefing' appears once more:

(a) Provision must be made for 'presetting' (i.e. preparative) commands which produce no immediate output but set a condition which will determine how subsequent output commands will be interpreted. These may be hardware or software interpreted, as with 'tab-setting' on typewriter or teleprinter.

(b) It is very inconvenient if a control character such as carriage-return cannot be referred to in the programming language without exciting the corresponding effect, so that 'neutralized equivalents' of these characters are required.

5. The environment division of Cobol introduced a number of issues that were ignored by its contemporaries. One important one is the designation of output organs in a programme by 'logical' references which must somehow be related at run-time to actual hardware devices. It will be convenient to use the phrase 'environment control' to cover these requirements, however met.

Historically, it must be remembered that Autocodes were intended in the first instance for mathematical work. In these cases intelligibility and ease of reading are important in the output, but unless facsimiles are to be included in a report, elegance, including all *paging*, is unnecessary. Moreover, Autocodes were most often intended for a restricted group of machines and therefore for a restricted variety of output systems. Usually Autocodes contain a NEWLINE *order* and are opaque to the corresponding character in the output, which serves as a statement terminator. A CAPTION *order* provides for output of a whole line as a literal. All other output is confined to the current line, which is built up by programming from three types of output — short literals, groups of spaces, and numbers in a specifiable format (e.g. '5 sig.fig., 2 integral'). The technique of format specification is sometimes *print*(x, 5, 2), and sometimes *print*(x,'*dd.ddd*'). With these facilities there is no difficulty in organizing a layout such as

TRIALS SIMULATION RESULTS
RUN NO.6   R = 500 YARDS;   T2 = 0.05 SECS.

T	X	Y
000.0	00000	00000
000.1	00216	00050
000.2	00405	00098

SIMULATION STOPPED BECAUSE OF EMERGENCY NO.12

but there is a lack of all higher-level facilities, including any ability to lay down a format in advance.

Fortran introduced the explicit format statement designed to specify a format which could later be called upon. In Basic Fortran a format description, or ⟨FD⟩, is one of the following,

nX	meaning n blanks (spaces)

nX   meaning n blanks (spaces)

nH$\langle$string$\rangle$ literal (n must be the number of characters in the string)

rIw r w-character integers

rF$w.d$ r real numbers of w characters, d digits after the point, and no exponent part.

rE$w.d$ the same but including an exponent part

Whenever $r = 1$ it may be omitted. To these full Fortran adds rLw for logical ($w-1$ blanks, then T or F), rAw for r w-character fields to be filled from the list (see below), and certain further varieties of real. The full syntax of a format statement (or$\langle$FS$\rangle$) is

$$\langle FS \rangle ::= \langle label \rangle FORMAT(\$0\{/\}\$0\langle spec\ gp\rangle\$0\{/\})$$
$$\langle spec\ gp \rangle ::= \uparrow 1\langle integer\rangle(\langle spec\ gp\rangle)|\langle FD\rangle\$0\{\langle sepr\rangle\langle FD\rangle\}$$
$$\langle sepr \rangle ::= ,| \$1\{/\}$$

i.e. the argument of FORMAT is a series of $\langle$FD$\rangle$ separated by commas or slashes and with provision for abbreviating repetitions by use of coefficients. The format statement is, of course, a monstrosity of the same sort as the Algol 60 switch, a declaration with initialization of a type of variable to which assignments cannot otherwise be made — in this case a string variable. Input/output statements take the form

$$\{READ|WRITE\}(\langle unit\rangle \uparrow 1\{,\langle format\ label\rangle\}) \uparrow 1\langle list\rangle$$

where $\langle$unit$\rangle$ is an integer specifying (by a correspondence established through an environment control) the input/output organ to be used, and the list specifies the variables (or states the literals) whose values are to be transferred. The latter may take forms like

$$'P = ', P, (R(S), S = 0, 1, N)$$

including recursive use of the loop specification. Of the two simplest forms

$$READ(\langle unit\rangle) \qquad WRITE(\langle unit\rangle)$$

the latter is meaningless, but the former can occur as a function designator. The list will be empty if the format is entirely literal, and the format can go by default when it contains no literals. It is assumed that input does, or output will, consist of *records* composed of *fields*, and in the formats, commas separate fields and slashes separate records. Elaborate rules provide interpretations, wherever possible, in cases of mismatch; broadly speaking (1) an excess of format information is skipped, (2) a deficit of format information is made up by repetition of the last item used, and (3) a slash in a format when there are still fields in the current record will cause these to be skipped. (Note that Algol 60 treats (2) by falling back on standard format, and PL/I by repetition of the *whole* format.) READ is a procedure with side effects in that it leaves input looking at the start of the *next* record after the one just read. There are three auxiliary procedures, BACKSPACE(⟨unit⟩), which steps input back to the beginning of the currently just read *record*, ENDFILE(⟨unit⟩) which writes an end of file mark, and REWIND(⟨unit⟩) which steps input right back to the beginning of the *file*.

Cobol assumes the existence of buffer areas containing the last-read or next-to-be-written record of each file, and of associated routines compiled in accordance with the information in the Environment and Data divisions. READ and WRITE orders are thus very simple, no formatting being involved. Every variable has its picture and format changes are effected by the MOVE verb. (The fact that arithmetic may actually be done in binary is not mentioned in polite society except through the euphemism USAGE IS COMPUTATIONAL.) Thus the contribution of Cobol may be said to be the development of the picture — with Fortran suggesting that '6A' may be preferable to either 'PICTURE IS AAAAAA' or 'SIZE IS 6 ALPHABETIC' — and the concept of environment control.

14.2 Algol 60 and Algol/IFIP

Fortran had the advantage of being developed for the machines of a particular company; Algol 60 essayed independence of machine characteristics over a much wider range, and therefore assumed that it was almost inevitable that in/out procedures would have to be written in machine code. For a long time it refused to provide even specifications for such procedures, but those holding this position were politically out-manoeuvred when I.S.O. made provision of explicit in/output a prerequisite for recognition of a language. Two sets of proposals were then issued, at such different levels as not to be rivals. An IFIP committee (1964) issued a set of seven 'primitives', with the aid of which anything more complicated could be built up in true Algol 60, and an ACM committee (Knuth, 1964) issued a set of proposals which expanded the Fortran system using all the virtuosity of Algol 60. The latter was then revised to include the former.

Because Algol 60 is so essentially a language for numerical work, the first two of the IFIP primitives are *insymbol* and *outsymbol*, both with three parameters. These are (1) an integer *channel* the meaning of which is established by environment control, (2) a string whose characters are implicitly mapped on to the integers 1, 2 . . . , and (3) a second integer variable whose value, by virtue of the mapping, is or becomes the value of the single character written or read. Algol 60 symbols not in the string will map on to zero and non-Algol symbols acquire an implementation-dependent association with a negative number. The third primitive is the integer procedure *length*(⟨string or string variable⟩), whose value is the number of characters in its parameter. (There are no free string variables in Algol 60, but bound string variables can occur.) The remaining four of the seven procedures are *inreal, outreal, inarray* and *outarray*, each with two parameters, a *channel* and a *source* or *destination* of appropriate type. These are not primitive in the same sense, as they can be written in terms of the first three with one exception — that for the last two another primitive would be required giving explicit access to information which must exist about the shape of an array whose name only is available as a parameter. (Indeed, an *'ininteger'* is so written in the report to show how it can be done.)

The IFIP procedures permit the accurate definition, in Algol 60, of the procedures actually required or available for in/output in a given context; it may be doubted whether they have ever been used practically. Who, for example, would willingly employ

```
procedure outstring(channel, string); value channel;
  begin integer i;
    for i := 1 step 1 until length(string) do
        outsymbol (channel, string, i) end;
outstring (1, 'GRAND TOTAL =');
```

when a procedure body in machine code for *outstring* would short-circuit most of the machinery involved? Their theoretical interest is more difficult to assess; they arise out of certain deficiencies of Algol, but is, in fact, a character-to-integer mapping procedure not likely to be required sooner or later even in a language which is not so numerically bound as Algol?

14.3 Algol 60/ACM

The wider ACM proposals have been largely ignored, which is a pity as they contain many features of interest. Some of these have been adopted in Algol 68. Others were *tours de force* which became unnecessary when the limitations of Algol 60 were removed. The crucial difficulties arose from two rules in particular. (a) A procedure with an Algol body has to be declared with a fixed number of parameters (and no type **list** exists to ease this); (b) When the type of a parameter is specified (and this is compulsory in some implementations) it cannot be varied from call to call, so that separate procedures are required for numerical and string outputs. To circumvent the first of these difficulties the ACM proposals used a technique which has always been available but little recognized, known as the *list procedure*. It depends only on the ability to write a function or procedure name as an actual parameter, and is therefore available in Fortran (though not in Basic Fortran). Where the rule requiring a fixed number of parameters would be broken by

    A1:   print(a, b);   print(x, y, z);

the list procedure technique attacks this situation thus:

procedure list1(X); **procedure** X;
begin X(a); X(b) **end**;
procedure list2(X); **procedure** X;
begin X(x); X(y); X(z) **end**;
:
:
A2: list1(print); list2(print);

The line labelled *A2* is legal and identical in effect with the more obvious but illegal sequence *A1*. Moreover there is nothing special about the list procedure, which can be written to include use of any facility normally available — for example

procedure list3(X, Q); **procedure** X; **boolean** Q;
begin integer i; **if** Q **then**
for i := 1 **step** 1 **until** n **do** X(V[i]) **end**;

It can also contain statements revising the previous basis of layout control.

The second difficulty was overcome by transferring all its problems to the library routines that could do things that could not be expressed in true Algol 60, such as branching on the type of a parameter.

Two levels of sophistication were provided for actual output calls. The more general was in the form

outlist(channel, layout, list)

formally identical with the Fortran scheme except that as both *layout* and *list* are *procedure* names, and not a statement label and an actual list, both occur as parameters. The less sophisticated provision was a higher-level facility consisting of a series of routines defined for $n = 0, 1, \ldots 9$ in terms of *outlist* thus

procedure output*n*(channel, formatstring, e1, ... e*n*);
begin procedure A; format(formatstring);
procedure B(P); **begin** P(e1); ... P(e*n*) **end**;
outlist(channel, A, B) **end**

We may observe that only a purist would insist on retaining the *n* in the identifiers, and it was even claimed as an advantage that 'small' compilers that ignore characters in an identifier after the fifth or sixth would not even notice it. Thus do languages evolve!

Before explaining how these procedures work, we must consider the syntax of a format string. This was expressed in BNF, but its historical significance will be clarified if we present it in modern notation using the rules

NOTION:: LETTER; NOTION LETTER.   (Spaces ignored)
NOTION option: NOTION; EMPTY.
NOTION sequence: NOTION; NOTION, NOTION sequence.
NOTION list: NOTION; NOTION, comma symbol, NOTION
  list.

The syntax of a format string is based on

  format string: open quote, format unit list, close quote; empty
    string.

(The empty string calls for a default format.)

  format unit: format item sequence; replication.
  replication: replicator option, open bracket, format unit list, close
    bracket.
  replicator: positive integer; letter x.

A replication is equivalent to its unit list repeated as many times as
the integer of its replicator. For the use of x see below.

  format item: alignment code; insertion item; TYPE pattern.
  insertion item: letter b; string.

The alignment codes are characters representing newline(/), new-
page(↑) and tabulate(j). A string represents its contents and letter
b a space. The arithmetic patterns have terminal productions
almost identical with Cobol pictures, but being based on productions
like

      digit code: insertion item sequence option, letter d.,

they also allow calls like

      output1(1, 'zzb'dollars'bddb'cents'', 2↑10)

the result of which would be

              _10_dollars_24_cents

going far beyond anything that Cobol or Fortran permit.
  It is to be noted that the types of e1 ... en are left unspecified,
as Algol 60 permits. Moreover the Algol user does not know what is
implied by the differences between a card punch and a typewriter.
Outlist sends the items on its *list* to its *channel* after editing them
according to its *layout*; in doing so it uses its *channel* to select an
appropriate system routine as the actual parameter to be passed on
in the call of *list*. These system routines must be generic in the sense
of Section 13.1.2. Prior to this, *outlist* calls its *layout*. Innocent of any
illegality at user level, *format* assigns the format string to a *hidden*
variable of type string. There are also routines

              format$n$(string, k1 ... kn);

185

these replace successive x-replicators in the string by the integer values of $k1 \ldots kn$ before the assignment, thus permitting dynamic determination of the replicator.

There are routines similar to *format* for defining margin settings, nominating 'on overflow' procedures, and so on. It is understood that calls of these procedures are only effective when made from within *outlist* (or *inlist*) — i.e. when they have been written by the programmer within a procedure which is elsewhere made a parameter of *outlist*. By the general rules of 'scope' in Algol, if a call of a procedure within a block (or procedure declaration) is valid and the procedure is not declared at the head of that block, then a similar call is valid in the encompassing block. However, calls of these procedures in 'open program' would produce no effect that could be detected except by output, and would be overridden at the next output call.

It is also necessary to be on guard against easy association of equivalence between idioms in different languages. Thus it is true that a call *nodata*(A) of the system defined **procedure** *nodata* (L); **label** L; . . . ;, is the Algol equivalent of the Cobol AT END GO TO A, in the sense that it is an alternative idiom more congenial to Algol syntax in general and with the same elementary semantics. But there are at least eight alternative variations of how L may be treated in complex situations. In the first place, is there *one* hidden L, or *one per file* (in Algol, *per channel*)? And alongside this, is the statement :

(a) an irredeemable initialization,

(b) a value for that (lexicographic) call only,

(c) an assignment to a label-type variable,

or(d) putting of the value on a pushdown list, popped up on leaving the routine from which the statement was made?

Cobol manages both (a) and (b) according to context. The Algol proposal is either (c) or (d). On which, depends the effect of, for example, calling *outlist* in the middle of a layout or list procedure.

14.4 Input/output in PL/I

PL/I has very elaborate arrangements for in/output, and it is unlikely that any brief account could avoid being misleading under some circumstances or other. Subject to this warning, we may say that it is based upon the following

$\langle i/o \rangle ::= \{READ|WRITE\}\langle xxx \rangle\langle data\ specification \rangle\langle option\ list \rangle;$
$\langle xxx \rangle ::= FILE(\langle name \rangle),|STRING(\langle name \rangle),|\langle empty \rangle$

The string alternative is used for all internal transfers which call for editing to be done, and the empty alternative implies use of a standard (input or output) file. With the string alternative the option list must

186

be empty. In other cases, one record is processed, mismatches being dealt with much as in Fortran unless the option list includes one of (a)

$$\text{CROSS} \quad \uparrow 1\{((\langle\text{integer exp} = n\rangle)\} \quad \uparrow 1\{\text{HOLD}\}$$

in which case $n-1$ record boundaries may be crossed and if HOLD is present there is no skip to the beginning of a new record, and (b) SEGMENT($\langle$character exp$\rangle$), which implies both CROSS and HOLD and uses the character expression as an intersegment marker (one segment being read or written). Other options permit the file to be used sequentially or searched on a key, permit input data to be simultaneously written on the standard output file, allow recognition of trailing zero suppression in fractions, and allow the source of a WRITE statement to be, not working space, but the buffer of a named input file.

The data description consists of a list of variables (including non-scalars) and associated formats. The latter are those required or expected in the file, and if they differ from the declared attributes of the variables some editing will be involved. There are four varieties of data description, corresponding to four modes of data transmission, examples of each are

List-directed: WRITE LIST(A*B,(M(I) I = 1 TO 5));
Data-directed: WRITE DATA (M);
Format-directed: WRITE('RESULT IS', X) (A, F(5,2));
Procedure-directed: WRITE$\langle$as above$\rangle$, CALL P;

In each of these examples the standard output file is used and the option list is empty. In *list-directed* transmission the items must be scalar; output format is controlled by the attributes of the scalars and a 'tab' separator, while input format is that of constants in the language (except, oddly, that two numbers of which the second is signed and *not* separated from the first by a blank is a complex number and this does not apply *within* the language). It is permitted, in a second bracket after the list, to nominate a different item separator. In *data-directed output* non-scalar names are permitted; if M is a matrix then WRITE DATA (M) is equivalent to

$$\text{WRITE DATA (((M(I,J) J = JMIN TO JMAX) I =}$$
$$\text{IMIN TO IMAX))}$$

(i.e. the later subscripts vary more rapidly). Each scalar item is output in the form '$\langle$name$\rangle = \langle$value$\rangle$'. On *input* this form is expected and the list can be used as a check or omitted, but names which may turn up without warning like this must be given a SYMBOL attribute on declaration so that the translator knows that it must compile a dictionary for use at run time. Not all the elements in the list need be found in the input at one read, nor need the order in which they occur agree with the list.

In *format-directed* transmission the format in the external medium is explicitly provided according to a code in which:

F refers to fixed-point layout
E   floating-point layout
C   complex layout
P   format defined by picture
A   string length
R   remote format (with the label of a FORMAT statement as parameter)
IF, etc,   the internal layout as declared for a fixed-point (etc) number.

Interspersed between these item-formats may be positioning formats SPACE, SKIP, GROUP, TAB (each with an optional parameter which is an integer replicator) or POSITION(⟨format list⟩) which repositions the external medium by going to the beginning of the record and recapping (without doing anything) the specified format. These positioning format-items may also be used as statements.

More complicated cases are dealt with by the *procedure-directed* option. A statement WRITE . . . , CALL X; is equivalent to WRITE . . . ; CALL X; with this exception, that the name of the file which is the object of the WRITE is placed on a pushdown list known as the current-file (normally empty), and the file at the top of this list can be referenced by PUT (for WRITE) and GET (for READ). On the return from X the list is popped-up. As an example, the situation described in Section 9.4, where one does not know which type of record is coming up next, can be dealt with in the following way (among others)

    READ FILE (COSTS FILE), (ITEM)(A(1)), CROSS(1) HOLD,
      CALL J;
      :
      :

J: PROCEDURE;
  IF ITEM = 'W' THEN DO; GET(WAGE_DETAIL)(A)26));
  . . . END; ELSE IF ITEM = 'P' THEN DO; GET(PURCH_
  DETAIL)(A(22); . . . END;
  ELSE SIGNAL BADCARD;
  END J;

There are no restrictions on the way calls of this sort may be nested.

Files must be OPENed and CLOSEd, and these verbs have options which deal with file-identification labels, and, in the case of OPEN, with much of the information which Cobol puts in the environment division, one result of which is to remove the inflexibility of the Cobol arrangements and make them alterable during the course of a run.

FETCH and DELETE are used to bring in library programs (to be subsequently invoked by a CALL statement) and to free the storage again when the process is finished with. These are interesting in that it is legal to write

FETCH('PROG' | | N)

which, since | | is the concatenation operator, will have the effect of converting the value of N to a string and concatenating it with 'PROG', and thus calling a routine with the name 'PROG*n*' (*n* an integer). One then uses the same trick in the parameter of CALL. But for some reason, the report makes it sound as if one is not allowed to do this with one's own routine names — a strange lapse from 'objective 1' since to allow the SYMBOL attribute to a PROCEDURE statement would seem to cover any difficulties. (Of course, one would then logically have to allow the same to *any* label, and this would raise more problems.) Another form of output is

DISPLAY(⟨string exp⟩) ↑ 1 REPLY(⟨string variable⟩)

which displays the expression on the monitor typewriter and, if the REPLY is included, suspends the program until the message is acknowledged with contents for the variable. This eliminates need for the ACCEPT verb of some languages. There are also separate PAGE and LAYOUT statements for presetting page-size, -heading, etc, and margins respectively.

SAVE and RESTORE statements, each with an item-list and optionally an integer-expression tag, write and read respectively on a 'dump file'. For each distinct variable this provides effectively one push-down list (untagged SAVEs and RESTOREs) and an unlimited number of single, numbered, reserve stores. The items must be scalars or *complete* arrays or structures. These are not strictly in/out statements unless these are held to include *all* transmission to and from *files* of any description. So far as list-processing is concerned, once again (as with CONTROLLED) a pushdown list is not an adequate provision, unless means are also available to explore its depths non-destructively.

14.5 CPL and Algol 68

In CPL, the philosophy of 'no side effects' made it necessary to provide

(a) a *procedure* with parameter x which assigns to x the *next* value on the tape, and holds a record of it, and

(b) a *function* whose value is the *currently recorded* input value and which does not have the side effect of advancing the tape.

The notational difficulties of Algol 60 appeared to be circumvented

189

in CPL by including **list** and **general** among the types, but **general** proved too hot to handle.

Algol 68 has introduced the word *transput*. It is true that everyone finds continual repetition of 'input and/or output', whether in full or abbreviated, to be clumsy, but elimination of clumsiness is no excuse for ugliness, and with the anglo-saxon *crossput* and such classical alternatives as *transport*, *transduction* and *transception* (cf. *transceiver*), available, it is a pity that the choice fell on such a misbegotten mongrel. On the other hand, when building St. Paul's cathedral in London, Sir Christopher Wren was forced to defer to critics who said that four pillars would not support the dome and he must have eight; three hundred years later it was discovered that of his eight pillars only four actually take the weight of the dome, the other four being a few inches short. In a similar way, despite IFIP (see Section 14.2) the description of the Algol 68 language is nearly as empty as the Algol 60 report of references to input and output. Where Algol 68 differs is that (1) *after* the language has been described, it is *then used* to define standard input and output procedures, much as the Algol 60 report could have defined *sqrt* in Algol 60 (but did not), and (2) format strings are provided with a distinctive syntax different from that of other strings and are known as format *texts*.

Transput in Algol 68 occupies a 64-page section of an 83-page chapter in a 226-page report. If this seems an excessive proportion it must be said that it is only an extreme example of a general trend indicative of a general malaise in this area, not confined to any one language or group of languages. (The solution in Omnibus is to provide transput of strings only, leaving conversion routines outside the language definition.) But the size of this section is also due to the fact that it provides a complete model of a filing system. A mode **file** is defined, with a field *text* of mode [][][]**char** (possibly with flexible bounds) and many other fields for system requirements like opening and write protection. The three suffixes of *text* allow for page, line and character-in-line numbers. The modes

mode simplout = **union(int, real, complex, bool, bits, char, []char,**
⟨**longs** of these⟩)
mode simplin = **union**(< corresponding **ref** modes including
ref string >)

include all for which direct conversion routines are provided, and two others, **outtype** and **intype**, supplement these unions by such modes structured or rowed from them as the program may require. A fifth mode, **format**, is represented in source language by a 'format text', the equivalent of the ACM format string. The standard prelude provides three 'ways of transput', plain, formatted and binary. It opens the standard files *standin* and *standout* on standard channels —

e.g. card reader and line printer — and makes available with these files six routines (two with alternative names)

read	readf	readbin
write *or* print	writef *or* printf	writebin

Each of these takes one parameter — the 'trans-thing' as we may call it, of type []union(⟨suitable types⟩). At one remove of convenience we may write

$$\begin{Bmatrix}\text{put}\\\text{get}\end{Bmatrix}\begin{Bmatrix}\langle\text{empty}\rangle\\\text{f}\\\text{bin}\end{Bmatrix}(\langle\text{file name}\rangle,\text{trans-thing})$$

instead. In a binary call, trans-thing is of mode []**intype** or []**outtype**; in plain or formatted calls these unions are supplemented by **proc(ref file) void** or **format** respectively. Because (⟨list of items with commas⟩) can, in a strong position, be coerced into a rowed mode, this is a legal form for trans-thing.

All of these routines are defined in the standard prelude in the form of Algol 68 procedures. Transfer functions, to **string**, for values of the other modes in **simplout** are defined, and also an operator **straightout** which converts any **outtype** not in **simplout** to a []**simplout** by recursive splitting (i.e. regarding successive fields or rows as distinct objects). Though technically available to the user, **straightout** may well be, in actual output, a reinterpretation rather than a manipulation; it is one of the few supporting routines with a body in English. The following abbreviation of *put* is instructive (note that **upb** x is 'upper bound of x'):

```
proc put = (ref file f, []union(outtype, proc(ref file)void)x)void:
    if file ok then for i to upb x do case x[i] in
    (proc pitem) : pitem(f),
    (outtype oitem) : ([]simplout y = straightout oitem;
                        for j to upb y do case y[j] in
                        (bits b) : bitsoutput(f, b),
                        (bool b) : booloutput(f, b),
                        etc., esac od
    esac od
    else undefined fi
```

In plain output the **proc** alternative allows for procedures to insert spaces, newlines and newpages, but the *TYPEoutput* routines also deal with line or page overflows when required.

Formatted transput is less simple, but is an object lesson in the handling of data structures. The following grammar, while inadequate as a complete description, brings out some important differences between the format text and the Algol 60 format string:

191

format text: dollar symbol, collection list, dollar symbol.

collection: TYPE pattern option, insertion; replication.

replication: insertion, replicator, open bracket, collection list, close bracket, insertion.

replicator: positive integer option; letter n, meek integral CLOSED clause.

insertion: literal option, alignment sequence option.

alignment: replicator option, alignment code, literal option.

literal: replicator option, strong string denoter coercee, literal option.

real pattern: zero frame sequence option, sign frame, digit frame sequence, point frame, digit frame option.

zero frame: insertion, replicator, letter z.

digit frame: insertion, replicator, letter d.

point frame: insertion, point symbol.

    etc.

Two of these differences are (1) lacking proper string quotes, two levels of embedding are obtained by use of the dollar symbol. We discuss this further in Section 14.8. And (2) instead of *format*n, the complete generality of a CLOSED clause is available for dynamic replication. It should also be noted that TYPE*pattern* is more general than its appearance suggests since it includes *integral and boolean choice* and other dynamically selected *patterns*. Internally, a format text is represented by an object of mode

$$\textbf{mode format} = \textbf{struc(flex } [1:0] \textbf{ piece } \aleph)$$

where $\aleph$ (aleph) is a private character; this is used to prevent the programmer from breaking into the object, thus allowing a more efficient form of storage than that expected by field selection routines. We shall simplify the discussion by assuming that **format** is simply []**piece** (and also by ignoring indications of suppression — i.e. making a decimal point 'understood' in card output). A piece is not, as might be supposed, an item from the collection list, but is a complete collection list in which all sublists (in replications) are replaced by pointers to other pieces; the first piece in a format is the whole format text and the remainder are its sublists. The internal structure is taken a stage further by the following mode definitions

  piece = **struc(int** current pointer, count, back pointer **c** all used by
        the traversing routine **c**, []**collection** c);

    collection = **union(picture, collitem)**;

    picture = **struc(union of patterns** p, **insertion** i);

    collitem = **struc(insertion** i1,
                proc int rep,
                int p **c** index of sublist in format **c**,
                insertion i2);

insertion = []**struc**(**proc int** rep,
                              union(**string**, **character**) sa)

and is completed by definitions of all the various patterns.

The fields of a **file** include two, **format** *format* and **int** *forp*, which are used in formatted output. The procedure *putf* begins thus

```
proc putf = (ref file f, []union(outtype, format) x)void:
  if file ok then for i to upb x do case x[i]in
  (format fitem) : (format of f := fitem;
                    forp of f := 1;
                    current pointer of (format of f)[1] := 1;
                    count of (format of f)[1] := 1;
                    back pointer of (format of f)[1] := 0),
  (outtype vitem) : ([]simplout values = straightout vitem;
                     picture picture; int j := 0;
                     while (j plus 1)⩽upb values do
                     bool incomp := false;
                     getnextpicture(f, false c = writemode to
                     c, picture)
                     etc.
```

That is, *putf* deals with the items in its trans-thing seriatim. If the first item is a format, this is copied to the *format* of the file and initialized, but if it is not, then any format left by a previous call will be picked up where that call left off; (*format* **of** *f*)[*forp* **of** *f*] is effectively a **ref piece**, and (*c* **of** *this*)[*current pointer* **of** *this*] is the next collection. Subsequent **format** items erase anything that is left of a previous one, overwriting it with a newly initialized format. An **outtype** item is straightened and its component **simplouts** matched against successive *pictures* obtained by traversing the format.

During this process insertions will have been encountered. Integer replicators and dynamic replicators will have been unified during compilation by proceduring both, and it is important to know when they are staticized (by calling the procedures). Consider a section of format text derived from

       TYPE picture, collitem, void picture, TYPE picture

and suppose that the first TYPE *picture* has just been implemented. Replacing the commas above by asterisks and expanding, we see that we are faced with

          * ins, rep, piece, ins * ins * patt, ins *

or structurally,

```
*[](prep,str), prep, piece, [](prep,str)* [](prep,str)*[](prep,frame),
A              B    C      D               E
    [](prep,str)*
         F
```

193

All the **proc int** *reps* (preps) from A to B are now called collaterally, then the insertions performed, after which a pushdown process is used to enter the piece. On return, sections CD, DE and EF are dealt with successively, in each case starting the section by calling *all* its preps collaterally.

14.6 Program input and portability

To ensure maximum utility, a language should be able on the one hand to handle as wide a variety of data as possible, while on the other it should impose no necessities that are beyond the means of small computers. PL/I recognized the implications of this when it decided to allow any character the equipment can handle in data, and therefore in (string) constants within a program, but to confine its syntactic requirements to a restricted character set based on old-style card practice. In fact, the small computer with only a tele-printer is often better off in this respect than the medium sized one with only card equipment, and it is one of life's ironies that specialists in natural linguistics, who ought to be using large character sets, are often condemned to machines of the latter type.

What we have termed old-style card practice is based on a 60-character alphabet with certain conventions for making do with 48. If we lay out our requirements thus

(1)   A . . Z
(2)   0 . . 9
(3)   . , - * / $ space
(4)   ( ) + = '
(5)   & @ % ♯ ?
(6)   ; : ⟨ ⟩ ! " _
(7)   [ ] ↑ ← ¢ | £ lower-case letters, etc.

then there is practically no equipment (other than such as substitutes £ for $) that does not provide the first three groups. The 'Fortran 48' is groups (1)–(4), and groups (1)–(3) with (5) constitute an alternative 48-set sometimes preferred in commercial work. (1)–(6) is the standard 60-character set. Newline (NL) does not occur because it is assumed to occur *between* cards. The make-do conventions are mappings of the extra characters onto pairs of characters from groups (1)–(3), e.g. ',.' for ';' or 'GT' for '>'.

Group (7) shows a number of additional characters which are frequently met with. A six-bit (seven with parity) paper tape code will provide 64 characters, but as it needs at least 'blank' (= null, not space), 'erased' and 'newline' in addition to its graphics, it can just manage to match the 60-character set and to add one further character. The ISO code is a seven-bit code and produces 128 characters; those mapping on to the integers 0–31 are used for control purposes

194

(including backspace as well as newline and null) leaving thirty-five available for new graphics; these are assigned to the lower case letters, the first five characters of group (7), and four 'locally defined' characters. Because the masking out of one bit which maps lower case on to upper case also maps _ on to @, six-bit codes often omit one of these and provide a second extra. Teleprinter sets often exceed 64 characters but are prevented the full ISO set by mechanical inter-locks that can 'make a proper charlie' out of any intelligent pro-grammer.

In addition to the characters capable of being input and output, there is a need for at least one character which a program can intro-duce into a string as a private character of its own. Its status in the programming language must be that of a system-defined manifest constant. Algol 68 selfishly provides one for its own grammar (letter aleph) but none for the user! Some implementations are based on 'a set of 64 graphics and nothing else, in strings'; for the reasons just stated this is not to be recommended.

Languages that use an extensive character set in their syntax require to be mapped on to the minimal one for use on small com-puters. A very recent IFIP report (Hansen and Boom 1976) makes interesting proposals for mapping Algol 68 in this way while main-taining the validity of three distinct conventions that already exist. Apart from features peculiar to Algol 68, these proposals are as follows (and there seems no obstacle to wider application):

(1) A set of 60 characters are defined as 'worthy' for the purpose. They include groups (1)–(3) above, but because of the import-ance of certain characters in Algol 68 they do not match the card-60 completely, preferring [,] and | to &, ? and !. (Hence **and** must be used for &.) They include both @ and _. Among the 'base' characters of the local implementation a set of 60 are chosen which either are worthy characters or represent them locally.

(2) Under all circumstances, .PR represents the pragmat symbol, provided that it is followed by a space or other character which is neither a letter nor a numeral. The pragmats .PR RES .PR, .PR POINT .PR, and .PR UPPER .PR introduce 'stropping regimes' in which bold type words become reserved words, words preceded by a point and words in upper case (contrasting with plain type in lower case) respectively.

(3) One underscore character may follow any plain letter or numeral.

(4) If an escape character is required (see next section) it should be the apostrophe.

These three regimes represent

begin goto end; end: skip end

by

    (1)   BEGIN GOTO END_; END_; SKIP END
    (2)   .BEGIN .GOTO END; END: .SKIP .END
    (3)   BEGIN GOTO end; end: SKIP END

respectively. Portability now requires only that a preprocessor recognizes all three pragmats, and will usually be simple to achieve except on equipment that automatically condenses the third to a single case. (In the first two regimes, in equipment possessing two cases, this condensation is assumed to occur except in strings, so that '.GOTO end; End:' would be valid.) In view of what we have said towards the end of Section 10.5, it is pertinent to remark that it is only the symbols used in the definition of the language, not the additional ones of the standard prelude, that are strictly reserved (i.e. not redefinable because they automatically mean something else).

There seems no reason why other languages that have character set portability problems should not adopt these principles. PL/I is defined in terms of the 60-character set; it has many words with special meanings but it reserves only those combinations that map it on to the 48-character set.

14.7 Data portability

A computer that cannot read and print the signs of the zodiac is ill equipped to deal with all the demands of the 20th century. To clarify the implications of this situation, let us define a primary peripheral as one that consists of a keyboard and a printer, linked by a single channel in which there is a local/on-line switch. Each key transmits a distinct signal to the channel. When the switch is at local, this transmits directly to the printer which interprets it. A 'valid' peripheral is one in which the character generated by the printer is always identical to the one engraved on the key. When the switch is on-line, the signals generated by the keys are sent to the computer and the signals received by the printer are ones generated within the computer (which may or may not consider itself bound to 'echo back' what it receives). A computer can handle the signs of the zodiac if it has a valid peripheral equipped with keys (a) for the signs themselves, and (b) for the characters required by the syntax of the language in which it will receive its instructions. These two sets may overlap completely, partially, or not at all.

Not all installations will want to do this, but for many purposes (though not all) it is desirable that a program developed in one place shall be useable elsewhere without requiring adaptation to the new environment. Such portability is something to be maximized — it can be maintained that

a language is only as good as the computers it is implemented on
a computer is only as good as the languages implemented on it

196

— but it can never be absolute, since nothing can make a program completely portable from a machine with only card peripherals to one with only paper tape equipment. There is no reason why a computer should not have two large valid primary peripherals that are identical except that where one has astrological signs the other has greek characters. Portability is now incomplete between these peripherals but only to the extent of requiring mental transcription of the sign into the greek letter or vice versa.

The essence of this situation is that the programmer is unconcerned about the form taken by a data character inside the computer, and the computer is equally unconcerned about the external form provided only that its identity will be preserved within the computer and its external form restored by a valid peripheral. It is quite otherwise with the characters out of which the program is built up; the computer must recognize these for what they are *even from diverse equipment*.

It is also possible that both valid terminals carry the same additional characters, but they are assigned differently to the keys. A program typed in on one terminal is now valid on the other *provided* that the alphabet of additional characters is asked for by the program as data, but not if it is contained within it as a string constant.

14.8 Theory of strings

There is a tragic, because theoretically fatal, omission in all of the codes we have been discussing, and until it is corrected the subject will remain a shambles. The author confesses that as a member of a standards committee that was asked whether the Algol 60 black words should be included in the ISO code, he was present when a unanimous 'Good heavens, no!' accidentally threw out the baby with the bath water by appearing to show no requirement for the string quotes. Yet string quotes are the perfect and the only workable interface between languages, and their inclusion in the ISO code, even at the cost of losing two locally defined characters, will become more and more desirable as languages develop, despite vested interests in other uses for these characters.

Sections 5.5.1, 5.6, 8.2 and 8.3 all discuss specialized uses of quotes but none of these penetrates to the real crux, which is that a string is a section of text in another (not necessarily different) language. An example is the introduction of machine code in Section 6.1. The interior of a string should be absolutely portable; that is, it should always be *immediately* parsable in terms of its *own unmodified* grammar. Since other languages also claim the right to include strings in their syntax, this imposes a recursive requirement that cannot be obtained except by *distinct, universally recognized*, opening and closing quotes.

The apostrophe and the so-called quote of the ISO code are

originally the single and double vertical half-lines of the typewriter, not the inverted commas of the printer. Without the latter one falls back on the clumsy system whereby alternate quotes are openers and closers and a special notation (called the *quote image*) is required for nested quotes. PL/I uses ′ for the quote and ″ for the quote image (so that ″″ is '"'); Algol 68 unforgivably follows suit (but using ″). On this system, quotes *n* deep require 2^n quote symbols. Not only is this clumsy but, what is far worse, one has to know how deep a string is before one can interpret it properly.

The language inside a string may be unknown or it may be defined by the syntactic position of the string. A string as a procedure body is in machine assembly language. A string as the second parameter of a transput procedure is in a language designed for the description of layout. Thus one language may dictate what other language an embedded string is in, but it should have no power to dictate any conventions to that language. In particular, a language may ignore layout; it has no right to impose this on the language of any embedded string.

It is sometimes convenient to adopt a compromise, which is that a language may impose a change of *representation* on embedded strings; this is what Algol does by its 'space in strings' character. The reason for this compromise in Algol is that it is *convenient*, however unsound it may be, to remove all layout characters from an Algol text during input, before any syntactic analysis, even the simple recognition of strings, is performed. The nearest that the author has found to a satisfactory application of this principle to quotes is to say that nested quotes are represented by square brackets. It is absolutely essential that the characters used for this purpose shall be ones that are *never* used unpaired; this is not true of round brackets, where the notation 1), 2) ... is sometimes used, but it seems sufficiently true at present of square ones. It is, of course, necessary to have means of removing the resultant ambiguity in the embedded text, which is why it is an unsound device, and doubtless the ungodly will lose no time in proposing a convention that upsets it.

It is the author's private belief that *no* programming language should include transput proposals to the level of the 60/ACM or 68 proposals, but that two (or three) independent compilers should be invoked whenever necessary, one defining the programming language and one the layout language (or the input and output languages independently). There is, however, one constraint on the practical application of this belief; in Algol 68 terms, if strings and string variables were to replace format texts, then conversion to formats (which would be the job of the layout language compiler) would have to be done at run time, at least in the case of strings synthesized by the program, and this might result in an unacceptable deterioration of efficiency.

Complete portability of string contents means that it should be possible, for example, to splice any tested piece of paper tape, whatever its origin, between opening and closing quotes in another piece. The resulting implications on layout are not always acceptable. There are three ways of overcoming this:

(1) The right way. A buffer language is defined. In this language codes are provided for newline, newpage, etc., substrings represent their own contents, and the true layout characters have no meaning.

(2) The compromise way. The outer language imposes a representation change on the quoted one, by defining an escape character. CPL used this method with the asterisk as escape.

(3) The wrong way. Undesirable layout characters are replaced by quoted codes. This can conflict with the needs of the inner language.

As an illustration, let us use the printer's double quotes as quote symbols and consider "

> It's time for bed.
> "Come", I said.

". This is obviously awkward. Coded the first way it might become "//12s "It's time for bed."/12s" "Come", I said."//". Coded the second way, the twelve spaces are a nuisance unless we can use the 'tabulate'. Using the apostrophe for the escape, we have "'n'n'tIt"'s 's time 's for 's bed. 'n 't "Come", 's I 's said. 'n 'n". The third way would give " "nn12s"It's "s" time "s" for "s" bed. "n" "Come", "s" I "s" said "n" ", and if I ever wanted to say "nnsss", the result would be catastrophic.

The scheme adopted by ICL for their Algol 60 looks at first sight like the 'wrong' way, but is not. Black letter words are apparently in quotes, e.g. 'END', and some other characters in strings are disguised in this way. But the true string quotes are '(' and ')' — black versions of the round brackets, if you like — and thus new characters. There are two ways of interpreting in this system, the one apparently used which is that certain sequence of characters beginning with the apostrophe are to be interpreted as single symbols (the Algol 60 black letter words are in fact single symbols) and a more fluent and flexible one in which the apostrophe acts as an on/off black-type switch. The former allows the apostrophe to be itself in most contexts, the latter requires a substitute to be found for it (the principle of the quote-image could be used).

The reader's attention is drawn to the way in which Macro-generator respects the principles set out here. Strings inside quotes are *always* copied *literally*; if they emerge from their quotes then, unless immediately output, they are subject to interpretation.

15

MISCELLANEOUS TOPICS

The foregoing chapters have, as it were, explored the main line of programming languages, in which three sources — machine languages, mathematical formalism, and the requirements of business data-processing — developed until they overlapped, while concurrently the mathematical theory of language became available to explain, co-ordinate, codify and control much of what was in the first place empirical in their practice. But there were also developments which, for one reason or another, lay out of the main stream, yet deserve mention.

15.1 Special purpose languages

A large number of languages of considerable variety have been produced for special purposes. Because every language must have a character set and an unambiguous, decidable grammar, and probably has at least a limited requirement for handling strings and numbers (English and Arithmetic, if you like), individual consideration of any of these languages is apt to involve much recapitulation of ground already covered, and any features of real interest, when arrived at, turn out to belong to the special nature of the intended application. The incorporation of new types and techniques into general purpose languages from PL/I onwards has diminished interest in languages of this sort (with often only rudimentary arithmetic facilities) nor has the author attempted to keep track of all of them, but they cannot altogether be ignored.

Comit (Yngve, 1961) and Snobol (Farber *et al*, 1964) are 'string processing' languages. Thus they may be thought of as procedure type equivalents to the function language Macro-generator. Since all lists can, by the use of brackets, be represented as strings, they might be regarded as a subset of list-processing languages, but compared with those mentioned in Section 12 they are more restricted, and consequently they are more efficient within their chosen fields, less efficient outside them. Their outstanding features are (1) the provision of an instruction to search a string for an incompletely specified substring such as 'The ⟨description⟩ cat' and to label the substring ⟨description⟩ for later reference, and (2) similar provision to replace a given substring by an alternative, possibly of a different length. These processes can be expressed by a modern general purpose language, but only by a level of analysis at source text level that is apt to introduce an unwelcome amount of housekeeping at machine level.

'Axle, An axiomatic language for string transformation' (Cohen and Wegstein, 1965) might be regarded as a third candidate for this group, but it also anticipated another development, the movement to popularize programming by the construction of decision tables (a program in Axle consists of two tables, an assertion table and an imperative table). As tables fall outside the concept of language which has been the main thesis of this book, we take this subject no further.

Two further groups, somewhat overlapping, are composed of (1) languages with special features for statistical processes and (2) simulation languages. The overlap arises when stochastic variables are involved and Monte Carlo methods become appropriate. The Multiple Variate Counter (Colin, 1961, 1963, 1964) is concerned primarily with the reduction of raw data from surveys, etc, to its statistical parameters. Montecode (Kelly and Buxton, 1962) provides for use of Monte Carlo methods for computations involving stochastic variables. Mention should also be made of Autostat (Douglas, 1960) and its extended form Opal (Pilling, 1963); the latter is a simulation language with provision for stochastic variables.

Simulation languages (Freeman, 1964) include GPSS, Simscript and CSL (see also Buxton, 1962), and the Elliott Simulation Package (Williams, 1964). The first three of these are IBM developments; GPSS caters for those who prefer to think in terms of block diagrams, Simscript for those requiring Fortran in the computational aspects, while CSL (a British development) suits problems with elaborate logical situations. The Elliott Simulation Package takes the form of extra facilities associated with the Elliott Algol compiler.

It is no disparagement on a simulation language to describe it as a conversion kit to turn some existing language into something bigger and better. (If anything, it is an implied criticism of the standard language.) The simulation which is carried out in these languages is that of real time processes such as queueing, workshop scheduling, chemical processes or military exercises. For a neat handling of such problems a master program which handles the time is required, and entries to this program must be by standard features of the language. Besides holding the variable which represents the time and making it available to other routines on a read-only basis, this program must maintain a diary into which other routines can write; in general, its mode of operation will be to advance the time to the next diary-entry, update variables which change continuously, and call the routine represented by the diary entry, unless the updating process

201

reveals an earlier, unforeseen event, in which case it advances the time only to the latter. (E.g. routine *heater on* could enter *water boiling* in the diary for 5 minutes later, or it could set a non-zero rate of change of *water-temperature*, in which case integration of the latter must never be allowed to carry it above 100°C.) Williams (loc. cit.) gives a complete program for a waiting room, several doctor, queueing problem, which illustrates the type of situation which is met in these languages.

The only development subsequent to those mentioned above has been Simula (Dahl *et al*, 1966 and 1970). This was designed as a new language taking in sufficient of the ideas of Algol 60 that it could be regarded as a superset of that language. It altered somewhat the concept of what a simulation language needs to do. In a simulation to investigate, for example, the cause of accidents on a certain stretch of road, it starts by considering cyclists, private cars, lorries etc., as *classes* of objects which must be *created* as they enter the section and destroyed as they leave it; moreover, such objects must be considered as *processes*. Algol 68 has allowed for this approach by the inclusion of semaphores and parallel processing; the author has no experience by which to judge whether its non-specialized approach implies overheads, but if it does, then a library prelude should be able to provide the Simula ethos within the Algol 68 syntax.

Control languages are closely related to simulation languages. On-line control languages have been developed for military purposes. Machine tool control languages are usually off-line; that is, a description of the work required is translated into the machine language of the tool, on tape, and the tape fed to the tool. The primary language contains provision for various descriptions — e.g. a circle in terms of three points or in terms of centre and radius. An early language in this class, Apt, was developed by R.A.E. Farnborough; information on the later ones is usually to be obtained from the manufacturers of the associated tool control equipment.

15.2 Open-ended languages

From time to time the announcement of a new language includes the claim that it is open-ended. This term is meant to imply possession of a property, supposedly shown by natural languages, by which they are able to describe possible changes in their own structure and then adopt them, at least temporarily, in order to deal with situations not envisaged when the language was developed. Usually it means something less fully developed than this, but it means at least that some of the normal constraints within the language can be removed by invoking some other construction in the language.

15.2.1 Macros

For example, claims have been made that macro-facilities render an assembly language open-ended. Assembly languages have a one-to-one relation between their statements and the machine instructions, and apart from labels each statement begins with an operation code drawn from the *finite set* provided by the hardware designer. Macro-facilities involve provision of a directive, the macro-definition, that removes the first of these constraints and, while retaining the syntactic restriction in the second, allows the user to *add to the set* of operation codes.

Machine level programmers distinguish between a closed subroutine, inserted into a program once only and called by a process that preserves knowledge of where to return to, and an open subneeded, of which a distinct copy is inserted at each point where it is routine. The earliest macro provisions simply allowed a single name (syntactically an operation code) to represent the whole of an open subroutine. Later, parameterized macros were introduced to allow variations between one copy and another, but usually only to allow the same sequence of operations on different operands. Embedding macros within macros was handled very gingerly at first.

Macro-generator showed that the semantics of macro-definitions and macro-calls could be powerful and safe, but instead of being used in this way it is more often considered as a language in its own right. Thus the author has used it to expand §IF,X,LT,Y,L; into

        LOAD X
        SUB Y   (omitted if Y is identically '0')
        SKIP IF POSITIVE
        JUMP L

on one machine, or to a corresponding sequence on another. However, few macro-assemblers allow manipulation of the operator (SUB, derived *via* §LT; from §∼2;) in this way, and still fewer permit one to allow for the fact that it is inefficient to demand subtraction of zero. The distinction between what is done at compile time and what is done at run time is vital here. If we try to implement the non-need to subtract zero at high level, we can hardly avoid something like **if** $x = 0$ **then** y **else** $y-x$, which saves a little subtraction at the cost of a lot of testing. A rudimentary form of what is required, known as conditional compilation, is found in a number of installations; this allows the compiler to be called with boolean parameters, and, depending on their values, certain parts of the source text may be skipped by the compiler. But some more generous facility for computation at compile time is required to secure real openendedness.

203

15.2.2 High-level openendedness

Higher-level languages have neglected the open subroutine principle on the whole, though Bamford (1976) has shown that (in the guise of 'manifest procedures') they can improve the efficiency of BCPL, and Napper (1967, 1968, 1976) has used Compiler-compiler to pursue the subject of high-level macros over a period of many years.

In the previous section we implicitly suggested that a macro-definition is a directive. There is a very narrow line between 'instructions to the compiler' and 'instructions to be obeyed at compile time'. PL/I, probably following certain local extensions to Fortran, introduced the use of '%' at the beginning of a line to indicate that the statement is to be obeyed, not compiled, at compile time. Originally intended for the purpose of providing a macro-facility, this feature is actually wider in its scope, and is a step towards true openendedness. When this facility is used, the source-text must begin with a '%DECLARE. . .' statement in which all identifiers to be used at compile time are declared (integer or character string), and possibly initialized; these are known as macro-variables. The remainder of the source-text is then converted into 'program text' by (1) copying plain text, (2) substituting values for macro-variables, and (3) obeying macro-instructions. Substitution can be recursive and obedience can generate loops by means of macro-labels, macro-conditionals and macro-'go-to's. Parameter notation is not used at the macro level; instead, the concatenation operator is used with string constants and variables. (This would involve our first example of the use of Macro-generator being written

% DECLARE VERSE, ANIMAL, SOUND (CHARACTER VARYING);
%VERSE = 'Old Macdonald . . . had some'||ANIMAL||. . .;
%SOUND = 'cheep';
%ANIMAL = 'chicks';
VERSE;

and so on.) During this process the source text remains unaltered. When its end is reached, macro-activity ceases and the program-text, which contains no macro-material, is then compiled. (So the true equivalent of Macro-generator would be a program which compiled a single print statement, and not as above.)

Radin and Rogoway make it clear that the use of the same language for macro-operation as is used for the program itself is a deliberate attempt at a first step towards an open-ended language, and they give an example in which string manipulation is used in an advanced way, namely, if a function $f(p,q)$ involves p being an expression and q its derivative, the work of derivation can be performed by the macro-facility. At the same time, the first-step character of this facility is clear from such features as the lack of block structure

204

at the macro-level (all macro-variables must be declared in the first statement of all), the fact that macro-parameters are handled by the **perform** technique of Section 11.1 and so on.

To allow any programmer to develop the programming language most congenial to himself is an extreme form of openendedness, but this was the claim made by Xpop (Halpern, 1964, 1966). Developed for use with Fap, the symbolic assembly language of certain IBM machines, it provided three groups of facilities

(1) A macro-facility to extend Fap itself
(2) Additional system facilities for use within the compiler
(3) Notation re-defining facilities.

The chief interest arises from the third group. Being designed for applications that included its use on-line by personnel unfamiliar with programming languages, Xpop contained provisions enabling the user to define his own preferred way of saying something. The 'canonical form' of a macro call is, after an optional label, the name of the macro (what was the label of the pseudo-operation MACRO in the definition) followed by its parameters separated by commas and terminated by a blank. The one unchangeable, anchor, feature of this is that the first word is the macro name. This ties the free, 'users', grammar down to the rule that every statement must begin with its imperative verb — probably the least restrictive rule which it is possible to impose from the point of view of user and compiler alike. For the rest, pseudo-operations exist by which (1) other character combinations can replace or supplement the comma and blank as separators and terminators, and (2) words can be defined to be noisewords — words to be ignored in looking for parameters. Furthermore, these words need not be altogether ignored — they can be defined (a) to represent an omitted parameter, or (b) to cue in parameters which may be out of order (e.g. if ADD adds the first parameter to the second, then if in ADD A TO B, TO is a cue to B, then ADD TO B, A will not be misunderstood on account of the inverted order). The omitted parameter feature, incidentally, is a curious one useful if correctly handled; if it existed in Algol, then the following would illustrate its use

$$\textbf{procedure } increment(x, y, 01); \textbf{ begin}$$
$$x := x+1; \quad y := y+01 \textbf{ end};$$

A call *increment(a,b)* would increment both *a* and *b* by unity, but a call *increment(a,b,c)* would increment *a* by 1 and *b* by *c*. In a situation like

begin real x, y, z;
      procedure proc(x,y,z) . . .
        :
        proc(a,,c); . . .

the absence of the second parameter in the call would cause any y in the procedure body to have the meaning which it would have if it were not a formal parameter, viz., here the real variable declared in the first line.

The PL/I feature acts by operating on the source program at compile time; the Xpop features also act within the compiled program. Many programs in regular use on the London Atlas were written in Compiler-compiler and anyone trying to unravel one of these was apt to find that it started by overwriting part of the Compiler-compiler itself and thus modifying it. This was true openendedness but in a machine-dependent form, requiring a knowledge of Atlas machine code on the part of the user. Is such ability to do compile-time modification of the compiler necessary to true openendedness, and if so, can it be done in a way that is both machine independent and fail-safe? It is not absolutely necessary to put the program part of the compiler at risk; some compilers are so written that only overwriting of tables is necessary. Nor need the compiler be a mystery, now that the practice is growing of writing the compiler for a language in the language itself (cf. BCPL and Pascal). (Omnibus will be compiled into an intermediate language immediately transcribable for the machine as a series of subroutine calls, and the compiler written in this language.) What is necessary is that certain of the *identifiers* used *in the compiler* shall be accessible to the user in 'obey at compile time' instructions; not merely those of procedures to be called, which is normal practice, of course, but some also of variables that can be assigned values, as well. On the interpretation of 'some' depends the balance between power and safety.

15.3 Subsets of English

From time to time the suggestion is made that we might make use of a subset of English for programming. In fact, this was one of the ideas behind Cobol. Looked at in this light, Cobol went completely off the rails. When we say that Basic Fortran is a subset of full Fortran, the idea in this statement is that anything done in Basic Fortran will be judged good full Fortran by any test made up for this purpose. No knowledge of the rules of Basic Fortran is necessary to make this test. But if we give a program in Cobol to a judge of good English (and there is no need for such a judge to have any knowledge of Cobol), it is probable that he will say that, though it makes use of English words, it is not in English, and it is certain that he will say that it is not *good* English. So Cobol is not a subset of English.

An example of a subset of English is Basic English (cf. Richards, 1943). The discovery of the existence of this useable subset was made in the 1920's by C. K. Ogden. Its vocabulary (word-list) is made up of

100 operations (verbs, prepositions and so on)
600 names (of things and abstract ideas)
150 qualities (adjectives)
? special names (proper nouns, technical terms and so on).

If the special names in any one work are kept under 150, the complete vocabulary for that work is kept under 1,000 words. As to the test, if you are a judge of good English and the writing in this section has your approval, then we have taken the test and come through with flying colours.

To see if something is in Basic English, the quickest way is to take a look at its verbs. Among the 100 operations are

be	come	do	get	give	go	have	keep	let
make	may	put	say	see	seem	send	take	will

and these eighteen are the only verbs in Basic English, though the number may seem greater because the forms ⟨noun⟩ing and ⟨noun⟩ed may be used anywhere where an adjective might go whenever the effect of doing so is good full English. It is less simple to be quite certain that one has not gone outside the range of the other operation-words, and less important over the names because of the power to take in special names. In this section we have gone outside only in

programming: giving a machine the details of what it is to do
subset: a group of things which is a part of a greater group. In making a comparison between two languages the 'things' are statements, not words (as is clear both from the Chomsky way of looking at a language and from the way a good judge does his work).
noun, verb, adjective: words which in full English have a sense of naming, doing or quality-giving.

and one or two (as *vocabulary*) whose sense is given at the first place at which they are used.

As Basic English is a language for all purposes, it is more than is needed for programming, even with the 1,000 word vocabulary limit, and its grammar (its rules for putting together statements) is almost as complex as that of full English. The chief profit to the learner is in the field of accidence, not syntax. (From now on we shall make use of any special names whose sense has been given earlier in this book.) It is not free from ambiguities (for example 'He took a picture from the window'). It is important, not as a possible programming language in itself, but (1) as a step in the right direction from the natural language side, and (2) because its small vocabulary (a) makes it more manage-able in machine studies of natural languages, and (b) is a help in getting the different questions which have to be answered separate from each other. As an example of (2a), McConologue and Simmons

207

(1965) give an account of a 'Pattern-learning Parser' which was quicker in learning when given material in Basic English (from Richards and Gibson (1960)) than when given material in normal English. (But the chief purpose of their work is in the field of machine translation, not in that of programming languages, because it was hoped that processes which give success quickly in a simple language will give success in the long run with other languages.)

It is worth the space of a single paragraph (in normal English) to conclude with the observation that while nothing can dim the technical achievement which Basic English represents, politically it met with catastrophe. There was a moment during the second world war when Churchill was interested in it as a world language, but copyright laws were invoked to preserve its purity, prevent the rise of dialects, and so on, and this killed it (politically) far more effectively than either the arguments or the ridicule of its opponents could do. There is a moral here somewhere for all who seek proprietary rights in programming languages.

15.3.1 Pronouns

Any attempt to construct a language which reads smoothly like a subset of a natural language very soon meets the fact that it cannot be done without pronouns. It would appear that the whole question of pronouns is a major bridge to be crossed in linking programming languages (as they now are) and natural languages. Their limited introduction into programming languages would have certain advantages. The nearest approach so far implemented is probably a feature of Nebula known as 'q' or 'quantity-in-hand'. This is a working variable whose value can be deduced from a knowledge of what happened in the previous statement. After an assignment, it is the value handed over. Therefore, if '$z := x; y := x+1$' is replaced by '$z := x; y := q+1$', the time of a second store access for x is saved. The second statement reads 'make z equal to x and y equal to *this* plus one'. Another move in this direction is the proposal by Hill (1965) to introduce **self** into Algol. This may only be used on the r.h.s. of assignment statements with a single l.h.s., and it refers to the l.h.s. Replacement of $x := x+1$ by $x := \textbf{self}+1$ has few advantages, but in

$$A[p-q,\ p+q] := \textbf{self} + 1$$

it avoids both rewriting and recomputing of a complicated expression. Should one take this further — e.g. $A[p-q,\ p+q] := B[\textbf{ibid}]+1$?

A comparison between verbal instructions such as 'Take x, increase it by 1 and store *it* in y', or 'Evaluate. . . ; multiply *this* by. . .', and any machine code equivalents will show a high correlation between use of pronouns in the natural language and retention of a result in an

208

accumulator (if possible) at machine code level. The chief difficulty in applying the principle of pronouns is the extent to which semantic considerations rather than syntactic ones are used in determining the antecedent of a pronoun. As an extreme example, consider the two sentences

(a) The committee considered that the meat was safe because it contained an adequate amount of preservative.
(b) The committee considered that the meat was safe because it found an adequate amount of preservative.

The antecedent of 'it' can only be determined by the verb which *follows* the 'it', and then only by knowledge of the fact that meat cannot find things, and committees do not (we hope) contain preservative. Yet both sentences on their own are perfectly clear.

15.3.2 Examples

A very interesting attempt to produce a language that is *really* a subset of English is Snap (Barnett 1969). The extent to which it is successful may be judged from the following program from Barnett's book, to allocate married couples to places around a dining table without putting any husband and wife together — from cards each with the name of a couple in the first twenty columns:

READ A RECORD. CALL THE 1-ST THROUGH 20-TH CHARACTERS OF THE RECORD THE NAME. COPY THE NAME AND CALL IT THE FIRST NAME. (LOOP START) COPY THE NAME, AND CALL IT THE PREVIOUS NAME. IF THE INPUT IS EXHAUSTED CONTINUE WITH THE FINALE, OTHERWISE CONTINUE AS FOLLOWS. READ A RECORD. PRINT "MR." THEN THE NAME. PRINT "MRS." THEN THE PREVIOUS NAME. REPEAT FROM THE LOOP START. (FINALE) PRINT "MR." THEN THE FIRST NAME. PRINT "MRS." THEN THE PREVIOUS NAME. EXECUTE.

The semantic advantages of using English are equally enjoyed by the use of certain practices that are not strictly languages. One is the process of stepwise refinement. An example is the use of the 'identifiers' *file ok*, *bitsoutput*, etc., in Section 14.5. These can be declared, or expanded *in situ*. (E.g. **if** *file ok* **then** ... becomes **if if** *fileexists* **then** *file open* **and** *write permitted* **else false fi then** ....) Stepwise refinement can be described as applying this process to *solve my problem*. Another is the semi-formal description of algorithms used, for example, by Knuth (1968) and exemplified by the algorithms in Sections 4.0 and 15.4.3.

15.4 Ross's Algorithmic theory of language

The main line theory of the interaction between syntax and semantics as presented here is not the only one to have been developed in a computer context, and we conclude with an alternative. In its distinction between right and left it has affinities with Floyd's precedence grammars (Section 7.5), but it goes much further on the semantic side.

In his *Algorithmic Theory of Language*, Ross (1962, 1964) aims at a decision algorithm for natural languages. He divides the terminal vocabulary into two representative groups which he calls *symbols* and *words*, but which we shall call *objects* and *operators* respectively, since (a) Ross's use produces an unfortunate inversion of the natural association of these terms when applied to programming languages, and (b) the two classes are very close to those distinguished by Ogden in Basic English. Thus a *symbol*, or *object*, is an item in the terminal vocabulary which stands for something in the external world, such as x, or *cost*, while a *word* or *operator*, is an item whose significance is more internal to the language and to the sentence syntax, such as '+', ';', **let** or **be**. In Chomsky terms he then assumes

$$\langle construct \rangle ::= \langle operand \rangle \langle operator \rangle \langle operand \rangle$$
$$\langle operand \rangle ::= \langle object \rangle | \langle construct \rangle | \langle nil \rangle$$

a highly ambiguous grammar from which the ambiguities are removed by methods which, superficially at least, are foreign to the Chomsky theory. As this grammar stands, it imposes the restriction that two objects cannot occur in succession in a terminal string. Natural languages do not altogether accept this restriction (even when punctuation is included), but formal compliance can usually be achieved by assuming the existence of implicit operators in certain standard situations. The converse case, of two operators in succession, is covered by the nil operand. It is worth noting that in English:

1. 'the' almost always has a nil left-hand operand, the exceptions being structures like 'Jack the Ripper'.
2. The commonest need for an implicit operator occurs between an adjective and its noun, or between adjectives when there is no comma.
3. Auxiliary verbs are operators, and so are some main verbs (including all the Basic eighteen); participles are objects when used adjectivally. Between these there is an area where there is room for debate.

The resolution of ambiguity is based on a dictionary of properties. This includes, for any object, a 'type', and for any operator (1) a type for the construct whose centre it is, and (2) a statement about the types it 'likes' to have on either side. When there are no alternatives, an operator can be used to denote the type it produces — e.g. we can use '×' to denote type *product* unless we wish to make finer distinctions such as real product and integer product. As an example, consider the rudimentary dictionary

	on its left	on its right
+ likes	+,×,),L, N	×,),L
× likes	), L	×,), L
:= likes	)*, L	:=, +, ×,), L
) likes	(only	N only
(likes	L, N	+, ×,), L

where L denotes a letter, and N denotes *nil*. This dictionary is sufficient to determine, for example, that

$$y := a \times b + c$$

must be interpreted in the sense $(y) := ((a \times b) + c)$, or, as Ross would express it, by the first of the following diagrams:

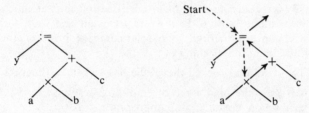

The interpretation $y := (a \times (b + c))$ is impossible because × does not like + on its right, and interpretations like $(y := a) \times (b + c)$ are impossible because × does not like := on its left. Note also that

'nil' on the left of '+' allows for unary '+',

+ on its own left only, but × on its own right only, will guarantee that + associates to the left and × to the right.

If round and square brackets are distinguished as in Algol, then both occur everywhere as shown except (1) each closer likes only its *own* opener on its left, (2) the asterisked bracket is only square (subscripted variables but not functions on the l.h.s. of assignments — unless *car*, *cdr* type functions have round brackets), and (3) a square opener does not like 'nil' on its left.

:= on the right of itself allows for multiple assignments, and maintains the rule that an assignee is a left-hand object.

This illustration is confined to simple numerical assignments; more generally, 'likes' may be dynamic — thus ':=' likes to have on its right the same type of quantity as is already determined to be on its left-hand side, the type of a '+' can be determined to be real or integer by inspection of the types of its operands, and types can be set by declarations.

211

It is fairly obvious that in simpler cases the 'likes' in the dictionary are equivalent to a set of productions. However, the $:=$ rule is equivalent to a *set* of productions which the CBN notation can only define by enumeration, thus lacking some flexibility and running the risk (as happened in Algol) that legitimate expressions may become illegal by reason of their accidental omission in the enumeration. The other dynamic type assignments also take in their stride the Λ-productions of Section 7.4.

Ross's full analytical procedure produces the additional information in the second of the above diagrams. Here, the arrows convey the order in which 'evaluation' must proceed, a dotted arrow implying a 'tactical excursion'. Thus, in our illustration, one starts by realizing that an assignment is called for. It takes place 'to' y, which is simple, but to find 'what' is to be assigned to y, one must first do a multiplication (of a by b), then an addition (of the result to c), and then we return to '$:=$', indicating that the assignment can now be completed and we can proceed to whatever comes next. Note that in Ross's concept, assignment is evaluation, just as much as is addition or multiplication. Evaluation seems an odd word to apply to most sentences in natural languages; compare, however, the process of obtaining the meaning of

The hand that rocked the cradle has kicked the bucket!

Here it is only the final stage of emotional response to which the word 'evaluation' seems at all inappropriate.

15.4.1 The parsing algorithm

The algorithm is a one-pass process, a feature very much in its favour, since passages in natural languages are certainly assimilated in one pass in most cases, and the exceptional cases are deprecated — one should not have to read a passage twice to understand it unless the sense itself is difficult to assimilate. A simple algorithm yields the first, or parsing, diagram and is expanded by grafting further stages on to it to yield the second, or precedence, diagram. The grafting process seems able to accept complication after complication without getting into a position in which it requires a second pass. The degrees of complication admitted may be held to define nesting classes of languages.

A preprocessor (all within the one pass) converts the true input into a series of pointers into the dictionary, and supplements those which point to operators with four tag-pointers, all initially pointing to 'nil' and destined ultimately to hold pointers from the tagged operator to

  (a) The word below it and to the left (the left-parsing pointer)
  (b) The word below it and to the right (the right-parsing pointer)
  (c) The word at the far end of a full arrow (the major precedence pointer) and

(d) The word at the far end of a dotted arrow (the minor precedence pointer).

The parsing algorithm, which sets the first two pointers, may be described as follows. Suppose the input string is ...(V)WXY ..., V having just been read. The algorithm is concerned with the top of a stack and with two other variables, M and N, the latter of which will contain V. Representing these as

Stack		M	N
P Q R S T		U	V

with T the top of the stack, then there occurs what is called 'a fight between T and V over U', with one of two possible results:

Result R: P Q R S   T V   U becomes the right operand of T; unload T.

Result L: P Q R S T V nil W   U becomes the left operand of V; stack V.

Following result L, if W is an object but not otherwise, a further input occurs leading to

P Q R S T V   W   X

(unless X is also an object, in which case it must be held back and an implicit operator inserted if possible, otherwise the input must be declared ungrammatical). The decision between these two results is taken on the basis of two tests:

TEST I: If T likes U on its right but
          U does not like V on its left ..... Result R?
          If V likes U on its left but
          T does not like V on its right .... Result L?
          If one of these, accept it; if neither then fail (input is ungrammatical), but if both, then go to Test II.

In Test II; made when both 'likes' in Test I are 'on', the choice is made in such a way as will forestall trouble later, namely,

TEST II: If V does not like T on its left ..... Result L
           Else if T does not like V on its
           right, then .... Result R

If neither of these criteria is sufficient to force a conclusion, then the situation remains officially ambiguous at this level. Ultimately the stack is cleared, and enough pointers will then have been set to determine the structure. A few remain holding 'nil'; thus in the analysis of $x := (a+b) \times c$, the left-hand pointer of '(' points to 'nil'– it would point to f in the analysis of $x := f(a+b) \times c$.

15.4.2 The precedence algorithm

The simplest precedence algorithm needs no further semantic information. It uses a private pointer which points initially to the first operator pointer in the input string. The setting of a precedence pointer is always made (a) *from* (i.e. in a tag of) the operator thus pointed to, (b) to point *to* an operator involved in a fight, (c) the private pointer then being altered to point to the latter. If the fight is 'over' an object, then no precedence pointer is set unless (a) the result of the fight is to set a right-hand parsing pointer, and (b) the left-hand pointer of the winner is also an object; in this case the minor precedence pointer is set to point to the winner. If the fight was over an operator, a major precedence pointer is always set to point to the winner (this pointer is usually the reverse of the parsing pointer set at the same time). The following sequence shows how this works out in the case of the sentence $y := a \times b + c$:

Stack	M	N	Result of I	II	Parsing ptr set	Precedence ptr set
nil	y	:=	L		y ← :=	
:=	a	×		L	a ← ×	
:=	b	+		R	× → b	:= − → ×
:=	×	+		L	× ← +	× → +
:= +	c	End	R		+ → c	
:=		+	End	R	:= → +	+ → :=

and the final state in the machine can best be represented by

Contents of loc:	0	1	2	3	4	5	6	7
point to:	Start	y	:=	a	×	b	+	c
Tag 'a' holds	nil		1		3		4	
'b'	nil		6		5		7	
'c'	nil		End		6		2	
'd'	2		4		nil		nil	

It has been necessary to describe the above in fair detail in order to make any sense whatever of Ross's extensions to wider classes of languages. His first step is the introduction of 'minor modifiers', which are words that can influence the meaning of operators occurring later in the sentence. Suppose one could write

$$; matrix\ y := a \times b + c;$$

then it is important *not* to arrange for the precedence to go straight to the heart of the matter (which is $:=$) without taking note of *matrix* first, since this affects the meaning of both $:=$ and the arithmetic signs. In this context, *matrix* will be an operator with a *nil* l.h.s., and the minor precedence pointer which the former rules would set from the first $;$ to the $:=$, must be broken in such a way as to call at *matrix* 'en route'.

214

The second step is the much bigger one of introducing likes and dislikes into the precedence-setting part of the algorithm. This involves another stack on which to keep completed fragments of the precedence chain which so far cannot be linked into anything bigger. For an intuitive perception of what this means, consider the idiom that gives compiler writers so much trouble,

begin . . . **end where** . . .;

It means that the syntax of any part of the contents of the compound statement can be sorted out as we scan it, and yet the result kept in suspense as regards its semantics until it is known whether any option has been stated. It permits the precedence chain to look ahead and treat the **where** as if it preceded the **begin**, like *matrix* in the previous paragraph. It provides a simple mechanism for single scan comprehension of sentences full of forward references such as

Although it was raining cats and dogs, and, falling being now apparently part of its nature, the barometer held out no prospect of relief, once he had put on his greatcoat and oilskins, the captain felt warm and dry inside and prepared to brave the elements indefinitely

— a style which may be deplored, but is used.

It will be seen that all of this leaves the original syntactic structure (as determined by the parsing algorithm) untouched, but consists of modifications with profound effects on the precedence chain. It would seem, therefore, that Ross is developing a 'structural semantics' midway between syntax and 'operational semantics'; a formalized 'semantic grammar' for getting out of a sentence the order in which it implies you do things independently of defining exactly what it is you do. This is not a process which can be carried to completion, however, if a language is self-defining even to the degree implied by Algol declarations.

15.4.3 Further comments

The elementary part of Ross's treatment, at least, makes no contribution whatever to one problem — that of determining when two different sentences have identical results (or meaning). For it is possible from his parse to reconstruct the original sentence by the following algorithm:

Start at the top of the diagram.
A: Move as many steps down and to the left as possible.
B: Print what you find.
   If there is a move of one step down and to the right, make it and go to A, otherwise

C: If there is a move of one step up and to the right, make it and go to B, otherwise

Move up and to the left as far as possible and go to C. If this is impossible, the process is complete.

Thus it is hopeless to expect the fact that two alternative word orders convey identical meaning (if they do) to declare itself in the two orders leading to the same diagram. But a number of avenues remain. (1) There may be — indeed there are — operators which are known to be symmetrical. (2) The sequence in the precedence chain may reveal equivalences. (3) In some situations a modifier can imply some implicit syntax change — a well-known case of this being those words which, when they start a sentence, cause inversion later on.

The concept of a fight is confirmed by some unpublished work of the author. Consider the structure 'The A of the B', where the alternatives for B include the structure itself. A recursive structure of this sort can be expanded without limit, in practice as well as theory. We have no difficulty in understanding

The election of the chairman of the committee of the society of the friends of the cathedral

nor is there any doubt that the structure is correctly interpreted by the recursive definition. It is the election of something, and that something is the chairman of something. It is not

The committee-etc's election-of-the-chairman

nor any other alternative structure. But now consider

The effect of the election of the chairman of the committee of the society of the friends of the cathedral was unfortunate

All our previous comments hold. But if *any* one of the *of*s is replaced by *on*, its effect is to take one right back to the word *effect* for a new link. My interpretation of this is that *effect* 'expects' both *of* and *on*. Having got its *of*, its expectation in that direction is satisfied, but the expectation of *on* remains until one of three things happens. (a) All expectations are cancelled by the end of the sentence. (b) If another word that expects *on* intervenes, a fight may occur. (c) But otherwise the expectation will exert itself as soon as an *on* appears. The second possibility, of a fight, led to a game. This is to start with a construction which is syntactically ambiguous, and with two cases of it which are unhesitatingly parsed differently, and then to modify the variables in it until the tensions are as nearly equal as possible. The results vary from the mildly amusing to the positively disconcerting. Two examples must suffice.

1. *The A of the B of the C.* In 'The election of the chairman of the committee', we clearly have the election of an officer, not an act

216

of the committee. In 'The knowledge of the law of the magistrates' we are unlikely to adopt the interpretation that the magistrates have a special law of their own, and we therefore adopt the admittedly unusual parse with little difficulty. Roughly equal tensions are mildly amusing in 'The Minister of the Interior of the Prince', and positively disconcerting in 'The lilies of the valley of the shadow of death'.

2. *Effect of* and *effect on*. The parsing naturally takes different courses in 'The effect of the election on the people', and 'The mayor of the town on the river'. To counteract the expectation created by *effect*, one needs a fairly close-bonding *on*, as in 'The effect of The Mill on the Floss', or 'The effect of the prisoner on the rack'. A case where equal tensions are held undecided pending further clues can be seen in the way an identical first phrase is differently analysed in the two sentences

> The effect of the paint on the wall is to make the wall waterproof.
> The effect of the paint on the wall is to reduce the value of the house.

— and even so, one is left with a probabilistic decision which could be reversed by features in a wider context.

Quantification of these ideas in a way which would enable an algorithm to be written would involve maintaining a table of expectations which have been awakened, and provision to make them decay with time (= distance along the scan). There is also required a much more complex theory of types than suffices for programming languages, since it is the type complexity of words like 'mayor', 'town', 'river' when compared with words like 'age', 'cost', 'time', which provides the spectrum of possible, but varyingly probable, readings of many English sentences. For this reason, the use of a subset of a natural language for programming is not as difficult a problem as some of the above considerations might suggest. All the same, it is quite difficult enough.

BIBLIOGRAPHY

This bibliography includes all the references from within the text of this book, and a few others. Attention is drawn particularly to the entries IEEE (August 1964) and Samet (1969), which contain extensive bibliographies for further reference.

Aho, A. V., and Ullman, J. D. (1972). *The Theory of Parsing, Translation and Compiling*, 2 vols, Prentice Hall, Eaglewood Cliffs, N.J.

Backus, J. (1959). 'The syntax and semantics of the proposed international algebraic language of the Zurich ACM-GAMM conference' in *Proc. Int. Conf. Inf. Processing*, UNESCO, June 1959, pp. 125–132. Reprinted in *Ann. Rev. in Automatic Programming*, Vol. 1, pp. 268–291 (Pergamon Press, 1961).

de Bakker, J. W. (1967). *Formal definition of programming languages*, Math. Cent. Tracts 16, Amsterdam.

Bamford, A. C. (1976). *Ph.D. Thesis*, University of Oxford.

Bar Hillel, Y., Perles, M. and Shamir, E. (1961). 'On formal properties of simple phrase structure grammars.' *Z. Phonetik, Sprachwiss. und Kommunikationsforschung, 14*. pp. 143–172.

Barnett, M. P. (1969). *Computer Programming in English*, Harcourt Brace and World, Inc., New York.

Barrett, W. and Mitchell, A. J. (1963). 'An extended autocode for Pegasus.' *Computer J., 6*, p. 237.

Barron, D. W., Buxton, J. N., Hartley, D. F., Nixon, E. and Strachey, C. (1963). 'The main features of CPL.' *Computer J., 6*. pp. 134–143.

Bobrow, D. G. (1963). 'Syntactic analysis of English by computer — a survey.' *Proc. 1963 Fall J.C.C.*, Spartan Books, Vol. 24 pp. 365–387.

Bobrow, D. G. and Raphael, B. (1964). 'A comparison of list processing languages.' *C.A.C.M., 7*, pp. 231–240.

Borko, H. (Editor) (1962). *Computer Application in the Behavioral Sciences*.

Brooker, R. A. (1956). 'The programming strategy used with the Manchester University Mk.I computer.' *Proc. I.E.E.*, Vol. 103B, Supplement, pp. 151–157.

Brooker, R. A., and Morris, D. (1960). 'An assembly program for a phrase structure language.' *Computer J., 3*, pp. 168–179.

— (1962). 'A description of Mercury Autocode in terms of a phrase structure language.' *Ann. Rev. in Automatic Programming*, 2, pp. 29–65 (Pergamon Press).

— (1963). 'A general translation program for phrase structure languages.' *J.A.C.M. 9*, pp. 1–10.

Brooker, R. A., McCallum, I. R., Morris, D., and Rohl, J. S., (1963). 'The Compiler compiler.' *Ann. Rev. in Automatic Programming*, 3, pp. 229–275 (Pergamon Press). See also an article in *J.A.C.M.*, 9, pp. 1–10 (1962).

British Standards Institution. 'Glossary of terms used in Data processing.'

Burkhardt, W. H. (1965). 'Metalanguage and syntax specification.' *C.A.C.M.*, 8, pp. 304–305. See also a letter in *ibid* p. 261.

Burstall, R. M., Collins, J. S. and Popplestone, R. J. (1968). *Pop-2 Papers* Oliver and Boyd, Edinburgh.

Buxton, J. N., and Laski, J. C. (1962). 'Control and simulation language.' *Computer J.*, 5, pp. 194–199.

Caracciolo di Forino, A. (1963). *C.A.C.M.*, 6, pp. 456–460.

Chomsky, N. (1956). 'Three models for the description of language.' *I. R. E. Trans. Inf. Theory*, 2, pp. 113–124.

— (1957). *Syntactic Structures*. Mouton, The Hague.

— (1959). 'On certain formal properties of grammars', *Inf. and Control*, 2, pp. 137–167. Also 'A note on phrase-structure grammars, *ibid*, pp. 393–395.

— (1962). 'Formal properties of grammars' in *Handbook of Mathematical psychology* (ed. R. R. Bush, E. H. Gelernter and R. D. Luce) Vol. 2, Ch. 12.; Wiley, New York.

Chomsky, N., and Schützenberger, M. P. (1963). 'The algebraic theory of context-free languages' in *Computer programming and formal systems* (ed. Braffort and Hirschberg), North-Holland Pub. Co., Amsterdam; pp. 118–161.

Church, A. (1941). *The Calculi of Lambda Conversion*. Princeton University Press.

Clarke, B., and Felton, G. F. (1959). 'The Pegasus Autocode.' *Computer J.*, 1, p. 192

Cohen, K., and Wegstein, J. H. (1965). 'Axle: an axiomatic language for string transformation.' *C.A.C.M. 8*, pp. 657–661.

Colin, A. J. T. (1961). 'MVC Mark 3: A general survey analysis program for Mercury.' University of London Computer Unit Internal Report.

— (1963). 'The MVC manual.' University of London Computer Unit Internal Report.

— (1964). 'The multiple variate counter.' *Computer J.*, 6, pp. 339–347.

Conway, R. W., Delfausse, J. J., Maxwell, W. L., and Walker, W. E. (1965). 'CLP — the Cornell List Processor.' *C.A.C.M. 8*, pp.

215–216. (Includes a brief account of CORC, in which CLP is embedded.)

Cooke, D. J. (1975). 'The pragmatic formalization of computing systems relative to a given high-level language', *Ph.D. Thesis*, University of London.

Cooper, D. C. and Whitfield, H. (1962). 'ALP, An autocode list-processing language.' *Computer J.*, *5*, pp. 28–31.

Corbato, F. J. (1963). *The Compatible Time sharing System and Programmers' Guide*. M.I.T. Press.

Currie, L. F., Bond, Susan, G., and Morison, J. D. (1971). 'Algol 68R' in Peck (1971).

Curry, H. B., and Feys, R. (1958). *Combinatory Logic*, Vol. 1 North-Holland Pub. Co., Amsterdam.

Dahl, O.-J., Myrhang, B. and Nygaard, K. (1970). *Simula 67 Common Base Language*, Pub. S-22, Norvegian Comp. Centre, Oslo 3.

Dahl, O.-J., and Nygaard, K. (1966). 'Simula, an Algol based Simulation Language', *C.A.C.M.*, *9*, pp. 671–678.

Dahl, O.-J., Dijkstra, E. W. and Hoare, C. A. R. (1972). 'Structured Programming', *APIC Studies in Data Processing No.8*, Academic Press, New York.

Davis, M. (1958). *Computability and Unsolvability*. McGraw-Hill.

Dickens, C. (1837). *The Posthumous Papers of the Pickwick Club*, Nelson Edition, p. 147.

Dijkstra, E. W. (1962). 'An Algol translator for the X1' in *Automatic Programming Bulletin*, No. 13, reprinted in *Ann. Rev. in Automatic Programming*, *3*, pp. 329–356 (1963).

— (1963). 'On the design of machine independent programming languages.' *Ann. Rev. in Automatic Programming 3*, pp. 27–42.

— (1968). 'Cooperative Sequential Processes' in *Programming Languages* (ed. F. Genuys), Academic Press.

— (1969). *Notes on Structured Programming*, EWD 249, Tech. Univ., Eindhoven, and see Dahl *et al*, (1972).

Douglas, A. S., and Mitchell, A. J. (1960). 'Autostat: A language for statistical programming.' *Computer J. 3*, p. 61.

Duncan, F. G. (1963). 'Input and Output for Algol 60 on KDF9.' *Computer J. 5*, p. 341.

Edelstein, L. A. (1963). 'Picture logic for Bacchus, a fourth generation computer.' *Computer J. 6*, p. 144. (No language here, but a new field that may call for one.)

Eickel, J., Paul, M., Bauer, F., and Samelson, K. (1963). 'A syntax controlled generator of formal language processors.' *C.A.C.M.*, *6*, pp. 451–455.

Elgot, C. C., and Robinson, A. (1964). 'Random access stored-program machines, an approach to Programming languages.' *J.A.C.M. 11*, pp. 365–400.

Farber, D. J., Griswold, R. E., and Polonsky, I. P. (1964). 'Snobol: A string manipulation language.' *J.A.C.M. 11*, pp. 21–30.

Feldman, J. (1964). 'A formal semantics for computer oriented languages.' Doctoral Dissertation, Carnegie Inst. of Tech.

Floyd, R. W. (1961). 'A descriptive language for symbol manipulation.' *J.A.C.M. 8*, pp. 579–584.

— (1962). 'On the non-existence of a phrase structure grammar for Algol 60.' *C.A.C.M. 5*, p. 483.

— (1963). 'Syntactic analysis and operator precedence.' *J.A.C.M. 10*, pp. 316–333.

— (1964). 'Bounded context syntactic analysis.' *C.A.C.M. 7*, pp. 62–65.

Foster, J. M. (1970). *Automatic Syntactic Analysis*, Macdonald and Jane's, London, and Elsevir, New York.

Freeman, D. E. (1964). 'Programming languages ease digital simulation.' *Control Engineering*, Nov. 1964, pp. 103–106.

Fries, C. C. (1952). *The Structure of English*. Longmans Green.

Garwick, J. (1964). 'Gargoyle, a language for compiler writing.' *C.A.C.M.*, Jan. 1964.

Gelernter, H., Hansen, J. R., and Gerberich, C. C. (1960). 'A Fortran-compiled list-processing language.' *J.A.C.M.*, 7 (1961), pp. 87–101.

Gilmore, P. C. (1963). 'An abstract computer with a Lisp-like machine language without a label operator.' pp. 71–86 of *Computer Programming and Formal Systems* (ed. Braffort, P., and Hirschberg, D.) North-Holland Pub. Co., Amsterdam.

Ginsberg, S., and Rice, H. C. (1962). 'Two families of languages related to Algol.' *J.A.C.M.*, 9, pp. 350–371.

Ginsberg, S., and Rose, G. F. (1963). 'Some recursively unsolvable problems in Algol-like languages.' *J.A.C.M. 10*, pp. 29–47. Also 'Operations which preserve definability in languages', *ibid*, pp. 175–195.

Goodman, R. (Editor) (1963). 'Automatic Programming Bulletin, No. 17.' Brighton Technical College.

Gorn, S. (1963). 'The detection of generative ambiguities in context-free languages.' *J.A.C.M.*, 10, pp. 196–208.

Greibach, S., (1964). 'Formal Parsing Systems.' *C.A.C.M. 7*, pp. 499–504.

— (1965). 'A new normal form theorem for C.F.P.S. grammars.' *J.A.C.M.*, 12, pp. 42–52.

Griffiths, T. V., and Petrick, S. R. (1965). 'On the relative efficiencies of context-free grammar recognisers.' *C.A.C.M. 8*, pp. 289–300.

Habermann, A. N. (1973). 'Critical comments on the programming language Pascal', *Acta Informatica*, 3, pp. 47–57.

Halpern, M. I. (1964). 'XPOP: a Meta-language without meta-physics.' *Proc. Fall Joint Computer Conf. 1964*, pp. 57–68.

221

— (1966): *Ann. Rev. in Automatic Programming* Vol. 5.

Hansen, W. J. and Boom, H. (1976). 'Report on the Standard Hardware Representation for Algol 68' for IFIP (WG 2.1), *Algol Bulletin No. 40*, pp. 24–43.

Heising, W. P. (1965). Report of American Standards Association, ASA Committee X3, published in *C.A.C.M. 7*, p. 10, ibid pp. 591–625, and *C.A.C.M. 8*, pp. 287–8.

Hendry, D. (1966). *The Provisional BCL Manual* (and other internal reports) University of London Institute of Computer Science.

Higman, B. (1963). 'Towards an Algol translator.' *Ann. Rev. in Automatic Programming*, *3*, pp. 121–162. Pergamon Press.

— (1968). 'Nonpareil, a machine level machine independent language for the study of semantics', ULICS Internal Report No. ICSI 170, University of London.

— (1974). 'The two faces of Chomsky', *Internat. J. of Math. Education in Sci. and Technology*, *5*, pp. 617–624.

— (1976a). 'The place of own variables in programming language theory', *Computer J.*, *19*, pp. 225–228.

— (1976b). *Omnibus Paper No. 2*, Dept. of Computer Studies, University of Lancaster.

Hill, I. D. (1965). *Algol Bulletin* No. 21, pp. 70–74.

Hoare, C. A. R. (1968). 'Record Handling' in *Programming Languages* (ed. F. Genuys), Academic Press.

Hornby, A. S. (1954). *A Guide to Patterns and Usage in English*. Oxford University Press.

Huskey, H. D. (1961). 'Compiling Techniques for Algebraic Expressions.' *Computer J. 4*, p. 10. See also *C.A.C.M. 3*, pp. 463–468 (1960) and *6*, pp. 649–658 (1963).

IEEE (August 1964). *Special Issue on Computer Languages*, IEEE Trans. El. Comp., EC-13, pp. 343–462.

I.F.I.P. 'Report on input/output procedures for Algol.' Reprinted in *C.A.C.M. 7*, pp. 628/630.

Iliffe, J. K. (1961). 'The use of the Genie system in numerical calculations.' *Ann. Rev. in Automatic Programming*, *2*, pp. 1–28.

— (1971). *Basic Machine Principles*, Macdonald and Jane's, London, and Elsevir, New York.

Iliffe, J. K., and Jodeit, J. C. (1962). 'A dynamic storage allocation scheme.' *Computer J.*, *5*, pp. 200–209.

Irons, E. T. (1961). 'A syntax-directed compiler for Algol 60' *C.A.C.M. 4*, pp. 51–55.

— (1963). 'The structure and use of the syntax directed compiler.' *Ann. Rev. in Automatic Programming*, *3*, pp. 207–227.

— (1964). 'Structural connections in formal languages.' *C.A.C.M. 7*, 67–71.

Iverson, K. E. (1962). *A Programming Language*. John Wiley and Sons, N.Y.

— (1964). 'A method of syntax specification.' *C.A.C.M.*, 7, pp. 588–589.

Jensen, K., and Wirth, N. (1973). *Pascal User Manual and Report*, Springer Verlag (2nd Edition 1975).

Kelley, D. H., and Buxton, J. N. (1962). 'Montecode — an interpretive program for Monte Carlo simulation.' *Computer J.*, 5, pp. 88–93.

Kleene, S. C. (1952). *Introduction to Metamathematics*. Van Nostrand.

Knowlton, K. C. (1965). 'A fast storage allocator', *C.A.C.M.*, 8, pp. 623–625.

— (1966). 'A programmer's description of L⁶', *C.A.C.M.*, 9, pp. 616–625.

Knuth, D. E. (1964a). 'A proposal for i/o conventions in Algol 60.' Report of A.C.M. committee, reproduced in *C.A.C.M. 7*, pp. 273–283.

— (1964b). 'Backus Normal form vs Backus Naur form.' *C.A.C.M. 7*, 735.

— (1967). 'Top-down Syntactic Analysis', Internat. Summer School, Copenhagen and *Acta Informatica 1(c)* (1971), pp. 79–110.

— (1968). *The Art of Computer Programming*, Addison Wesley.

Kuno, S., and Oettinger, A. G. (1962). 'Multiple path syntactic analyser.' *Proc. IFIP Congress*, North-Holland, Amsterdam, pp. 306–312.

— (1963). 'Syntactic structure and ambiguity in English.' *Proc. Fall J. Comp. Conf.* pp. 397–418. Spartan Books, Baltimore.

Kuno, S. (1965). 'The predictive analyser and a path elimination technique.' *C.A.C.M. 8*, pp. 453–462.

Landin, P. (1964). 'The mechanical evaluation of expressions'. *Computer J.*, 6, pp. 308–320.

— (1965. 'A correspondence between Algol 60 and Church's Lambda-notation.' *C.A.C.M. 8*, Part I: pp. 89–101, Part II: pp. 158–165.

— (1966). 'The next 700 programming languages', *C.A.C.M.*, 9, pp. 157–166.

Leavenworth, B. M. (1964). 'Fortran IV as a syntax language'. *C.A.C.M.*, 7, pp. 72–79.

Lindsey, C. H., and van der Meulen, S. G. (1971). *Informal Introduction to Algol 68*, North-Holland, Amsterdam.

Lucas, P., and Walk, K. (1969). 'On the formal description of PL/I', *Ann. Rev. in Automatic Programming*, 6, p. 3.

Markov, A. A. (1952). 'The Theory of Algorithms', *Trudij mat. Inst*, 38, p. 176.

McCarthy, J. (1960). 'Recursive functions of symbolic expressions and their calculation by machine, Part I.' *C.A.C.M.*, 3, pp. 184–195.

— (1962). *LISP.1.5 Programmer's Manual* (revised 1966) M.I.T. Press, Cambridge, Mass.

— (1963). 'A basis for a mathematical theory of computation' in *Computer programming and formal systems*, Amsterdam, North-Holland Pub. Co. See also 'Towards a mathematical science of computation' in *Proc. IFIP Munich Conf. 1962*, North Holland, 1963.

McConologue, K., and Simmons, R. F. (1965). 'Analysing English syntax with a pattern learning parser.' *C.A.C.M.*, *8*, pp. 687–698.

Mendelson, E. (1963). *Introduction to Mathematical Logic*, D. van Nostrand, Princeton, N.J.

Metcalfe, H. H. (1963). 'A parametrized compiler based on mechanical linguistics.' *A.C.M. Nat. Conf.* Denver, Ohio. Reprinted in *Ann. Rev. in Automatic Programming 4* (1964) pp. 125–165.

Miller, G. A. (1965). Presidential address in The Advancement of Science, Vol. XXI, No. 93, p. 425.

Napper, R. B. E. (1967). 'Some proposals for Snap, a language with formal macro facilities', *Computer J.*, *10*, p. 231.

— (1968). *The Revised Compiler-compiler*, Dept. of Computer Science, U. of Manchester (2nd edition 1973).

Napper, R. B. E. and Fisher, R. N. (1976). 'Alec, a new extensible scientific programming language', *Computer J.*, *19*, p. 25.

Naur, P. (1960). 'Report on the Algorithmic Language ALGOL 60.' *C.A.C.M.*, *3*, p. 299 or *Numerische Mathematik 2*, p. 106. Revised report (1963) in *Computer J.*, *5*, p. 349, *C.A.C.M.*, *6*, pp. 1–17, or *Ann Rev. in Auto Prog.*, *4*, p. 217. For Algol 58 see Backus (1958).

—(1964*a*). Algol Bulletin No. 18, pp. 26–43.

— (1964b). 'The design of the GIER Algol compiler', *Ann. Rev. Automatic Programming*, *4*.

Newell, A. (1961). *Information Processing Language-V Manual*. The Rand Corporation. See also Newell, A., and Tonge, F. M., *C.A.C.M.*, *3*, p. 205.

Opler, A. (1965). 'Procedure-oriented language statements to facilitate parallel processing.' *C.A.C.M.*, *8*, p. 306.

Oettinger, A. G. (1960). *Automatic Language Translation*. Harvard University Press, Cambridge, Mass.

Paterson, J. B. (1963). 'The Cobol Sort Verb.' *C.A.C.M.*, *6*, pp. 255–258.

Peck, J. E. L. (editor; 1971). *Algol 68 Implementation*, North Holland Publishing Co., Amsterdam.

Perlis, A., Smith, J. W., and Evans, A. (1959). 'TASS.' Computation Centre, Carnegie Inst. Tech.

Perlis, A. J. (1964). 'A format language.' *C.A.C.M.*, *7*, pp. 89–96.

Pfeiffer (1960). *Fortune*, May 1960, p. 153.

Pilling, D. (1963). 'C-E-I-R OPAL Language.' C.E.I.R. (U.K.) Ltd, Internal report.

Quine, W. V. (1960). *Word and Object*. New York, John Wiley and Technology Press.

Rabinowitz, I. N. (1962). 'Report on the Algorithmic Language FORTRAN II.' *C.A.C.M.*, *5*, pp. 327–337.

Radin, G., and Rogoway, H. P. (1965). 'NPL: Highlights of a New Programming Language.' *C.A.C.M.*, *8*, pp. 9–17.

Randell, B. (1963). Private communication.

Richards, L. A., and Gibson, C. (1960). *English Through Pictures*, Bk. I., Washington Sq. Press Inc., N.Y.

Richards, I. A. (1943). *Basic English and its uses*. London, Kegan Paul.

Richards, M. (1973). *The BCPL Programming Manual* The Computer Laboratory, Cambridge, England.

Rose, G. F. (1964). 'An extension of Algol-like languages.' *C.A.C.M.*, *7*, pp. 52–60.

Rosen, S. (1964). 'A compiler building system developed by Brooker and Morris.' *C.A.C.M.*, *7*, pp. 403–414.

Ross, D. T. (1959). 'The design and use of the APT language for automatic programming of numerically controlled machine tools.' *Proc. Comp. App. Symposium*, *ITT Res. Inst.*, Chicago, Ill., pp. 80–99.

— (1962). *On the Algorithmic Theory of Language*. ESL-TM-156, Elec. Systems Lab., M.I.T., Cambridge, Mass.

— (1964). 'On context and ambiguity in parsing.' *C.A.C.M.*

Rossiter, A. P. (1939). 'The growth of Science' (in *Basic English*). Pelican Books.

Samelson, K., and Bauer, F. L. (1960). 'Sequential formula translation.' *C.A.C.M.*, *3*, pp. 76–83.

Sammet, Jean E. (1969). *Programming Languages*, Prentice Hall Inc., Englewood Cliffs, N.J.

Schuman, S. A. (1975). (editor for IFIP WG 2.1). *New directions in Algorithmic Languages*, Inst. de recherche d'informatique et d'automatique, Rocquencourt BP5, 78150 Le Chesney.

Scott, D. and Strachey, C. (1972). 'Towards a mathematical semantics for computer languages' in Microwave Res. Inst. Symposium series, Vol. 21, Polytech. Inst. Brooklyn.

Seegmüller, G. (1965). 'A proposal for a basis for a report on a successor of Algol 60', Bavarian Acad. Sci., Munich.

Shavell, Z. A. (1965). 'The use of Fortran in subroutines with Cobol main programs.' *C.A.C.M.*, *8*, pp. 221–2.

Shaw, C. J. (1963). 'A specification of Jovial.' *C.A.C.M.*, *6*, pp. 721–736. Also 'Jovial, A programming language for real time command systems'. *Ann. Rev. in Automatic Programming*, *3* (1963), pp. 53–119.

Snidvongs, K. (1975). 'An investigation into an operator basis for mathematical semantics', *Ph.D. Thesis*, London.

Sproull (1964). Cited from Ref. 6 of Datamation, Dec. 1964, p. 48.

Steel, T. (1964). 'Beginnings of a theory of information handling.' *C.A.C.M.*, 7, pp. 97–103.

Steiner, G. (1975). *After Babel*, O.U.P.

Strachey, C. (1965). 'A general purpose macrogenerator.' Cambridge University Math. Lab. Report No. 65/1, reprinted in *Computer J.*, 8, pp. 225–241.

— (1963). See Barron *et al* (1963).

Strachey, C. and Wilkes, M. V. (1961). 'Some proposals for improving the efficiency of Algol 60.' *C.A.C.M.*, 4, pp. 488–491.

Tajiri, K. (1965). 'The use of Cobol subroutines in Fortran main programs.' *C.A.C.M.*, 8, 223–4.

Tocher, K. D. (1960). *Handbook of the General Simulation Program*. United Steel Co., Dept. Op. Res. Report No. 77/ORC 3/Tech.

Wegner, P. (1971). 'Data Structure Models in Programming Languages', *SIGPLAN Notices*, 6, 2, pp. 1–54.

Weizenbaum, J. (1963). Symmetric List Processor, *C.A.C.M.*, 6, 524–544.

Wesselkamper, T. (1972). 'A mathematical model of the computing process in a high level language'. *Ph.D. Thesis*, London.

van Wijngaarden, A., *et al* (1969). 'Report on the Algorithmic Language Algol 68', *MR 101* Math. Cent. Amsterdam and *Numerische Mathematik 14*.

— (1974). 'Revised Report on the Algorithmic Language Algol 68'. Tech. Report TR 74–3 Dept. of Computer Sci., Univ. of Alberta, Edmonton, and *Acta Informatica 5*, (1975) Fasc 1–3, pp. 1–236.

Wilkes, M. V. (1964). 'An experiment with a self-compiling compiler for a simple list-processing language.' Camb. Univ. Math. Lab. Tech. Memo 63/1, reprinted in *Ann. Rev. in Automatic Programming*, 4, pp. 1–48.

Williams, J. W. J. (1964). 'E.S.P. The Elliott Simulator Package.' *Computer J.*, 6, pp. 328–331.

Wirth, N. (1963). 'A generalization of Algol.' *C.A.C.M.*, 6, pp. 547–554.

— (1965). 'A proposal for a report on a successor to Algol 60' *MR 75*, Math. Cent. Amsterdam.

— (1971a). 'The programming language Pascal', *Acta Inf. 1*, pp. 35–68.

— (1971b). 'The Pascal Compiler' *ibid*.

— (1971c). 'Program development by stepwise refinement', *C.A.C.M. 14 (4)* pp. 221–227.

— (1974). 'On the design of programming languages', in Rosenfeld, J. L. (editor), *Information Processing 74*, North Holland.

— (1976). 'Programming languages, what to demand and how to assess them', Symposium on Software Engineering, Queen's University of Belfast.

Wirth, N. and Weber, H. (1966). 'Euler, a generalization of Algol and its formal definition' *C.A.C.M. 9(1)*, pp. 13–25 and 89–99.

Woodger, M. (1963). 'The description of a computing process. Some observations on automatic programming and Algol 60.' *Ann. Rev. in Automatic Programming, 3*, pp. 1–16.

Woodward, P. M., and Currie, L. F. (1972). *A User's guide to Algol 68R* (2nd edition 1974), London, H.M.S.O.

Woodward, P. M., and Jenkins, D. P. (1961). 'Atoms and lists.' *Computer J., 4*, pp. 47–53.

Yates, F., and Simpson, H. R. (1960). 'A general program for the analysis of surveys.' *Computer J.*, Part I: *3*, p. 136; Part II, *4*, p. 20.

Yngve, V. H. (1961). *Comit Programmer's Reference Manual*, and *Introduction to Comit Programming.* M.I.T.

INDEX

Names of languages are in capitals, names of people in italics. Other entries may be to definitions, special uses of terms in specific languages, or to general discussion; it has not been possible to distinguish these. f (ff) mean that most of the reference is on the following page (pages).